# VLAD
## THE IMPALER

*Pace voua, morti nostri*
Rest in peace, our dead.

# VLAD
## THE IMPALER

IN SEARCH OF THE REAL
## DRACULA

M.J. TROW

SUTTON PUBLISHING

This book was first published in 2003 by
Sutton Publishing Limited · Phoenix Mill
Thrupp · Stroud · Gloucestershire · GL5 2BU

This paperback edition first published in 2004

British Library Cataloguing in Publication Data
A catalogue record for this book is available from the
British Library

ISBN 0 7509 3522 7

Typeset in 11/12pt Sabon.
Typesetting and origination by
Sutton Publishing Limited.
Printed and bound in Great Britain by
J.H. Haynes & Co. Ltd, Sparkford.

# Contents

# ACKNOWLEDGEMENTS

I would like to offer my sincere thanks to everyone involved in the creation of *Vlad the Impaler*: to Jacqueline Mitchell and the team at Sutton, for their unfailing support and kindness; to Andrew Lownie, friend and literary agent *extraordinaire*, for his tireless effort; to my colleagues Brian Bond and Trevor Pine, for their scholarly advice and expertise; to the library staff at the School of Slavonic Studies, London University; to the proprietors of the pictures featured, for permission to use their photographs; to Taliesin Trow whose advice on filmography was invaluable, but most of all, as always, to my wife Carol, a busy writer herself, who did more than anyone else to shape this book.

Europe at the time of Vlad the Impaler, c. 1460

SCOTLAND
ENGLAND
WALES
HOLLAND
DENMARK
TEUTONIC ORDER
POLAND
BRANDENBURG
GERMAN PRINCIPALITIES
SILESIA
MORAVIA
BAVARIA
AUSTRIA
TYROL
STYRIA
SWISS CONFEDERATION
BURGUNDY
LOMBARDY
VENICE
GENOA
PAPAL STATES
FRANCE
NAVARRE
ARAGON
CASTILE
GRANADA
PORTUGAL
MEDITERRANEAN SEA
NAPLES
SICILY
PAPAL STATES
SERBIAN STATES
BOSNIA
HUNGARY
MOLDAVIA
WALLACHIA
OTTOMAN EMPIRE
BYZANTINE EMPIRE

The principalities of Wallachia, Transylvania and Moldavia during the reign of Vlad the Impaler

# 1

# THE GAPING GRAVE

His face was a strong – a very strong – aquiline, with high bridge of the thin nose and peculiarly arched nostrils; with lofty domed forehead and hair growing scantily around the temples, but profusely elsewhere. His eyebrows were very massive, almost meeting over the nose and with bushy hair that seemed to curl in its own profusion. The mouth, so far as I could see it under the heavy moustache, was fixed and rather cruel-looking, with peculiarly sharp white teeth; these protruded over the lips, whose remarkable ruddiness showed astonishing vitality in a man of his years. For the rest, his ears were pale and at the tops extremely pointed; the chin was broad and strong and the cheeks firm though thin. The general effect was one of extraordinary pallor.

Jonathan Harker's *Journal*, 5 May 1897

He was not very tall, but very stocky and strong, with a cold and terrible appearance, a strong and aquiline nose, swollen nostrils, a thin and reddish face in which the very long eyelashes framed large wide-open green eyes; the bushy black eyebrows made them appear threatening. His face and chin were shaven but for a moustache. The swollen temples increased the bulk of his head. A bull's neck connected [with] his head from which black curly locks hung on his wide-shouldered person.

Niccolò Modrussa, *c*. 1470

These two descriptions, one from a work of fiction, the other from real-life observations, are of the same man. They were written four hundred years apart and reflect the theme of this book: the huge gulf between one of the greatest creations of the modern horror story and a fifteenth-century warlord who still courts today the controversy that surrounded him in his own lifetime.

Count Dracula as described by the solicitor's clerk Jonathan Harker is the legendary king of the vampires, born of the fertile mind of Bram Stoker in his 1897 novel. The Count has his literary predecessors, as we shall see later, but it was essentially Stoker's variant that survived, as revenants do, to become the anti-hero of stage and screen in the years that followed its publication. Max Schreck, Bela Lugosi, Christopher Lee, Gary Oldman – we shall meet all these impostors.

Niccolò Modrussa's man was very different, the living, flesh-and-blood Vlad Dracula, known as Ţepeş, the Impaler. Modrussa, the pope's ambassador to the court of the king of Hungary, met him when he was under house arrest, probably at Buda in the summer of 1470. Vlad was no mere count, but a *voivod* or warlord and a prince of Wallachia, in what is today Romania. He is still referred to there as Ţepeş, the Impaler, and seen by the Romanians almost as a badge of pride, a freedom-fighter and national hero. The sobriquet Dracula, meaning son of the dragon, is explained by the fact that his father, also Vlad, was invested in the chivalric Order of the Dragon by the Holy Roman Emperor in 1431, and the title passed to his eldest surviving son. In medieval Wallachian, the suffix 'a' denotes son of.

How a medieval warlord became the most famous vampire in the world is at the heart of this book and the physical descriptions from Stoker and Modrussa are surprisingly similar. That Stoker dipped into Romanian history and folklore cannot be doubted. He may have read Modrussa's memories of Vlad or even seen a copy of one of the portraits of the Impaler that still exist today. And certainly there are intriguing parallels between the man of fiction and the man of substance, the undead and the living, which cannot be coincidental. Vlad Ţepeş ruled as prince of Wallachia three times in the space of a quarter of a century, the third time returning from an imprisonment and exile which had lasted twelve years. He came back, as it were, from the dead, to claim his inheritance, rather as Count Dracula continued to rise from his grave. As a military leader, Vlad was known to favour night attacks, with his most spectacular against the invading Ottoman Turks in the summer of 1462. So, Stoker's Dracula operates only at night and shuns the sun. Traditionally, the only means of destroying a vampire, which Stoker employs via a vampire-hunting Dr van Helsing in the novel, is to drive a stake through its heart and hack off its head. The driving of stakes – impalement – was Vlad's favoured method of torture, and gave rise to his nickname, Ţepeş. Decapitation was also a common execution method during his three reigns. There is, too, something of the undead about Vlad III Dracula, son of the dragon. To celebrate him, a commemorative stamp was printed in 1976, the four hundredth anniversary of his death. Today, he is at the heart of a tourist industry struggling to establish itself after the grim communist years of the *conducator* Nicolae Ceauşescu, himself perhaps a quirky reflection of Vlad in terms of his dictatorial powers and the appalling body count for which he is allegedly responsible. Before his overthrow and execution at Christmas 1980, Ceauşescu said smugly to his Health Minister, 'A man like me comes along only once every five hundred years.' Was his predecessor, five hundred years earlier, Vlad Dracula, the Impaler?

Tradition has it that Vlad Ţepeş is buried in the island monastery of Snagov, one of several he endowed in his role as prince of Wallachia, and one he almost certainly fortified as an excellent strategic refuge at a time when war and invasion were the constants of life.

Snagov strikes its visitor in different ways. When journalist Victoria Clark visited the monastery ten years after Ceauşescu's overthrow, she was rowed across the lake through mist and reeds to meet Father Emilian Poenaru of the Orthodox Church, the monastery's curator. She was told by her guide, 'Please don't start asking questions about Dracula. Father Emilian is sick of all that tourist stuff.'[1] Father Emilian, however, was hospitality itself, offering coffee, peanuts, pickled peppers and cold meat. He also smoked Marlboro Lights and whiled away his non-guiding hours by knitting! Six years earlier, ghost-hunter and photographer Simon Marsden had had a rather different experience:

> All was dark [he remembered] save for the flickering of candles that at intervals lit up the rich gold and silver of the many icons. Then, as I neared the altar, the small, dark figure of a nun appeared from behind a pillar and stared at me. 'Was this Dracula's grave?' I stammered. She did not reply, but continued to stare, I felt, straight through me.[2]

There was an Oriental rug over the great stone slab and a rather awful vase with Vlad Țepeș' portrait stencilled onto it, together with a sinister-looking chalice.

But Marsden and Clark were looking at the hollow shell of what may have been the Impaler's last resting place. And, intriguingly, their different agendas evoked different memories: Clark, researching the Orthodox Church, encounters a jolly priest with modern, Western habits, irked by the visitors' fascination with the Impaler; Marsden, the occultist, sees monsters in the shadows and the weird behaviour of the nun:

> I walked to the door, turned once more and saw [her] making strange signs over the grave, gesticulating and waving her arms as if in a trance.[3]

One of many legends of the Impaler is that, trapped in a loveless marriage, he wandered the streets of his capital, Tîrgoviste, picking up prostitutes on the way. So, too, Carol II Hohenzollern, king of Romania when archaeologists first came looking for Dracula's grave had his string of mistresses.

The insufferable Carol had many of the worst traits of Nicolae Ceaușescu and some of Țepeș, lending an eerie suggestion that a similar fate overtakes the rulers of Romania no matter when they live. He ran his own extortion racket, receiving monthly fees from casinos and nightclubs. He had shares in all the major companies and grabbed one million pounds in compensation when Stalin annexed Bessarabia from him, not for the country's Treasury, but for his own coffers. In 1938, having smuggled a vast fortune out of the country into his personal banks, he proclaimed a royal dictatorship (the '30s was, after all, the decade of dictators) and declared unofficial war on the country's 800,000 Jews. Forced out, as Ceauşescu would be fifty years later, he fled Romania, with his mistress Lupescu and nine railway carriages of loot. Like Vlad Ţepeş', Carol tried to play a double game against opponents who were far stronger and Fates who were just as unkind. And, like Vlad Ţepeş', he lost.

In 1931 the Commission on Historic Monuments appointed an archaeologist, Dinu Rosetti, and a genealogist, George Florescu, to excavate the island of Snagov as part of a national survey of historic buildings, concentrating on the area around the chapel, which was the core of the medieval monastery. Their findings were written up as *Diggings Around Snagov*, and they uncovered foundations of buildings, bones and pottery shards which indicated that the island had originally been a Bronze Age settlement. Its lake, one of the deepest in the country, was not only a source of fresh water, but provided fish for food and a natural defence against attack.

The archaeological team found clear evidence that Snagov was not only a monastery, with its chapel, dormitories, cells and chapter house, but that it was fortified against ravaging armies, with buttresses, trenches and thick walls. It must have been, in fact, a small town in the Impaler's time, with its own treasury, mint and printing press. And the bastions reaching to the water's edge gave comfort to boyar and peasant alike, both of whom could hide within the sanctuary of the Orthodox Church.

The original monastery at Snagov was endowed in the fourteenth century, but the largest of its three chapels, that of the Annunciation, was built by Vladislav II of the Dăneşti family, the Impaler's enemy, in 1453. It was probably Ţepeş' himself who was responsible for the later fortifications of the island, although no documentary evidence for this has survived.

Rosetti and Florescu found on the island an unprecedented number of skeletons with their skulls missing. One rational explanation is that these were victims of political assassination, and perhaps torture, but the conflict in which they died is less easy to discern. It was Vladislav's island before it was the Impaler's, and in 1462 it was captured by Radu cel Frumos (Rudolph the Handsome), Vlad's brother, who fought with the Turks against Vlad.

Tradition told the team that Dracula was buried, in keeping with his rank and honour as prince of Wallachia, near the altar. The archaeologists were trying to answer the question that Simon Marsden was to pose: was the altar slab Dracula's grave? The slab itself may once have borne inscriptions and frescoes typical of medieval Romanian tombs, but over the centuries the constant trampling by monks, soldiers, prisoners and vandals had removed all trace.[4]

The team knew that Snagov had undergone several transformations since Vlad Ţepeş time. The Turks burned part of the settlement towards the end of the 1462 campaign, and storms and earthquakes had brought about the collapse of the Chapel of the Annunciation. One of the ornate doors, with carvings of saints from the fifteenth century, is now in Bucharest Museum of Art. Despite the monastery's reputation in the seventeenth century as a centre of culture and learning, it had declined by the nineteenth, when Paul Kiselev, Governor-General of Wallachia, converted the place into a prison. By 1867 it had closed down and the locals helped themselves to anything they could find, which probably involved grave robbery and the exhumation of bodies in search of valuables.

Under the slab, the team found disappointment. Whether this grave had been robbed, like so many other graves, from those of ancient Egypt to that of the actor Peter Cushing, the Abraham van Helsing in a string of Dracula films, or whether it never contained a body in the first place, the huge dank hole merely contained piles of animal bones and pottery shards, which proved to be of Iron Age date.

Near the door of the church, however, was a tomb that looked all the more promising because it had clearly not been touched. Its position was odd and implied that this burial was a deliberate act of contempt: it was the same size as the slab near the altar, which suggested that this was the grave of someone of importance, and it was some way from the spiritual centre of the church, in a place where all visitors would walk on it. This time, however, the grave yielded information. In it was a wooden coffin, all but rotted, which had been wrapped in a pall whose purple plush and gold embroidery were still discernible. If this was the casket of Ţepeş, then the body inside gave the lie, at least in one sense, to the vampiric condition. Far from it being 'incorrupt' and hideous, with blood seeping from nose, ears, eyes and mouth, there was no head at all and the torso and limbs were mere bone.

The dressing of the dead is a fascinating subject. The body near the door at Snagov was wearing the rotted fragments of yellow and brown silk brocade, and the sleeves, clearly once crimson, were fastened with large silver buttons and cords typical of the fifteenth century. From the position of the sleeves it was possible to tell that the arms were not crossed over the breast, the common European symbol of piety and the position of bodies in other graves excavated at the site, but instead the right hand rested near the hip, as though holding the hilt of a sword. The problem with this interpretation is that throughout Europe to be left-handed was considered at best unlucky and at worst a manifestation of the devil. Whoever was buried in the doorway at Snagov would surely have been right-handed and would have worn the sword on the left. 'The clothing of the dead', says Mike Parker-Pearson,[5] 'constitutes a hall of mirrors, representations of representations, in which things may not be entirely what they seem at first.'

And the civilian clothes raise all sorts of questions. If this *was* Vlad Ţepeş, and if he died according to tradition (see below), he would surely be wearing plate armour, either the workaday 'harness' in which he was killed or a more elaborate, ceremonial suit put aside for the purpose.

Near the skeleton, Rosetti and Florescu found a battered crown with cloisonné inlay representing claws of terracotta colour, each claw holding a turquoise. All the known portraits of Vlad Țepeș show him wearing an ornate cloth cap, with cloisonné beads or pearls. There are no representations of his crown as *voivod* of Wallachia.

Other items, which were again clearly fifteenth century in date, included a small cup, with its fascinating echoes of the golden chalice legend, and a buckle with a gold thread decoration. Most intriguing of all was a ring, once probably attached to the dead man's sleeve. Rosetti speculated, having found similar examples in Nuremberg, that this was a love-token, specifically a fitting for a lady's colours, the heraldic scarf carried by medieval knights in tournaments. It is likely that both Țepeș and his father, Vlad Dracul, competed in such events, but Rosetti went further and saw the ring as part of the Order of the Dragon into which Vlad Dracul was invested at Nuremberg on 8 November 1431. A variety of representations of the dragon exist in Europe today. One, in the Bayerische Nationalmuseum in Munich, is of gold fabric, in trapunto work (quilting) and was probably sewn directly to a garment. Another, this time in metal, is preserved in the Kunstgewermuseum in Berlin. What is common to all the examples shown in D'A.J.D. Boulton's authoritative work on orders of chivalry, *The Knights of the Crown*,[6] is that the dragon's tail forms a circle. Is this the significance of the 'ring' found in the Snagov tomb?

Two years after the excavations at the Romanian monastery, two allegedly medieval skeletons were being examined in London. Dr Laurence Tanner, Keeper of the Monuments at Westminster Abbey, and Professor W. Wright, President of the Anatomical Society of Great Britain, were called upon to make a detailed study of the two sets of human remains found by workmen in the White Tower in 1674 and interred as the likely 'Princes in the Tower' four years later. I use this example of archaeological analysis because of its resonance with the Snagov work. Tanner and Wright found both animal and human bones in the urn. This is almost certainly because the collection of the bodies in 1674 was done carelessly, and included all sorts of debris. The English experts had an edge over their Romanian counterparts in that they were, respectively, a doctor and a dental surgeon. However eminent Florescu undoubtedly was as a genealogist, his expertise in the archaeological excavation of a grave was minimal. Moreover, in the 1930s archaeology was still largely an amateur science – it was only twenty years after the Piltdown find had taken in virtually the whole archaeological community, and not until 1953 that it would be revealed as a hoax.[7] Analysis was in its infancy too: Tanner and Wright were able to tell by an examination of the teeth that one body was between twelve and thirteen at the time of death and the other between nine and eleven. They could even tell that the elder child suffered from a painful condition of the jaw, probably the bone disease osteomyelitis. What they could not tell was the sex of the children, or the age of the bones.[8]

To be fair to Florescu and Rosetti, they probably intended to carry out further investigations into the Snagov bones. But this was not possible: the finds were placed in the History Museum in Bucharest, and, with the invasion of Romania by Hitler's Panzer Divisions in October 1940, a party of convicts was given the task of removing the Museum's contents for safekeeping to the mountains at Valeni de Murte, to be looked after by Nicolae Iorga, the country's foremost historian. Somewhere on the journey the finds disappeared, and despite rumours of their existence in various parts of the world, nothing has been forthcoming. In the 1980s, Dracula experts Raymond T. McNally and Radu R. Florescu approached the Romanian government to fund an American-Romanian archaeological team to continue where Rosetti and Florescu had left off in the 1930s. No serious reply was received.

It may be, as legend suggests, that the empty tomb in front of Snagov's altar originally did house Ţepeş' body and that it was removed to the door tomb or elsewhere for any number of reasons. A similar excavation was carried out years later at the Impaler's stronghold of Curtea de Argeş. Here, in the local church, it was the peasant tradition to light candles to the right of the altar only. Excavation has revealed the tomb of an earlier Wallachian prince there. Perhaps, then, Ţepeş' remains were removed by Orthodox priests appalled by the legend of the Impaler's cruelty or by the fact that he probably embraced the Catholic faith during his captivity in Hungary, if not earlier. Equally, it is possible that Ţepeş' body was allowed to rot in the forests where it lay. History, after all, is written by the victors. Richard III of England was hacked and stripped after Bosworth, and although he was eventually given a Christian burial, his body was dug up during the Reformation and his bones thrown into the River Soar in Leicester. In similar fashion, Oliver Cromwell, whose head, like the Impaler's, may or may not have been separated from his body, was disinterred two years after his death and the bones dragged through London's streets before finding a final unmarked resting place, probably somewhere under what today is Connaught Square. Given the Impaler's murderous reputation, at Snagov and throughout Wallachia, it was perhaps inevitable that his original tomb should be desecrated, or, at the very least, that the body should be moved.

But if the body at Snagov is that of Vlad the Impaler, how did it get there?

> Dracula's army began to kill [the Turks] and to pursue them without mercy. Then out of joy Dracula ascended a mountain in order to see how his men were killing the Turks. Detaching himself from the army, one of those around him, taking him for a Turk, hit him with a lance. Dracula, seeing that he was being attacked by his own men, immediately killed five of his assassins on the spot with his own sword. However, many arrows [another translation is lances] pierced him and he died in this manner.[9]

So runs the earliest Russian account of the death of Vlad Ţepeş. Its probable author was Fedor Kuritsyn, who arrived at the Court of King Matthias Corvinus at Buda in Hungary some time in the year 1482, as an envoy of Ivan III, Grand Duke of Muscovy. In many ways it is likely that Ivan's purpose in sending Kuritsyn was to open 'the window on the west', rather as Tsar Peter the Great was to do in 1689. The culture of the Renaissance, originating in Italy and spreading north and west to the rest of Europe, had reached Hungary by the middle of the fifteenth century; but it had not filtered further east. Ivan's nucleic state of Muscovy was to expand to become one of the greatest powers in the world by the twentieth century, but it needed friends in these early stages.

Probably working through an interpreter called Martinco, Kuritsyn mixed among the nobility in the court of Matthias Corvinus, and met the dead Impaler's widow and Mihnea, Vlad's eldest son by his previous marriage. Obsessed with the legends circulating about the Impaler, Kuritsyn visited Transylvania, where the man was born, and Wallachia, which he ruled, in a kind of fact-finding pilgrimage. He went to Braşov, whose townspeople Ţepeş had impaled in their thousands, and to Bistriţa, which also had reason to hate him. By the spring of 1484, Kuritsyn was at Suceava, capital of the Moldavian warlord (and Ţepeş' cousin), Stefan cel Mare (Stephen the Great).

Here the Russian envoy met not only Stefan, who had known Vlad Ţepeş since boyhood, but Maria Voichita, the daughter of the Impaler's brother, Rudolph the Handsome. Most importantly, Kuritsyn interviewed ten soldiers who had served with Stefan as the Impaler's Moldavian bodyguard near Bucharest eight years before at the time of the Impaler's death. It is likely that the account on page 10, with all its infuriating non-sequiturs, came from these soldiers and was included in the *Povest o Dracule* (The Story of Prince Dracula) in 1486. The actual document, now in Leningrad, is dated 1490 and was in fact drafted by Efrosin 'the sinner', a monk from the monastery of Kirillov-Belozersky who, judging by his comments, was less of a fan of Dracula than was Kuritsyn.

Another version of the Impaler's death comes from the Austrian chronicler, Jacob Unrest:

Dracula was killed with great cunning, because the Turks wished to avenge the enmity which he had borne against them for so long and also the great damages inflicted upon them. They hired a Turk as one of his servants with the mission of killing him while he served him. The Turk was apparently instructed to attack Dracula from the back. He was then to cut off his head and bring it back on horseback to the sultan.[10]

11

There is no clear evidence as to precisely where Vlad Ţepeş died. That it was near Bucharest and Snagov is certain, and the date was probably close to Christmas 1476. Legend has it that he died in a clearing in the dense forest of Vlasia, although mention of his having been killed on a mountain and his body having been found in a swamp does not accord.

The possible finding of his body by the monks of Snagov makes sense if Ţepeş died in battle. Routinely, after such clashes, it was the work of priests not only to bury the dead but to record the names of the famous who had fallen. No such listing exists for Vlad Ţepeş. The version that reached Frederick the Holy Roman Emperor in Vienna read, 'The captain named by King Matthias, Dracula, together with 4,000 men was butchered by the Turks.'[11] That number of corpses, even if not literally accurate, would have attracted the vultures that wheeled in the Carpathian skies. According to legend, the Impaler's body, pierced, bloody and headless, was carried through the forest and buried in the altar space of the church at Snagov; but who stripped the body of his armour, who washed the congealed wounds, who clothed the Impaler in the robes of the Order of the Dragon (if that was what they were) is not recorded.

In an age in which God's justice was still poetic and when 'murder will out', Ţepeş' end was almost preordained. In the Russian Orthodox accounts:

Dracula loved the sweetness of the earthly world much more than the eternal world, and he abandoned Orthodoxy and thereby forsook the truth and the light and accepted darkness.[12]

This book is an attempt to find that light and that truth again. It does so by peeling back the layers of legend to assess Vlad Ţepeş the man rather than Dracula the vampire monster.

# 2

# INTERVIEWS WITH VAMPIRES

We have seen that Vlad the Impaler, with his lance-riddled, headless corpse, has all the makings of the legendary Count created by Bram Stoker. The literary Dracula will be discussed in Chapter Three, but today's society, especially the young, reading less and watching more, have been brought up on a diet of films rather than books. The legend of the vampire has endured by adapting to new technology, and has once again leapt across time. The creature has become, in the words of vampire expert Tony Thorne, 'the shadowless, reflectionless, caped, fanged, garlic-and-crucifix-fearing, daylight-shunning cliché'.[1]

It is easy to see how, after his death, the Impaler transformed from tyrant to demon. His very name in Romanian, 'Dracula', means both son of the Dragon and son of the Devil, and his fearsome reputation as a slaughterer of thousands could easily be equated with the night-hunting demons that are part of Romania's folklore and spiritual past. Today's films, assuming that the celluloid Dracula is played out, inevitably veer away from the Count and his native Transylvania to create ever-more sophisticated variants on the vampire myth.

The best vampire films are based on novels or short stories, whereas it is the visual, overtly pornographic celluloid image that has most power over a modern audience. 'Video nasties' and 'shock horror' have long since replaced the 'penny dreadfuls' and the Gothic novel in the index of the macabre.

The most recent 'classic' of the vampire cinema is, arguably,

*Interview with the Vampire: the Vampire Chronicles*,[2] based on the novels of Anne Rice. Perhaps the most lavish 'dead undead' film to date, it focuses on the vampire Lestat, played by an elegantly pale Tom Cruise – 'exquisitely miscast' according to Thorne[3] – who takes us through two centuries of his 'life', centring on the murky night people of Paris and New Orleans.

'Drink from me and live forever' said the film's posters, but most critics were unimpressed by its intended longevity. The London *Evening Standard* wrote:

> For fear, it substitutes disgust. It's such a dishonest, hypocritical film. Largely an exercise in sado-masochism, it uses the traditional trappings of vampire legend as licence for its own fixation on an array of modern perversions it would be hard to get permission to show if they were performed in modern dress and contemporary times.[4]

Presumably the perversions that film critic Alexander Walker is referring to are the inevitable obsession with blood, the homoerotic subtext of the relationship between Cruise and Brad Pitt and the potential paedophilia involving the little girl vampire played by Kirsten Dunst. Interestingly, even though *Interview* does not feature Dracula at all, an even vaster array of perversions has been laid at the Impaler's door, as we shall see. Joe Queenan's comment was that the film was 'best thought of as a lycanthropic *The Odd Couple*', and it was noticeable that in the Academy Award and Bafta nominations, credit was given to the music and photography, not the writing, direction or performance.

The criticisms of *Interview* and the storyline of the film itself expose the problem for vampire film-makers in the twenty-first century: the audience has seen it all before and it is difficult to find anything new to say. With our jaded cinematic appetites, cloyed by years of television repeats and videos 'to rent and buy', are we seriously going to be frightened and shocked by a traditional vampire film? Directors and screenplay writers are, inevitably perhaps, bound to look for something else, something more pulse-quickening, to draw their audiences. If the straightforward bite to the neck no longer works, what if the bite belongs to Tom Cruise and the neck to Brad Pitt? The star element adds a dimension of the exotic and the forbidden which is actually an attempt to recreate the impact of Bram Stoker's original Dracula novel, and strangely takes us back to the repellent and shocking tales that were already circulating about the Impaler during his lifetime.

With this problem in mind, and moving back in time as we remove the layers of legend, film producers, mostly from Hollywood in the 1970s and '80s, created vampire stories that were modern in their setting, 'alongside the yuppie, the geek, the trailerpark and the shopping mall'.[5] *Interview*'s brooding nineteenth-century New Orleans backstreets have a sinister surrealism of their own, but that very surrealism means that it cannot frighten us in the same way as the folksy 1980s town of *Salem's Lot* or the tawdry fairground in *The Lost Boys*. And the ability to frighten lies at the heart of our understanding of Vlad Țepeș. Exaggerated though his crimes have been, there is no doubt that he used his shocking notoriety to establish and maintain his regime in Wallachia. For centuries, Romanian mothers have quieted their restless children with whispers of his name.

*Salem's Lot*,[6] originally a two-parter made for American television, was based on a novel by horror writer Stephen King and a screenplay by Paul Monash. The hero is a famous writer, played by David Soul, who returns to his home to find that it is infested with vampires, the undead victims of the mysterious Mr Barlow, a hideous gigantic ghoul brought to life by the sinister James Mason: 'You'll enjoy Mr Barlow – and he'll enjoy you.' Although it cannot compare with *Interview* in terms of budget or scope, *Salem's Lot* is a genuine attempt to implement the terror process by making the setting mundane. Bram Stoker did the same thing by bringing his undead Count to the prosaic Yorkshire fishing village of Whitby.

*The Lost Boys*,[7] whose screenplay is by Janice Fischer, James Jeremias and Jeffrey Boam, has as much to do with gang warfare, teenage status and the attention-seeking of

America's disaffected youth as with vampirism. As director Joel Schumacher said in an interview at the time of the film's opening:

> Vampires bring up a lot of stuff. In the Victorian period, when people lived such repressed lives, a lot of sexual fantasies were lived out through these stories. But I don't think our movie deals with any of those things at all. I think it just says, 'Hey! There are still Vampires, they just dress better!'[8]

However we rate *The Lost Boys* and *Salem's Lot*, both were serious attempts to return the concept of spine-chilling to a genre that was waning; a genre in which, without Dracula or the shadowy figure of the Impaler, the purpose was lost. Before these two films, as we peel back the layers of time, vampire film-makers had gone in two directions, the comic and the pornographic. In 1972 the first black horror film was made, with the Shakespearean actor William Marshal as *Blacula*.[9] The product of a pre-politically correct era, in which American Negro stars were big box office *because* they were black, the film attempted to link Transylvania in the early nineteenth century with an unlikely visit by an African prince to 1970s Los Angeles.

Going for the comic jugular with a more slapstick approach was Roman Polanski's *The Fearless Vampire Killers* or *Pardon Me Your Teeth Are In My Neck*,[10] released in 1967. *Halliwell's Film Guide* is dismissive: 'Heavy, slow spoof . . . most of which shows that sense of humour is very personal; a few effective moments hardly compensate for the prevailing stodge.'[11] The critic Tom Milne found the film 'an engaging oddity'; its blue screen Carpathian Mountains and polystyrene snow were certainly not to everyone's taste. Tony Thorne reminds us, however, that there is more to Polanski than this. The director had endured the horrors of a Nazi concentration camp as a child and two years after the release of *Vampire Killers*, its female lead (and Polanski's wife), Sharon Tate, would be decapitated by the deranged 'family' of serial killer Charles Manson. Her unborn baby died with her in a barrage of sixteen stab wounds eerily redolent of the impalements of Vlad Ţepeş. One of the killers, Tex Watson, said, appropriately, 'I am the devil come to do the devil's work.' Another, Susan Atkins, claimed to have drunk Sharon Tate's blood – 'It felt so good the first time I stabbed her. When she screamed at me, it did something to me, sent a rush through me and I stabbed her again . . . it was like a sexual release, especially when you see the blood. It's better than a climax.'[12] Although it is unlikely that Manson or his followers were sophisticated enough to equate Polanski's work with the deeds of the Impaler, the vicarious thrill of such blood letting and the notion of doing the devil's work have obvious echoes of Vlad Ţepeş.

Even more of a flop than *Vampire Killers* was *Dracula: Dead and Loving it*,[13] written by Mel Brooks on the strength of his hugely successful *Young Frankenstein*. 'You'll die laughing,' promised the film's hype, 'Then you'll rise from the dead and laugh once more.' Former 'heavy', turned comedian, Leslie Nielsen, starred as the Count, complete with ludicrous silver wig, and the plot was actually quite close to Bram Stoker's novel. *The Sunday Times* was unimpressed, finding it as 'thin as bat wing'.[14]

If comedy was not the natural home of the vampire film, what about pornography? There was certainly a pornographic element in Stoker's novel and in many of the literary works that preceded it. To many, the tortures enjoyed by Vlad Ţepeş have heavy erotic overtones, depending on the motives ascribed to them. Two vampire films in recent years had sections left on the cutting-room floor after the censors had taken over. Both from 1970 and considered pure sexploitation, *The Vampire Lovers*[15] and *Lust for a Vampire*[16] attempted to breathe titillation into a tired theme. *The Vampire Lovers*, directed by Roy Baker, was based, apart from the opening dream-like scene, entirely on Sheridan Le Fanu's *Carmilla*, which pre-dated Stoker's novel. It is worth remembering that before the vampire of fiction became 'distorted by the overwhelming influence of that middle-aged gentleman, Count Dracula,'[17] it was 'again as a *femme fatale*, a lady, that she was cast.'[18] Jimmy Sangster's *Lust for a*

*Vampire* was not actually a sequel to Baker's work, but it took the idea of vampire and sex-goddess a stage further.

Most of the sex-vampire films of the 1960s and '70s were French – such as Jean Rollin's *La Vampire Nue*, with its elements of nudity, blood and sadomasochism. We are increasingly drifting away here from that 'middle-aged gentleman' and still further from his fifteenth century original, but the films of the previous generation were altogether more faithful.

For many, the archetypal vampire films were made by the British company, Hammer, which by Hollywood standards was a tiny film studio, housed at Bray, on the Thames. The success of its vampire films turned Hammer into the biggest money-spinner in the British film industry. Founded in 1947, the studio specialized in low-budget B features, with a price tag of under £20,000. The stock sets were immediately recognizable, as was the stable of actors who filled the minor roles. The undoubted star of the Hammer series, however, was the 'tall, dark and gruesome' Christopher Lee, who first played Bram Stoker's malignant Count in *Dracula*[19] in 1958. Lee was a natural. As David Pirie writes,[20] Lee is:

> himself an aristocrat of Italian origin and claims to be able to trace his family tree back to the Emperor Charlemagne. His slightly demonic good looks and tall statuesque physique made him ideal for the role and after nearly ten years of supporting parts in movies, he put everything into it.

Lee himself sums up the cinematic Dracula brilliantly:

> He offers the illusion of immortality, the subconscious wish we all have for limitless power, a man of tremendous brain and physical strength with a strange dark heroism. He is either a reincarnation or he has never died. . . . He is a superman image with an erotic appeal for women who find him totally alluring. In many ways he is everything people would like to be, the anti-hero, the heroic villain . . . part saint and part sinner. Men find him irresistible because they

cannot stop him and, to women, he represents the complete abandonment to the power of a man.[21]

As horror expert Christopher Frayling put it in a Radio Scotland feature, *The Usual Suspects*, in December 1997:

> . . . gorgeous Christopher Lee coming slowly towards you across the carpet, with this incredible voice saying, 'I am here. You have called me, my dear, and I am here.' They [Dracula's victims] just throw back the covers and seem to say 'Have me! Have me!' And he does.[22]

Journalist and horror expert Basil Copper was particularly impressed by Lee's blood-filled eyeballs (a red contact lens technique which Lee himself thought overdone) and 'particularly his agonies in disintegration'.[23]

No less distinguished was Peter Cushing as Professor van Helsing, the vampire-hunter and a force for good, an altogether more suave character than Bram Stoker's creation, doomed to spend his life with immense courage and folkloric knowledge before driving the inevitable stake through Lee's heart. There were no official complaints about this violence in late '50s Britain, although audiences were equally thrilled and appalled by the erotic overtones of Lee sinking his fangs into all-too-welcoming throats and Cushing driving home his whitethorn spike with a mallet. 'Who will be his bride tonight?' the film's posters asked.

Of all the later productions on the vampire theme, *Dracula, Prince of Darkness*,[24] released in 1966, stands out. Film critic Judith Crist dismissed it at the time as 'run-of-the-coffin stuff . . . only for ardent fangs-and-cross fans', but this ignored the rather more tempestuous background to its creation. Lee was not keen to 'resurrect' the role eight years after his first appearance, but censorship problems also accrued. Richard Matheson's vampire novel, *I am Legend*, was due to be filmed by the company until the British Board of Film Censors warned that it would ban such a production if it went ahead. *Prince of Darkness* was therefore a much more timid effort than it might otherwise have been.

Vampire films have always walked a fine line, exemplified by the friction between mid-twentieth-century caution, even pomposity, of the BBFC and the boundary-pushing creativity of Hammer's boss, James Carreras, 'king of nausea'. The no-go areas for the BBFC in 1912, the year of its creation, were nudity and portrayals of Christ. In America things had been much more lax, but the Hays Office, a self-regulating studio watchdog, clamped down severely in the 1920s, so that, unusually, attitudes towards vampire films were more or less in accord on both sides of the Atlantic.

From where had Carreras, Fisher and Hammer obtained their inspiration? From Stoker, clearly, but a series of limp sequels throughout the 1930s and '40s were descendants of the best-known Dracula of them all, Bela Lugosi. As Basil Copper wrote:

[Lugosi's] Dracula . . . showed the powerful effect a serious approach to the vampiric could have on mass audiences. This, coupled with acting of integrity, impressive art work and the intelligent use of sound and atmosphere proved that the theme, though inherently distasteful to the person of average intelligence and sensibility, could thrill without becoming repulsive. This was an artistic approach which might well have been noted by those who followed.[25]

Hollywood's Universal Studio was then outside the giants of the industry, with only the critically acclaimed *All Quiet on the Western Front* to its recent credit. The cut-throat economic competition between West Coast studios in the mid-'20s and the potentially catastrophic advent of sound nearly broke the company, but its boss, the German immigrant Carl Laemmle, survived by making low-budget westerns and comedies, which played in the less prestigious theatres. Perhaps because of his mid-European background, Laemmle took the idea of the 1927 Broadway play *Dracula*, intending to give the lead to Lon Chaney, the most celebrated horror film star of his day. When Chaney died of cancer in 1930, actors Ian Keith, Conrad Veidt and William Powell were considered for the role before it was finally awarded to Lugosi, whose Broadway theatricality was transferred to celluloid.

Bela Lugosi Blaske has become a character of legend himself. He was probably born in 1884 in Lugoj, in the Banat region of Romania (then a Hungarian province) and was brought up in Hungary, arriving in America some time in 1919. The fact that the character of Dracula was played by a Hungarian outraged patriotic Romanians in 1931. He claimed to have been a Hussar officer in the Austro-Hungarian army, but this is unsubstantiated. His English was poor and in minor parts, as in MGM's *The Thirteenth Chair*, he had to learn his lines phonetically and clearly often had no real understanding of what he was saying. He was admirable, however, in introducing pure Transylvanian evil to American audiences. As Tony Thorne nicely observes:

> The Magyar actor actually brought a little bit of Hungary to Hollywood, itself a place that was deliberately and wilfully ignorant of the rest of the planet, even though many of its founders were refugees from the Vampire's homelands.

Lugosi's delivery of 'I am Dracula. I bid you welcome'[26] has been much parodied over the years, contrasting sharply with Christopher Lee's public school sang-froid and also with Stoker's original,[27] in which a much more subtle Dracula shakes Jonathan Harker's hand, saying 'Welcome to my house. Come freely. Go safely. And leave something of the happiness you bring.'

Because of the power of the stage-play and the problems of censorship in what was, after all, a delicate area of sexual seduction,[28] much of the real action happens off set, with creepy shadows, cobwebbed vaults and bat motifs in abundance. Basil Copper wrote:

> The opening of the production could hardly be bettered; the Count's lair, the dark, malodorous vaults, with the camera passing slowly past the melancholy scene . . . bones

protruding from a shattered coffin; a rat gnawing listlessly at them . . . the coffin-lid lifts, a hand gropes. . . .

Thanks to Garrett Ford's clumsy screenplay and Lugosi's own limitations as an actor, there is little ambiguity and very little charm. As David Pirie rightly says:

He [Lugosi] is a thug and as such his capacity to threaten is drastically limited . . . His exaggerated gestures and diction stand out with dazzling clarity from the pale and more modern shadows with which he is surrounded, making that looming malevolent shape into the ultimate stereotype of all heavies. As a personality, as a phenomenon, as a star, he was remarkable. As an influence on the emergent horror film, struggling for freedom from stage melodrama, he was disastrous.[29]

There are fascinating echoes here of the real Vlad Ţepeş, whom many historians have dismissed as merely a 'thug'. This assessment, as we shall see, is naïve: the Impaler's 'capacity to threaten' was enormous.

Like many associated with the name of Dracula, Lugosi's career went downhill after making the film. Trapped in the ultimate of stereotypes, he resorted to recreating the Count (with no venom at all) in silly comedies like *Abbott and Costello Meet Frankenstein* in 1948 and *Old Mother Riley Meets the Vampire* in 1952. He claimed to be a heart-throb in his native Budapest, although there is no evidence for this, and he died a largely forgotten morphine addict in 1956, the year in which his native country attempted to throw off the yoke of Russian Communism. He had pleaded to be taken into care while still continuing to play small parts in minor films, virtually sleepwalking through the scenes. He was buried in the black, scarlet-lined cloak he had worn in *Dracula*. Reputed to have made over $600,000 from his film career, Lugosi died with only $3,000 to his name.[30]

The directorial creator of the Lugosi film was Todd Browning, who had worked with Lon Chaney and others in the silent-film industry. Browning was a cinematic genius in his own right, but he was working in the decade that produced the first,[31] best and still the most truly frightening vampire film ever made, *Nosferatu*.

What terrifies in this film is the central performance delivered by Max Schreck. Because 'Schreck' means 'fright' and the actor was so heavily made up, it was assumed for years that his was a one-off creation; and, like Lugosi, Schreck became as much a legend as the Count himself. In fact, Schreck had appeared in a number of other classics of the German silent cinema, though never with such effect. David Pirie explains our fascination with the man:

> The well-groomed, demonic vampire of Stoker [and one might add of Lugosi and Lee] is transformed into a skeletal, contorted monster, who shuffles with senile purpose in and out of frame . . . He resembles an animated corpse . . . the long fingers tapering away into little sticks of bone and nail; the broad, domed, hairless scalp with grotesquely pale skin; the mongoloid pointed ears, staring eyes and gap-toothed mouth.

Klaus Kinski's recreation of this role in 1979 in *Nosferatu the Vampyre*,[32] although stylish and slick, does not hold a candle to the original.

There is little of Stoker and nothing of the Lugosi/Lee tradition in *Nosferatu*. The vampire of folklore[33] has no shadow and no reflection: Schreck has both. There is no billowing cloak, there are no bloody fangs and almost no sexual atmosphere at all. Yet Schreck is compelling, unutterably creepy, to the extent that the recently made *Shadow of the Vampire*,[34] a fascinating movie about the making of *Nosferatu*, has Willem Dafoe as Schreck actually *being* a vampire.

In some ways, *Nosferatu* was a typical film of its time. It was made cheaply and quickly by the Prana Company of Berlin, at a time when that city was in a state of anarchy as a result of a lost war, the grip of economic chaos and the street-fighting engendered by the Kapp Putsch. Chaotic, demoralized Germany longed for escapism from the reality of

Weimar, and silent greats such as *Waxworks, Metropolis* and *The Cabinet of Dr Caligari* fed this need. *Nosferatu*, the work of director F.W. Murnau and photographed by Fritz Wagner and Gunther Krampf, was of the same stable, although its sets lacked the power of those mentioned above.

It was the links with Dracula that caused Murnau and the Prana Studios the greatest problems. Although 'the Count' is called Orlock and his coffin-laden ship puts into the German port of Bremen rather than the Yorkshire port of Whitby, its uncredited similarities to Bram Stoker's novel were sufficient to infuriate his widow, Florence, who promptly set out on the litigation warpath.

Realizing the extent of Prana's plagiarism two months after the film's release in March 1922, Florence successfully challenged the studio, which kept appeals going for three years before declaring bankruptcy. In July 1925, a destruction order was passed on all copies of the film; despite this, prints made from an original negative were being shown in American cinemas four years later. The irony is that Florence Stoker had no real objection to her husband's work being filmed. She gave the green light to Hamilton Deane's Broadway play in 1927, and is believed to have approved Lugosi's film version four years after that. What annoyed her was that Henrik Galeen's script had taken liberties with the original and made no reference to Bram Stoker anywhere.

Before *Nosferatu*, there were perhaps a dozen vampire films, some of which have survived the ravages of time, damp, dust and studio collapse. There are twenty-four such survivals made between 1896 (*The Devil's Castle*) and 1922 (*The Blonde Vampire*). Most of these, however, were a mish-mash of horror, and the 'vamp' was a heroine of the type made famous by the actress Theda Bara, a *femme fatale* intent on seducing men rather like the succubus of witchcraft and demonology. The film poster for Bara's *The Kiss of the Vampire* (1916) read, 'She just wanted to ruin her victims and then laugh at them. She was bad!'

Daniel Farson wrote of female vampires:

She is described as voluptuous and wanton, irresistible, heartlessly cruel. Like the male vampire, she has full red lips – supposedly the result of sucking blood, but also traditionally regarded . . . as a sign of excessive sensuality. Even the pure must succumb to her macabre charms.[35]

Before the invention of moving pictures, Dracula was played many times on stage. Inevitably, the anti-hero is essentially Stoker's and bears as little relation to Vlad Ţepeş as his celluloid counterpart.

The most famous portrayal of Dracula on stage was the one first performed in the rather unlikely setting of the Grand Theatre in Derby, in June 1924. An Irish actor-manager, Hamilton Deane, had been trying for years to turn his friend Bram Stoker's novel into a play, and eventually did so himself. His Count was the 22-year-old Raymond Huntley, a regular and reliable British film and television actor for many years afterwards. Deane himself played van Helsing, but Huntley was most impressed by the actor playing Renfield, an inmate from an asylum who falls under the Count's hypnotic spell: 'The outstanding performance . . . I would say, was that of an actor named Bernard Jukes – since dead – who played the fly-eating lunatic.'[36] As the curtain fell on the first night, Deane himself appeared front of house to send a suitable chill up the spines of the departing audience, saying, 'Remember, there are such things.'[37] With success on his hands, on St Valentine's Day 1927 Deane took the play to the Little Theatre, London, where it enjoyed one of the longest runs in theatrical history. For the Broadway version, American writer John L. Balderstone collaborated with Deane – although some accounts claim the two men detested each other – and the show opened at the Shubert Theatre, New Haven, Connecticut in the September of the same year. After Broadway, it toured the States for two years with Lugosi in the lead role, breaking all previous records.[38]

Attempts to make films of the *real* Dracula, Vlad Ţepeş, the Impaler, have appeared only rarely in the West. An interesting piece, *In Search of Dracula*, was made in 1972, with Christopher Lee looking very like the descriptions and portraits of Vlad with his well-known scarlet cap and sweeping black moustaches. But this was a documentary, interspersed with scenes from various Hammer versions, and was quite surreal. A version of Vlad's life was made, probably in Germany, in 1920 but it has not survived and we had to wait until 1992 for *Bram Stoker's Dracula*[39] to make its appearance. Francis Ford Coppola directed Gary Oldman as the Count, but in this version the action starts in wartorn fifteenth-century Wallachia, with Oldman as the Impaler cursing God and becoming a vampire as a result. Over a map of Wallachia and Transylvania, the shadow of the crescent thrusts north-west and a narration tells us of 'A Romanian knight of the Sacred Order of the Dragon, known as Dracula.' In a surreal battle sequence, with silhouettes against a fire-red sky, Oldman's Dracula skewers and impales Turks with his lance. His wife, given the fictional name Elizabeta, believing her husband has been killed, commits suicide by flinging herself from her castle tower into the river below.

Speaking Romanian and furious that Elizabeta is dead, Dracula renounces God, hacking his priests to death in front of an altar and vowing, 'I shall rise from my own death.' He drinks a chalice of the blood that is now flowing freely from the crucifix on the altar, and the credits roll – '*Bram Stoker's Dracula*' – even though nothing we have seen so far has anything to do with Bram Stoker.

The film flashes forward four hundred years, by which time Oldman had transformed into the better-known Count, complete with black cape and rather ludicrous Leslie Nielsen-style silver wig. His accent is pure Lugosi, however, and there is something quietly sinister in his delivery. We hear the wolves howling as he turns to the camera with the inevitable, 'Ah, the children of the night.'

*Dark Prince: The Legend of Dracula* (2001) is of a different genre altogether. It is not a vampire film at all, but an attempt to portray the life of the Impaler as authentically as appeals to a modern audience will allow. Written intelligently by Tom Baum, and directed by Joe Chappelle, the storyline remains true to the various legends of Vlad Țepeș, and was filmed on location in Romania with its idyllic, painted churches and the brooding majesty of its mountains.

Much of the film is in flashback, with a smoulderingly handsome (but amazingly clean-shaven!) Rudolf Martin as Dracula, explaining to a tribunal of the Orthodox Church that he is, in fact, more sinned against than sinning. We are introduced to Vlad Dracul, Dracula's father, and his slippery younger brother, Radu. The circumstances of the brothers' imprisonment by the Turks are inaccurate, but intriguingly we see our first impaled victim in the Turkish camp.

Sultan Murad, slicing Radu's chest with a dagger and licking his blood, displays homosexual leanings towards the boy (which has some basis in fact, although in connection to his son Mehmed), and Dracula is allowed to return to Wallachia, determined to take revenge on the treacherous boyars (nobles) who killed his father by burying him alive.

Snagov monastery is correctly shown on a lake, and the famous legends of the golden cup, the feast of the boyars and the nailing of the Turkish emissaries' turbans to their heads are all portrayed. Even János Hunyadi, king of Hungary (an unlikely role for former Who singer Roger Daltry) is shown in his ambiguous relationship with Vlad, although his son Matthias Corvinus, who actually imprisoned Dracula in the 1460s, is not mentioned at all.

The love interest is provided by Lydia, the daughter of a double-dealing Wallachian boyar, her marriage to Dracula, the birth of their son and her suicide – she leaps to her death because she cannot live with his barbaric cruelty. Dracula consistently denies committing the excesses with which he is usually credited, but one of the nastiest scenes in the film is the famous story of his eating a meal, surrounded by the dying victims of his impalement. Filmed under a cloudless blue sky, with the flies of summer droning around the still-bleeding corpses, the scene has an air of grim reality.

Far more evil than Dracula, who is ambiguously portrayed as either messiah (the patriotic Romanian version) or anti-Christ (the view of the rest of the world), is Stefan, the Orthodox priest who, we learn, has spent years trying to kill Dracula because he believes him to be the anti-Christ. In the film it is Stefan who engineers Vlad Dracul's death and conspires with Radu and the Turks to bring Dracula down. Vlad is finally killed in the monastery at Snagov, but reappears 'incorrupt and entire' as a result of being excommunicated by Stefan, and so unfit to rest in a Christian grave.

Most examples from the Vampire cinema have Dracula as their central character. Whether he is villain or hero, messiah or anti-Christ, and whatever the role of van Helsing is in relation to him, is still a subject for debate. For both viewers and film-makers, Dracula is the archetypal vampire of the silver screen; but his immediate origins lie in the literature of an Irish civil servant turned theatrical agent, Abraham Stoker.

# 3

# BRAM STOKER'S DRACULA

Abraham Stoker is the unlikely creator of one of the world's most enduring monsters. He was born in 1847 in Clontarf, County Dublin, the son of a third-class clerk in the Chief Secretary's office in Dublin Castle; the family was thus rooted in the Protestant Ascendancy that continued to dominate Irish history until the Troubles and partition in the years following the First World War. Ireland was a land of country estates, owned by often-absentee English landlords, whose affairs were run by less-than-scrupulous bailiffs. Three years before Stoker's birth, a blight had hit the staple potato crop so that the 'praties' turned black and spongy in the ground. The result was famine, an estimated one million dead from starvation and disease, a further million leaving the land through emigration, mostly to the United States, Canada and mainland Britain. Devastation on this scale has no parallel in recent western history, and the Irish were numbed as a result. When Stoker was a year old, William Smith O'Brien's 'rebellion' in Dublin turned out to be an ill-planned and half-hearted affair, a pale shadow of earlier attempts to throw off the English yoke, and easily controlled by army patrols. Many fighting men were dead or had emigrated, nursing their grievances like bloody wounds.

As was not unusual in the Victorian period, Stoker's father was considerably older than his mother (a pattern he would repeat in his own marriage). Abraham senior was forty-eight when his third child was born, and his wife, Charlotte, thirty. All Stoker's brothers became doctors, William, the eldest, being knighted for his services to surgery in 1895. Charlotte was an inveterate charity worker, visiting workhouses and supporting women's rights at the dawn of feminist militancy.

For the first six years of his life, Stoker was largely bed-ridden, and as a child found walking difficult. In view of his robust adulthood, it is possible that the cause was psychosomatic. But his affliction may have led to his passion for reading: he certainly immersed himself in Gaelic folklore, with its female vampires, the *Leannan-sidhe*.[1]

At Trinity College, Dublin, Stoker obtained an Honours degree in Mathematics, became president of the Philosophical Society and won the college's athletic championship. He also met Oscar Wilde and was a frequent visitor at Wilde's parents' house in Merrion Square. Called to both Irish and English bars, Stoker rather prosaically followed both his father and grandfather into service at Dublin Castle – 'the gingerbread castle of the viceroy', as Christopher Frayling calls it.[2] Here he worked as a junior civil servant, and his first book, taking for its subject *The Duties of the Inspector in Petty Sessions*, was published in December 1879. It really is as dull as it sounds and serves to point up the curious paradox of the Count's creator. How could the man who wrote *Dracula* have written this?

Two years earlier, Stoker had met the actor Henry Irving, an encounter that undoubtedly changed his life. Part of Stoker's curious personality is that he seemed intent on courting the attentions of men whose standing was truly great, drawing on their skills in the way a vampire drains his victims. For years he carried on a correspondence with the American poet and pacifist Walt Whitman, whose literary output at the time included subjects like homosexuality, which were taboo in nineteenth-century America and Britain.[3]

Irving had been a clerk in his early life, as had Whitman and Stoker, but had first trod the boards in Sunderland when Stoker was nine. His London debut was made at the St James's Theatre in 1866, but his Shakespearean triumphs at the Lyceum – *Hamlet* (1874), *Macbeth* (1875) and *Othello* (1876) – made him the greatest tragedian of his generation. Even so, when Stoker gave up the Dublin castle post to become his manager at the Lyceum, his mother was appalled. His pension had gone and he now worked for a 'strolling player'. The acting profession had supposedly been made respectable by David Garrick a century earlier, but Charlotte Stoker's attitude is proof enough that there were those who were less than impressed. Until the 1820s 'strolling players' risked a six-month jail sentence.

Stoker's career took another direction in 1878. He married the 'exquisitely pretty' Florence Balcombe, formerly Oscar Wilde's sweetheart and, many years later, the woman who would make life difficult for F.W. Murnau and the Prana Studio over copyright issues in *Nosferatu*. Their only child, Noel, was born a year later. Florence was the darling not only of literati like Wilde and Stoker, but artists like Burne-Jones and Walter Osborne, anxious to capture her Pre-Raphaelite, *fin de siècle* beauty.[4]

*Dracula* was seven years in the making, and was in many ways the culmination of the short stories on supernatural themes that Stoker had begun writing in the '70s. The first of these, *The Chain of Destiny*, appeared as a four-parter in *The Shamrock* in 1875 and was very much in the mode of his later short stories like *The Burial of Rats* and *The Judge's House*, published posthumously by Florence in 1914. These were overripe tales that would seem ludicrous today, although some writers place Stoker as a 'minor master' in the field. The 1890s has the reputation of being a 'naughty' decade, one that saw homosexual charges brought against Oscar Wilde, the illicit publication of the sexual 'biography' *Walter: My Secret Life* and a decadence which would resurface in Weimar Germany twenty years later to produce the extraordinary cinematic offerings of directors like Murnau.

What strikes one as odd, even parochial, about *Dracula* is Stoker's use of the minutiae of his own life. His family holidays in Cruden Bay, Scotland, and Whitby, Yorkshire, all eventually found their way into the book. He made copious notes and buried himself in local libraries, soaking up the legends and folklore of each area. Significantly, F.K. Robinson's *Glossary of Words Used in the Neighbourhood of Whitby* gave him 'barguests':

Terrifying apparitions, taking shape human or animal . . . some say barguest signifies castle-spectre . . . whether dog or demon, glares with large eyes 'like burning coals' . . . it is a harbinger of death to those who happen to hear its shrieks in the night.[5]

This was an era of heightened interest in the supernatural. The Victorian fad for spiritualism was waning and would not be resurrected until the appalling slaughter of the Western Front left families desperate for contact with their dead loved ones. The controversy over burial versus cremation was all but resolved, and the fascination with expensive, black-robed funerals was in decline, but the sinister and the macabre were still as popular as ever, as the ghost stories of M.R. James and Algernon Blackwood suggest. It may well be that for Stoker, *Dracula* had its origins in the over-generous helping of dressed crab he had for supper, which he believed gave him nightmares in 1890; but it was the whole fascination with the unknown that led to the full-blown novel.

Originally called *The Dead Undead*, the book was published as *Dracula* by Constable in June 1897. It had a print run of 3,000 and was priced at six shillings. Its reissue in 1901 was in the form of a sixpenny paperback with a yellow cover and a truly bad drawing of a cloaked, white-haired count descending a tower in Castle Dracula. Charlotte Stoker raved over the first edition:

My dear, it is splendid, a thousand miles beyond anything you have written before and I feel certain will place you very high in the writers of the day . . . No book since Mrs Shelley's *Frankenstein* [see below] or indeed any other at all has come near yours in originality or terror – Poe[6] is nowhere. I have read much but I have never met a book like it at all. In its terrible excitement it should make a widespread reputation and much money for you.[7]

The book's narrative has a surprisingly modern feel, expressed through the journal jottings of several of the main characters, all of them reacting to the fiendish Count himself.

Jonathan Harker, the solicitor's clerk, goes to Castle Dracula in Transylvania to conclude a property purchase of Carfax Abbey on behalf of the Count. While there, he learns that Dracula is a vampire – one of the undead – and is imprisoned while the Count sails for England. When the ship arrives, drifting into Whitby harbour, all the crew are dead, except of course for the Count, asleep in his coffin below deck. Dracula vampirizes Lucy Westernra, the flirtatious friend of Harker's fiancée, Mina Murray, and despite the efforts of Lucy's three suitors and the return of Jonathan from Transylvania, they cannot save the girl who haunts Highgate Cemetery in search of lost souls. Even the learned Professor van Helsing cannot prevent this, but concentrates instead on saving Mina from Dracula's attentions. Pursuing the monster back to Transylvania, van Helsing, Harker and Lucy's suitors drive a stake through Dracula's heart and lift the terrifying curse as the Count's body crumbles to dust.

As with the later landmark vampire films, the critics' reception of Stoker's book was less than adulatory. *The Athenaeum* found the book 'wanting in the constructive art as well as in the higher literary sense'. *Punch* wrote that it was 'the very weirdest of weird tales'. The *Bookman* damned with faint praise – 'we read nearly the whole with rapt attention'.[8] Thirty years later, occultist Montague Summers found the first sixty pages the best, believing that:

> many pages could have been compressed . . . It is hardly possible to feel any great interest in the characters; they are labels rather than individuals.[9]

Like any literary work that has caught the public imagination and survived, *Dracula* has been dissected over and over again, and meanings given to its passages that Bram Stoker probably never intended. Maurice Richardson sums up best, perhaps: *Dracula* is 'a kind of incestuous, necrophiliac, oral-anal-sadistic all-in wrestling match'.[10] Christopher Frayling notes that it is possible to interpret the story in a variety of ways, as Freudian allegory, Marxist 'cosmic racial conflict', feminist gender politics and so on. The literary expert James Twitchell[11] wrote that *Dracula* was successful because it represented:

> sex without genitalia, sex without confusion, sex without responsibility, sex without guilt, sex without love – better yet, sex without mention.[12]

Stoker's own sexuality is a blank page. The gorgeous and adorable Florence seems to have withdrawn her favours after Noel's birth; this may have sent Bram into the beds of a number of young actresses keen to secure plum roles at the Lyceum. The late Dan Farson, himself a descendant of Stoker's, claimed in his biography of his forebear that the theatrical agent died of tertiary syphilis. A more recent biography by Barbara Bedford doubts this. The death certificate, issued on 20 April 1912, days after the legendary *Titanic* went down, clearly says 'locomotor ataxia' which is consistent with the strokes he had suffered in the weeks before his death. Stoker died at home, and there are no other medical records surrounding his last illness, but Farson contends that 'locomotor ataxia' is Edwardian medical-speak for syphilis, in that its euphemistic vagueness covers a multitude of sins and that polite society was just too nice to be more specific. If Farson is right, then Bram Stoker, like F.W. Murnau, killed in a car crash in Hollywood, and Bela Lugosi, a shadow of his former success, is another victim of the curse of Dracula. Tony Thorne wonders whether either the 'closet homosexual' or 'duplicitous, syphilitic frequenter of prostitutes' portrayal of Stoker is correct, seeing him more as a rather dull, hard-working family man. In a BBC broadcast for Radio Scotland,[13] Christopher Frayling had an altogether more interesting view:

> There isn't a single photo of Bram Stoker smiling . . . but there's something going on underneath. There's something about Bram Stoker that doesn't quite fit. None of the biographies have cracked him . . . They are the eyes of a frightened man.[14]

In one respect, Stoker's mother was wrong in the letter she wrote to him shortly after *Dracula*'s publication. The book did not make him a fortune. He left only £4,700 in his will – a comfortable sum, certainly, but not what Charlotte Stoker would have expected. Never again would her son produce anything as successful as *Dracula* and not even he could accept, hand on heart, her comparison with Mary Shelley. The reality was that Stoker's upbringing and contacts had paved the way for *Dracula* over the course of a lifetime.

One of the most important of these contacts in our search for the real Vlad Ţepeş was Hermann Bamburger, who used a number of aliases but is usually (and briefly) referred to in the Stoker biographies as the orientalist Arminius Vambery. He appears in an aside of van Helsing's in *Dracula* itself: 'I have asked my friend Arminius, of Buda-Pesth University . . . he must indeed have been that Vovode Dracula who won his name against the Turk.'[15] Vambery was born to orthodox Jewish parents in March 1831, four hundred years after Dracula, in the village of St Georghem, then in Hungary. Short, and, like the earlier 'vampire', Lord Byron (see below), with a serious limp, he was a diligent, parsimonious social-climber and an incurable name-dropper. He was also a gifted linguist, possibly fluent in at least sixteen languages and he travelled widely throughout Afghanistan and Turkestan, invariably with a donkey and disguised as a Dervish, using the name of Hadji Rashid. He had no sense of humour, bore grudges and got progressively more tetchy as he got older.

He reached London in 1864 and promptly fell in love with the city, Britain and its Empire. His travelogues were hugely popular in an era when such books were snapped up, as were his two autobiographies. His lecture tours, too, were sell-outs. Although, he advised the nascent British secret service on matters relating to Russian aggression in Turkestan, it is unlikely he was a 'spy' in the usual sense of the term. Vambery first met Stoker at Sandringham in April 1889, where both men, together with Henry Irving, were the weekend guests of the Prince of Wales, whose favourite country house Sandringham was. A whole chapter on Vambery duly appeared in Stoker's biography of Irving in 1906.

Much of the correspondence between the two men has been lost to time, but it is likely that Vambery discussed his native Hungary with Stoker and probably suggested the books he should consult in the reading room of the British Museum when researching the background to his novel. Emily Gerard's *Land Beyond the Forest* (1888), for instance, gave Stoker the physical decription of Transylvania that he needed – as Christopher Frayling has remarked, Stoker himself 'never went further East than Whitby'.[16] Vambery was working in October 1889 on the papers of Matthias Corvinus, the Hungarian king who imprisoned Vlad Dracula in the 1460s. *The Times* wrote:

> The Hungarian commission, which has been sent to Constantinople with Professor Arminius Vambery to explore the archives of the Imperial Library, has already made the important discovery of three volumes which belonged to the library of Matthias Corvinus.[17]

It is likely that Vambery also suggested that Stoker read William Wilkinson's *Account of the Principalities of Wallachia and Moldavia*, written in 1820 when Wilkinson was British Consul in Bucharest. This book, in turn, was based on Oxford scholar Richard Knolles's work *The Generall History of the Turkes* (1603), in which the 'notable but cruell prince' Vlad Dracula receives several pages of description. Vambery may well have pointed Stoker in the direction of the English translation of Sebastian Munster's *Cosmographia*, a sixteenth-century 'best-seller' which talked of 'der streng ja tyranisch man Dracula'.[18] Vambery's colleague at Budapest and at Constantinople was Dr Franknoi, an acknowledged expert on the reign of Matthias Corvinus and the Draculas of Wallachia.

Stoker gave only the barest essentials of Vlad Ţepeş' history in his novel. He may have been intrigued by the name Dracula or Vambery's stories of barbarous cruelty that were associated with it, but the fact that his description of Vlad's lineage is reasonably accurate indicates that he intended his undead Count to be associated with the Impaler himself.

We know from Stoker's notes, preserved in the Rosenbach Museum in Philadelphia, that he originally meant to set the story, not in Vambery's Hungary or Emily Gerard's Transylvania, but in Styria, in his day a duchy in the Austro-Hungarian Empire. He was intrigued by this area, which he had read about in J. Sheridan Le Fanu's famous story, *Carmilla*.

Joseph Sheridan Le Fanu was a grand-nephew of the playwright and Whig acolyte, Richard Sheridan, and was born into the same Protestant Ascendancy as Stoker, but in 1814, when Robert Peel was Chief Secretary for Ireland. Sheridan's brother, William Richard Le Fanu, was Commissioner of Public Works at Dublin Castle during Stoker's father's time. His son, Thomas, worked in the office next to Bram Stoker's, and the aspiring novelist published his first short story, *The Crystal Cup*, in the *Dublin Evening Mail*, of which Sheridan Le Fanu had been editor. It was while Stoker was still at university that he read *Carmilla*, in which the vampire is a female and a lesbian, Countess Karnstein. Stoker must have been impressed by this, not only considering Le Fanu's Styria for his *Dracula* setting, but keeping the same sense of dreamy *ennui* used by Le Fanu: 'Think me not cruel,' [says Carmilla] 'because I obey the irresistible law of my strength and weakness . . . In the rapture of my enormous humiliation, I live in your warm life and you shall die – die, sweetly die – into mine.'[19]

It is likely that Le Fanu, like Stoker, was familiar with the Irish Gaelic folklore of the *Leannan-sidhe*, but other literary forces were at work on him as an impressionable young man.

*Varney the Vampire or the Feast of Blood* hit a horror-hungry public in the winter of 1846, when potato famine was ravaging Ireland. England was shaken by the repeal of the infamous Corn Laws and the collapse of Robert Peel's government. It was a hungry time in every sense, with unemployment barely under control and gangs of navvies roaming the countryside building thousands of miles of track in what was erupting as 'railway mania'.

The authorship of *Varney* is still in dispute a century and a half later. One tradition holds that it is the work of Thomas

Preskett Prest, a hack who churned out dozens of novels, some of them over a thousand pages long, with delectable titles such as *The Goblet of Gore*, *The Skeleton Clutch* and *The Secret of the Grey Turrett*. Even so, Prest's name is known today for the creation of *Sweeney Todd*, the Demon Barber of Fleet Street. Another contender for the authorship of *Varney* is James Malcolm Rymer, a Scottish engineer who turned to the lurid 'penny dreadfuls' of his day as a potentially more lucrative career. Writing in *The Vampire* in 1928, occultist Montague Summers expressed no doubts at all on the authorship: 'Who Rymer might be I cannot tell. *Varney the Vampire* was written by Thomas Preskett Prest.'[20] Also known as Errym and Merry (by which we may conclude that *all* the variants are pseudonyms) Rymer was paid one penny per line by his publishers, Edward Lloyd of Shoreditch. His description of the vampire has rather more in common with Schreck's Orlock than Stoker's Dracula:

> The figure turns half round and the light falls upon the face. It is perfectly white – perfectly bloodless. The eyes look like polished tin; the lips are drawn back and the principal feature next to those dreadful eyes is the teeth – the fearful-looking teeth – projecting like those of some wild animal, hideously, glaringly white and fang-like. It approaches the bed with a strange, gliding movement. It clashes together the long nails that literally hang from the finger ends. No sound comes from its lips. Is she going mad – that young and beautiful girl exposed to so much terror?[21]

Bram Stoker was born in the year that *Varney*'s 868 pages and 220 chapters beguiled a fascinated readership. Sheridan Le Fanu was already thirty-two. And whether it was Prest or Rymer who penned *Varney*, the author was working in the teeth of fierce criticism from the more sophisticated middle classes who worried that the 'penny dreadful' posed dangers to an easily seduced youth. The Dime Novel in America and the Newgate Novel in Britain were believed to have the same effect – they were the 'video nasties' of their day.

If we go back in time to before the publication of *Varney*, we have a number of writers using the term or the idea of the vampire. In America, Edgar Allen Poe introduced readers to a succession of female vampires without using the word vampire at all. Ligeia, Marella, Berenice and Madeleine Usher all fell into the succubi category, female spirits who seduced men as they slept, while in France, Théophile Gautier introduced a female vamp in *La Morte Amoreuse*, in 1836. Alexandre Dumas *père* set his *Pale Faced Lady* in the Carpathian Mountains, within whose 'horseshoe' Stoker would build Castle Dracula sixty years later. In Britain, Charlotte Brontë's Bertha Rochester is described as 'that foul German spectre – the Vampyre'.[22]

Interestingly, consciously or otherwise, these writers were drawing on older traditions still, particularly the Byronic vampire created by Dr John Polidori.

Europe opened its ports again after Napoleon Bonaparte's defeat at Waterloo. Tourists, intrigued to see what had become of Paris in the days of the 'beast', flocked to the French capital and beyond. A rather unlikely group of rebel poets and their entourages ventured further east, through the Swiss Alps to Italy, and, more specifically, to the Villa Diodati in the shadow of the 'haunted' Jura Mountains. The events of the night of 16 June 1816 have assumed a terror of their own, culminating in the *film noir Gothic* directed by Ken Russell and dubbed by one critic 'the thinking man's *Nightmare on Elm Street*'.[23] Staying first at the Hôtel d'Angleterre, the company rented a number of villas on the shores of Lake Geneva, but it was at the Diodati that the famous thunderstorm kept the group indoors. Trying to outscare each other like the overgrown schoolboys they were, Byron and Shelley decided to write ghost stories, building on the literary traditions of the Sensational and Gothic novels still in vogue.

George Gordon, the sixth Baron Byron, would probably have been taken into care had he been born today. On the poet's death, the artist John Constable wrote, 'The world is rid of him, but the deadly slime of his touch still remains.' Byron's father was the feckless, eccentric Captain 'Mad Jack' Byron, a compulsive gambler who had blown his own and his wife's fortune by the time the future poet was born. His mother, Catherine, was a bitter and vulgar woman given to fits of violent temper that left their mark on young George. Educated at Harrow and Trinity College, Cambridge, the young man led the life of a Georgian rake, excelling at swimming and boxing, and (perhaps unusually then for a Cambridge undergraduate) read voraciously. In 1809, despite the war raging across the continent, Byron, with poems already published in the influential *Edinburgh Review*, went on the grand tour, that strange blend of culture, drinking and sex which served as a rite of passage for many young men of the aristocracy and gentry. While soaking up the sights and culture of Spain, Malta, the Southern Balkans and the Aegean, he wrote *Childe Harold*, and returned as a gloomy man of mystery, impressing large numbers of fluttering ladies of society with his pronounced limp and striking good looks. The darling of London society in the days of the Prince Regent, he famously jilted the unbalanced Lady Caroline Lamb, married and left Anne Millbank, a wealthy heiress, and got out of England amid rumours of sexual flings with Augusta Leigh, his half-sister. He was known to have experimented in homosexual behaviour. It was in these enforced travels that he reached Diodati, where he met Shelley.

Percy Shelley was in his own way as subversive and rebellious a character as Byron. 'Mad Shelley', the 'Eton Atheist', wrote a Gothic novel in 1810 and at University College, Oxford, dressed and behaved outrageously before his expulsion from the university for publishing the pamphlet *The Necessity of Atheism* in 1811. Eloping with sixteen-year-old Harriet Westbrook, he wandered the Lake District, advocating Catholic Emancipation and falling in love with Mary Godwin. She, too, was sixteen and they, too, eloped before returning to London to face financial disaster. But they were on the road again by 1816 and had reached Diodati.

On the night of the storm they read excerpts from a book of ghost stories called *Fantasmagoria*:

Twelve o'clock's the Time of Night,
That the Graves, all gaping wide,
Quick send forth the airy Sprite
In the Church-way path to glide.

While it was Shelley who became hysterical and had to be sedated with cold water and ether, and it was Mary Shelley who created the monster of modern science in *Frankenstein* as a result of the storm, it fell to the other male member of the party, Byron's physician John William Polidori, to create the Vampire, Lord Ruthven. In two senses, Ruthven was based on Byron. The poet had gone into print three years earlier with *The Giaour*:

But first on earth, as Vampyre sent,
Thy corpse shall from its toils be rent;
Then ghastly haunt thy native place,
And suck the blood of all thy race;
There from daughter, sister, wife,
At midnight drain the stream of life;
Yet loathe the banquet, which perforce
Must feed thy livid, living corpse.
Thy victims, ere they yet expire
Shall know the demon for their sire . . .
. . . Yet with thine own best blood shall drip
Thy gnashing tooth and haggard lip;
Then stalking to thy sullen grave
Go – and with Ghouls and Afrits rave,
Till these in horror shrink away
From spectre more accursed than they.

But the more direct source for Polidori was the vampiric fragment that Byron produced at Diodati and which he later added to his poem 'Mazeppa'. And there were other links: Ruthven resembled Byron in that he was an arrogant libertine and seducer of gullible young women. Ironically, Polidori set Ruthven's 'death' in Greece, where Byron himself would die of marsh fever eight years later.

The darkly handsome Polidori was as highly strung as

Byron and Shelley, but lacked their talent. The young doctor, ridiculed as 'Polly-Dolly' by the arrogant Byron, was in some senses very like Bram Stoker: both men wrote of vampires and both men were overawed by the greatness of others. There is even a tangible link – Stoker knew Polidori's nephew, the poet Dante Gabriel Rossetti, who was a neighbour of the Irishman in Chelsea. Where they differ is that Polidori bore grudges. Educated by the Benedictines at Ampleforth and obtaining a medical diploma from Edinburgh University, Polidori had already specialized in the field that both Shelley and Stoker feared. He had published his dissertation in the year before the stay at Diodati, *The Psychosomatic Effects of Sleepwalking and/or Nightmares*. He also kept a diary of his time with Byron, not published until nearly a century later, which made it clear that the doctor became paranoid because he was constantly the target of Byron's barbs. Nor did he appreciate Shelley, finding him 'bashful, shy, consumptive . . . separated from his wife, keeps the two daughters of Godwin, who practice his theories [of free love]'.[24] Shelley's sister Claire became Byron's mistress. Eventually, during the summer that *The Vampire* was created, Polidori challenged Shelley to a duel. The rebel and atheist laughed it off, but Byron stepped in: 'Recollect, that although Shelley has some scruples about duelling, I have none, and shall be, at all times, ready to take his place.'[25]

By September, Polidori had had enough, but he was in fact dismissed by Byron before he could leave of his own accord. He drifted from Milan to Florence to Pisa and then back to England, where he briefly hung out his shingle in Norwich. In the meantime, in April 1819 his expanded short story, *The Vampire*, was published in the *New Monthly Magazine*, based on the manuscript he had left behind in Geneva. Wrongly attributed to Byron – the German writer Goethe believed it to be the poet's finest work – the novella was hardly a success. Byron was furious that the hack piece should have been attributed to him – 'Damn the Vampyre', he roared at his publisher, John Murray. 'What do I know of Vampyres?'[26]

In keeping with many of those associated with the vampire myth, John Polidori's end was tragic. Renting rooms in Great Pulteney Street, London, he lived as a recluse and became increasingly deranged. He was found dead in his room on 27 August 1821. He was twenty-five. The Coroner's Inquest was reported in *The Times* on 11 September, concluding:

> There being no further evidence adduced to prove how the deceased came to his death, the jury, under these circumstances, returned a verdict of – Died by the visitation of God.

Shelley the atheist would not have accepted this statement, and clearly neither did Byron:

> When he was my physician he was always talking of prussic acid, oil of amber, blowing into veins, suffocating by charcoal and compounding poisons. . . . It seems that disappointment was the cause of this rash act.[27]

If Polidori's patent suicide was the result of the *The Vampire*'s failure, it was a little ironic. The play had already appeared on the French stage eighteen months before his death as *Lord Ruthven ou les Vampires*, and it had toured far more widely than the much later *Dracula* play, appearing in theatres as far apart as Venice and Baghdad! When Alexandre Dumas went to see it in Paris at the Théâtre de la Porte-Saint-Martin, three rival productions were running on other stages in the French capital. 'How the theatre applauded,' Montague Summers paraphrased Dumas in 1928, 'the lean livid mask of the Vampire, how I shuddered at his stealthy steps.'[28]

And Polidori might have taken some pride in the fact that one of the lines in *Le Vampire* ran, 'Vampires . . . they come to us from England . . .'

The literary genre in which Polidori, Byron and Mary Shelley were working in the 'haunted summer' of 1816 was that of the Gothic novel. Chris Baldock in *The Oxford Companion to Crime and Mystery Writing* defines such a work as one which 'arouses terror and dread, typically involving enclosed settings such as old castles or mansions and emphasising themes of imprisonment, persecution and decay'.[29] Poetry, as well as prose, became absorbed with these ideas. Edward Young, rector of Welwyn in Hertfordshire, wrote *Night Thoughts* in the 1740s, occasioned by the death of his wife. The tone reflected gloom and doom, as did the 'churchyard school' of poetry initiated by the Scottish preacher Robert Blair in the same decade. From *The Castle of Otranto* written by Horace Walpole in 1764 to Charles Maturin's *Melmoth the Wanderer* in the year that *Le Vampire* appeared on the Paris stage (1823), the genre was enormously popular. In the context of the central theme of this book, the word Gothic fits like a glove, signifying both medieval and barbaric – although the storylines of Walpole, Maturin and above all of Anne Radcliffe are usually set in sixteenth- or seventeenth-century Europe and are obsessed with the Inquisition and the corruption of the Catholic Church. Mary Shelley's *Frankenstein; or the Modern Prometheus*, published in 1818, is one of the few examples of the type that has stood the test of time, although most literary experts see Stoker's *Dracula* as a late flourishing of the genre. The horror element present in the Gothic novel is again typified by Polidori's Lord Ruthven, Rymer's Sir Francis Varney and Stoker's Count – 'Female middle class innocence is pitted against an aristocratic and erotic past returned to haunt the living . . .'[30]

It was essentially the Romantic movement that gave birth to the literary vampire in the late eighteenth century, and thus examples can be found in Britain, France and Germany. In the German states, Ossenfeller wrote *The Vampire* as early as 1748, Burger *Lenore* (the name at least stolen by Poe) in 1773 and Goethe *The Bride of Corinth* in 1797. In Britain, many of the great writers of the day, and especially the poets, used the vampire theme: Coleridge in *Cristabel*, Shelley in *Cenci*, Keats in *The Eve of St Agnes* and *La Belle Dame Sans Merci*. And Robert Southey in *Thabala the Destroyer* (1797) wrote:

When Moath, firm of heart,
Perform'd the bidding, through the vampire corpse
He thrust the lance; it fell,
And howling with the wound,
Its fiendish tenant fled.

John Stagg's *The Vampyre* was written six years before
Diodati:

> With blood his visage was distain'd,
> Ensanguin'd were his frightful eyes,
> Each sign of former life remain'd,
> Save that all motionless he lies.[31]

But the oldest double reference to the twin themes of this
book, Dracula the myth and Vlad Ţepeş the man, can be
found in Robert Browning's *The Pied Piper of Hamelin*:

> In Tartary I freed the Cham,
> Last June from his huge swarms of gnats;
> I eased in Asia the Nizam
> Of a monstrous brood of vampire bats.

Thus boasts the Piper before tackling Hamelin's acute
rodent problem. More mysteriously, and possibly alluding to
the 'dancing mania', that inexplicable epidemic, chorea,
which gripped parts of Europe in the Middle Ages and may
partially explain the Children's Crusade of 1212:

> And I must not omit to say
> That in Transylvania there's a tribe
> Of alien people that ascribe
> Their outlandish ways and dress
> On which their neighbours lay such stress,
> To their fathers and mothers having risen
> Out of some subterraneous prison
> Into which they were trepanned
> Long time ago in a mighty band
> Out of Hamelin town in Brunswick land,
> But how or why, they don't understand.

# Vlad the Impaler

Stoker, Polidori and other vampire writers were drawing, consciously or otherwise, on earlier literary forms. They were also drawing on history and legend: the folklore of the vampire for ever linked via Stoker with Vlad Țepeș, the Impaler.

# 4

# VAMPYR

The ghostly psychic terrain of the vampire is a nocturnal
dreamscape of crossroads, foggy burial-grounds and
graveyard paths, dark forests, windy heights, desolate
heaths, lonely marshes where spectral will-o-the-wisps
hover over black, moonlit pools and flicker around the
weathered stones of ancient tombs.[1]

The atmosphere of the vampire folk-myth cannot be better
summed up. Elements of all the above pepper the literary
vampires from Polidori to Stoker to Rice. But the vampire is
no mere literary device: it comes to us from belief. Scientific
secular culture dismisses such things with the contempt
inherent in words like myth and superstition. Less than a
hundred years ago, certain people in Eastern Europe *knew*
that vampires were real. Ironically, it was another myth, that
of the efficacy of Communism, which drove the vampire out.

Chambers' *Etymological Dictionary* of 1885, which predates Stoker's *Dracula* by twelve years, defines the vampire
thus: 'in the superstition of Eastern Europe, a ghost which
sucks the blood of its sleeping victim'. In this sense, the
vampire is synonymous with the succubi, the night-haunting
demons believed to be real by the Catholic and Orthodox
Churches, and the subject of Papal bulls dating from the time
of Vlad Ţepeş. (In 1885 the word 'vamp', far from meaning
the *femme fatale* of the early twentieth century, meant only
the upper leathers of a shoe or boot.)

The vampire of folklore is found universally in pre-

Christian times and in non-Christian countries, but it survived long after Christ's Church imposed itself on superstitious societies throughout the world.

As Montague Summers wrote:

> Throughout the whole vast shadowy world of ghosts and demons, there is no figure so terrible, no figure so dreaded and abhorred . . . as the vampire, who is himself neither ghost nor demon, but yet who partakes the dark natures and possesses the mysterious and terrible qualities of both.[2]

In similar vein, the cynic Voltaire,[3] one of the most rational products of the Enlightenment, wrote:

> What! Is it in our eighteenth century that vampires exist? Is it after the reigns of Locke, Shaftesbury, Trenchard and Collins?[4]

Voltaire should not have been surprised. The eighteenth century has been dubbed the age of reason, but it also saw the rise of the Gothic novel, a continuing belief in the reality of hell-fire and the infamous poltergeist activity in Cock Lane, London, and Samuel Wesley's rectory at Epworth, Lincolnshire. The Cock Lane ghost manifested itself in Clerkenwell in 1761 in the form of 'Scratching Fanny', but was in fact poltergeist activity focused on 11-year-old Elizabeth Parsons. Dr Samuel Johnson was one of the 'committee of gentlemen' appointed to investigate. Fifty years earlier, similar activity centred on the younger sister of future Methodist leader, John Wesley. Although both cases are today regarded as hoaxes, at the time they were thought to be proofs of pure evil. Scholars like Johann Zopfius and Karl von Dalen wrote of vampires as matters of factual reality when Voltaire was already a young man. In *Dissertatio de Vampyris Serviensibus*, published at Halle in 1733, they defined the species:

> Vampires issue forth from their graves in the night, attack people sleeping quietly in their beds, suck out all the blood

from their bodies and destroy them. They beset men, women and children alike, sparing neither age nor sex. Those who are under the fatal malignity of their influence complain of suffocation and a total deficiency of spirits, after which they soon expire. Some who, when at the point of death, have been asked if they can tell what is causing their decease, reply that such and such persons, lately dead, have arisen from the tomb to torment and torture them.[5]

The most authoritative eighteenth-century work on vampires was published in 1746 by Dom Augustin Calmet, a prolific writer of the Benedictine order. His *Traité sur les Apparitions des Esprits et sur les Vampires* examined the 'horrid attacks' of vampires and described the traditional methods of killing them. The work was not a product of gullible superstition, however. Calmet noted that most of the vampire stories came from Eastern Europe:

> where people, being badly fed, are subject to certain disorders occasioned by the climate and the food, and augmented by prejudice, fancy and fright, which are capable of producing or of increasing the most dangerous maladies.

The folkloric vampire has two overlapping definitions. The first, and older, tradition is of the night-haunting ghost of a wizard or witch (the Turkish word *uber*, from which vampire is derived, literally means a witch who threatens whole communities). The second, the variant that Stoker used (though physically it was more obvious in Murnau's *Nosferatu*), was the tradition of the walking corpse, the revenant who has led an evil life and cannot find rest in the grave.

The origins of the vampire myth take us into paganism and shamanic spirituality, in which the dark, because it could not be explained or even readily understood, was filled with nameless terrors against which men must protect themselves. The shamans or witch doctors of the hunter-gatherers of Paleolithic society probably went into trances not unlike those of aboriginal tribesmen or Haitians under the grip of voodoo today. The trance symbolized death, and the spirits of the dead could walk again through the shaman. There are links, too, with the sensation of flight and the concept of shape-shifting.

The idea of flight is associated with late medieval witchcraft in which thousands of terrified, tortured people 'confessed' to flying to the sabbat (the meeting of witches with the Devil) on goats, horses and broomsticks. Much of this was nonsense, the result of the excruciating torture mechanisms of the Inquisition, but it may also have its root in religious ecstasy and trance-like states, with or without the narcotic, hallucinatory addition of hedgerow plants like hemlock. 'Root of hemlock, digg'd in the dark' is one of the ingredients of Shakespeare's witches' cauldron in *Macbeth*. Ingested, it was highly toxic, but mashed to a paste and smeared over the skin, it entered through the pores into the bloodstream and became a powerful hallucinogen.

In Eastern Europe in particular, the shape-shifting metaphor links the vampire with the werewolf. According to Ukrainian and Russian folklore, wolfmen will simply become vampires unless exorcized. Ian Woodward records that:

In Siberia, the vampire and the werewolf are known collectively as one creature, the vulkodlak and these are most active during the bleakest winter months. At their annual gatherings they strip off their wolf skins and hang them on the nearby trees. If any of them succeeds in getting hold of another's skin and burning it, the vulkodlak whose skin it was will be freed for ever from its fiendish enchantment.[6]

The sexual element and the use of fangs is common to both vampire and werewolf, and in medieval and early modern Europe it was not unusual for child rapists and serial killers to be accused of lycanthropy, perhaps because of the mangled state of their victims' corpses.

The lasting significance of vampiric folklore is borne out by the huge following of Anne Rice's books, especially in her native America. But such folklore had a frighteningly real side too. In 1993, the *Eventmental Ziliei*, one of Romania's most widely read newspapers, told its readers to prepare for St Andrew's Day, 30 November, by smearing their windows and doors with garlic to ward off werewolves and other 'children of the night'. This may have been reported in the *Independent* tongue in cheek, but there is no evidence that this was the case in the paper's home in Bucharest.

Even more telling was an incident in Stoke-on-Trent in January 1973. PC John Pye was called to investigate the death of Demetrios Myicuiria, a Polish immigrant in his seventies at 3, The Villas, in a Victorian terrace in the heart of the Potteries. Old people die alone commonly enough, abandoned by friends and family years before, but there was something odd about this particular death. Pye noticed, by the light of his torch, that salt had been scattered around the room and especially around the old man's bed. There was also a bag of salt between his legs and on his pillow, and a number of containers in the room were full of a mixture of salt and the dead man's urine.

The inquest reported at first that Myicuiria had choked to death on a pickled onion found wedged in his windpipe. Closer examination revealed that the 'onion' was in fact a clove of garlic. Garlic, salt and the crucifix are the traditional symbols of good against evil. The coroner said:

> This man genuinely believed . . . I've been a lawyer for a long time, dealing with courtroom cases of all kinds. I've seen all sorts of depravity, all sorts of nonsense, but I can visualize what was behind this man. A lot of evil had happened to him [he had lost everything during the Second World War] . . . I am convinced, even after this inquest, that this man was genuinely afraid of vampires and [was] not trying to kill himself.[7]

In the following year tales of the Highgate vampire reached the press. Highgate Cemetery is the burial place of the great and good of high Victorian society (and includes the unlikely tomb of Karl Marx, whom many Victorians regarded as neither great nor good). The older part of the cemetery became the focus of disturbing events after reports of a seven-foot vampire seen prowling the Gothic tombs.[8]

Nearly a hundred vampire-hunters under the loose leadership of the High Priest of the Occult Society, David Farrant, descended on Highgate – the result was an orgy of tomb-smashing, with iron stakes being driven through corpses. Farrant's home was searched by the police, who found salt, crucifixes and voodoo dolls in his apartment. He was officially charged with offering indignity to the dead, 'to the great scandal and disgrace of religion, decency and morality'.[9] Defending himself, Farrant lost and the judge gave him five years.

More recently (2002), and more disturbingly, a German couple, 23-year-old Manuela Ruda and her husband David, were found guilty of ritual vampiric murder. The trial, held at Bochum, in Germany's industrial heartland, produced weeks of lurid and graphic testimony which would not be out of place in any vampire-flick and which no Victorian 'penny-dreadful' writer would have been allowed to publish. Learning the art of devil-worship and blood-sucking in Scotland and England, the pair, appearing in the dock with shaven heads and wearing chains, admitted freely that they killed Frank Haegen and carved a Satanic star on his chest with a razor. Haegen died as a result of sixty-six slash wounds from a machete and demolition of his skull with a sledge-hammer. Prosecutor Dieter Justinsky tried his best to sum up the enormous callousness of the crime:

> I have never, ever, seen such a picture of cruelty and depravity before. They simply had a lust for murder . . . and . . . believed they would achieve immortality as vampires.

Manuela Ruda confessed in court, 'For the last two and a half years I have had Satan in my soul.'

And the Rudas may be the tip of a pernicious iceberg. There are an estimated 6,000 hard-core devil-worshippers in Germany today.

Belief in vampires is evident in the earliest Indo-European nomadic cultures that came out of the steppelands north of the

Caspian Sea some 3,000 years before Christ. Migrating bands of these peoples spread east into the Urals and Asia Minor, along the Indus and the Ganges into India and west along the Danube into the heartlands of the Balkans and what was to become Germany. They brought with them the mythology of the 'Terrifying Sovereign', god of death and magic, recognized in the teachings of Zoroaster and the cult of Mithras, in the eternal battle between good and evil. Many of the tribal groups produced warrior elites believed to be at one with the dead and with the wolves that prowled the European forests. Bram Stoker was drawing on this mythology when he described Jonathan Harker's horse-drawn coach rattling through the Borgo pass on its way to Castle Dracula:

> All at once the wolves began to howl as though the moonlight had had some peculiar effect on them. The horses jumped about and reared and looked helplessly around with eyes that rolled in a way painful to see; but the living ring of terror encompassed them on every side . . .

It is this ancient culture and its links between the dead, the undead and the wolf that gives us the lycanthropic vampire of Eastern Europe. Names vary: in Slovenia, we have *vukodlak*, in Poland, *wilkolak*, in Romania, *varcolac*, in Albania, *vurvolak* and so on; but the origin is the same: the original slavonic *velku dlaka* literally translated means wolf-coat.

There is also the classical tradition, which accounts for the obsession with succubi and incubi in the late medieval Christian Church. Lamia was the queen of Libya who was one of the many earthly conquests of Zeus. Long-suffering Hera, Zeus's wife, tired of his constant infidelities, killed the children of the liaison. In despair, Lamia, made hideous by Hera's magic, prowled the night for other children to kill. In the Hebrew language she became Lilith, the screech-owl, a Babylonian night-spirit and the first wife of Adam, and by the thirteenth century had been transformed into a vampire. In 1214, Gervase of Tilbury[10] wrote in *Otia Imperialia* that the Lamia 'disturbs the minds of sleepers and oppresses with weight' crushing their chests with a power intended to kill. A more likely scientific explanation of Lamia's assault is the comparatively common sleep apnoea, in which a sleeper literally stops breathing until reduced oxygen tension in the tissues makes them wake, with a gasping intake of breath. This oxygen-starvation can also cause hallucinations, vivid dreams and night-terrors, tying in with the variously imagined visitations of the vampire. Nicholaus of Cusa,[11] Professor of Theology at Prague and Heidelberg universities in the early fifteenth century, believed that *lamiae* were demons in the guise of old women (hence their general association with witches) who kidnapped children and roasted them over fires.

The infamous bull of Pope Innocent VIII,[12] *Summis desideratus affectibus*, which appeared on 9 December 1484, gave the full weight of the Catholic Church to the Inquisition, unleashing a wave of terror which saw the deaths of thousands of innocent victims across Europe.

Innocent wrote:

It has lately come to Our ears not without afflicting Us with bitter sorrow, that in some parts of Northern Germany . . . many persons of both sexes, unmindful of their own salvation and straying from the Catholic Faith, have abandoned themselves to devils, incubi and succubi . . .[13]

and proceeded to list dozens of disasters that their infidelity had caused. 'Our dear sons Henry Kramer and James Sprenger',[14] Professors of Theology of the Order of Friars Preachers were then unleashed onto an unsuspecting world. Between them, they wrote *Malleus Maleficarum* (Hammer of the Witches), eight years after the death of Vlad Ţepeş, a tome which the gullible and terrified world of the Reformation and Counter-Reformation was all too eager to accept as truth.[15]

Although the witch craze as it developed in the sixteenth century was largely a Western European phenomenon, creeping no further east than Nuremberg, the notion of incubi and succubi is closely tied with the Eastern European belief in vampires. 'Incubi' in Latin means to lie on, and this was precisely what the night demons were believed to do. They were linked with the 'familiars', the devil's agents, shape-

shifters who fed on witches' blood; and they were also linked
with the idea of the nightmare: they were demons whose
origins were in latent sexuality or even nocturnal emissions.
William Caxton's *Chronicle* describes their activities:

> That fiend that goth a-night
> Women full oft to guile,
> Incubus is named by right;
> And guileth men other while,
> Succubus is that wight.[16]

The philosopher and friar, Francisco-Maria Guazzo,[17] an
experienced judge in witch trials, produced his *Compendium
Maleficarum* (Handbook of Witches) in 1608. He wrote:

> [The incubus] can assume either a male or female shape;
> sometimes he appears as a full-grown man, sometimes as
> a satyr . . .[18]

Thomas Aquinas,[19] writing nearly four centuries earlier (in
his *Summa Theologica*), was trying to work out the science
behind the hysteria:

> Nevertheless, if sometimes children are born from
> intercourse with demons, this is not because of the semen
> emitted by them, or from the bodies they have assumed,
> but through the semen taken from some man for the
> purpose, seeing that the same demon who acts as a
> succubus for a man becomes an incubus for a woman.

Not until the late seventeenth century was the existence
of incubi and succubi, taken for so long to be scientific fact,
challenged. De Saint André, physician to Louis XV of
France, wrote:

> The incubus is most frequently a chimera, which has no
> more basis than a dream, a perverted imagination and very
> often the invention of a woman . . . To conceal her sin, a
> woman, a girl, a nun in name only, a debauchee who

affects the appearance of virtue, will palm off her lover for an incubus spirit which haunts her.[20]

Although De Saint André can be accused of much the same misogyny that characterizes the authors of, say, *Malleus Maleficarum*, his jibes at least put the incubus issue into perspective.

In Eastern Europe, where the Greek Orthodox rather than the Roman Catholic Church held sway, the vampire was treated differently, and certainly not as a demon in the conventional sense that Aquinas, Kramer, Sprenger and Pope Innocent VIII had understood the term.

James Dickie commented in 1971:[21]

Most mysterious and intriguing of all occult phenomena, the vampire, whatever his social status in life, becomes in death the expression of sadistic erotomania at its intensest. He is the hyphen between life and death: through his agency death poaches upon the reproductive function peculiar to the living. All the evidence amassed to prove the existence of the vampire contributes not an iota to his understanding, for in spite of all efforts, he remains an indecipherable hieroglyphic in the language of the Unseen.[22]

Nigel Jackson in *The Compleat Vampyre* lists no less than sixty-five variants of the vampire–werewolf that feature in European folklore. 'There was once a time,' runs a Romanian folktale, 'when Vampires were as common as blades of grass, or berries in a pail and they never kept still, but wandered round at night among the people.'[23] This book includes only those with relevance to the areas known to Vlad Ţepeş.

South of the Danube, where Vlad Ţepeş carried out his forays against the Turks in the summer of 1462, Serbian folklore tells of the *dhampir*, the offspring of a vampire and a living woman. With the psychic ability to detect vampires, the *dhampir* often took the role of *kresniki*, individuals born with a white caul which signified their ability to do good in the world. Bram Stoker's hero, van Helsing, represents this role, although he is blessed with scientific knowledge rather than pure folkloric skills. Stoker says in *Dracula*, 'He is known everywhere that men have been [in] the wake of the berserker Icelander, the devil-begotten Hun, the Slav, the Saxon, the Magyar . . .'[24]

The Serbian *dhampir* fulfils the role of the cunning woman in Western Europe, a devotee of white witchcraft whose skills were sought to ward off evil. There are examples of cunning practice happening in Serbia into the late 1950s.

In Dracula's native Romania, the *dschuma* was a night-haunting hag whose appearance presaged a cholera epidemic. Naked and wailing like the *Bean-Sidhe* of Irish Gaelic folklore with which Stoker was familiar, the *dschuma* could only be assuaged by the offering of a red shirt, woven in silence in one night by seven old women, and hung out before dawn for her to collect.

In Bulgaria, the first territory across the Bosphorus that the Ottoman Turks would invade in their western conquests, the *krvoijac* was a vampire which rested in its grave for forty days. After that time, with magical powers enhanced, it broke free of its coffin and prowled the night in search of blood.

In Bosnia, the vampire variant known as a *vampir* was thought to be especially active in times of typhus epidemics. It may have been this type that Byron was writing about in *The Gaiour*, in that these vampires returned from the grave to drink the blood and have sex with their still-living partners. Belief in the vampire was especially strong among the gypsies of Bosnia, irrespective of whether they were Orthodox Christian or Muslim. Nigel Jackson notes that as in many areas of the Balkans, ethnic genocide and war have recently combined to destroy many of the old myths. They have doubtless been replaced by new ones.

Westwards, in Hungary, where János Hunyadi and Matthias Corvinus would both seek to make their mark on Vlad Ţepeş' Wallachia, the vampire variant was the *kiderc nadaly*, whose despatch, unusually, was a nail driven through the temple.

To the south, in Albania, where, in the Impaler's time, the great Skanderbeg kept the Turks at bay, the vampire was called *liougat* or *kulkutha*. The German traveller J.G. von

Hann reported in *Albanesische Stuckein* in 1854 that *liougats* were 'dead Turks, with huge nails, who, wrapped up in their winding sheets, devour whatever they find and throttle men'.[25] A common belief among various Slavic gypsy groups was that the *liougat*'s enemy was the wolf and that a wolf wound was fatal to the *liougat*, ending his night-prowling for ever.

In Ţepeş' own Romania, the *moronii* were the undead, predatory vampires who stole blood, youth and beauty and targeted chickens and bees (the Carpathians are famous for honey production). Oddly human and very like the witches of Western Europe, they were organized in covens and carried out necrophiliac orgies in graveyards. They could change shape and had powers over animals and the weather, attributes also applied to western witches. They were easily distinguishable, however, by their chicken-clawed feet.

A variant in Vlad Ţepeş' Principality of Wallachia was the *murony*, able to change its shape, typically to that of a cat, toad, spider, hound or blood-sucking insect. Its physical appearance in the grave was repellent and was recreated by Murnau in *Nosferatu*. Its fingernails were long and blood seeped from its eyes, nose, mouth and ears. The only method of certain despatch was a stake of whitethorn or iron driven through the forehead.

Specific to Transylvania, 'the land beyond the forest', was the *nosferat* (plural, *nosferatu*). The folklorist Heinrich von Wlislocki described this creature over a hundred years ago:

> The *nosferat* not only sucks the blood of sleeping people, but also does mischief as an incubus or succubus. The *nosferat* is the still-born illegitimate of two people who are similarly illegitimate. It is hardly put under the earth before it awakes to life and leaves its grave never to return. It visits people by night in the form of a black cat, a black dog, a beetle, a butterfly or even a simple straw. When its sex is male, it visits women; when female, men. With young people it indulges in sexual orgies until they get ill and die of exhaustion. . . . It often happens that women are impregnated by the creature and bear the children who can be recognized by their ugliness and by having hair all over

the whole body. They then always become witches, usually *moronii*. The *nosferat* appears to bridegrooms and brides and makes them impotent and sterile.

Romania seems to have been at the centre of vampire belief in Eastern Europe. In 1845, at a time when folktales were being collected and printed for the first time, A. and A. Schott noted the wolf-coat tradition of the *prikolitsch*, a living man who attacked domestic animals in the guise of a black dog. Such animals have their echoes in Western European folklore too – the barguest of which Stoker wrote, Shriker and Black Shuck.[26]

The *streghoi* in Wallachia and the *strigoii* in other parts of Romania were those most closely associated with the *lamiae* of Greek and Roman mythology. The word means 'screech owl' (Lilith), a bird long associated with magic and occult wisdom. Their favourite human targets were babies in their cradles. They were also vampire-shamans, often with auburn hair and blue eyes[27] and born with a caul. They were variously believed to have their eyes open constantly in their graves and assume the appearance of lights like will-o'-the-wisps that floated over graveyards and forests. These lights are found in mythology the world over,[28] but the name itself probably reflects the Roman army's occupation of the area under the Emperor Trajan, during the two invasions that extended the Roman Empire in the first century.

Most terrifying of the Romanian vampires was the *varcolac*, the Wolf-coat. As described by the Romanian scholar G.F. Ciausanu:

> *Varcolaci* because their spirit is *varcolaci*. They are recognized by their pale faces and dry skin and by the deep sleep into which they fall when they go to the moon to eat it . . . The redness is the blood of the moon, escaping from the mouths of the *varcolaci* and spreading over the moon.[29]

There was a tradition that the *varcolaci* were the souls of unbaptized children, and that they took the shape of dogs, wolves and dragons (*drakul* in Romanian). Professor Cyprien Robert claimed that:

> The *voukodlak* [sic] sleeps in his grave with open, staring eyes; his nails and hair grow to an excessive length, the warm blood pulses in his veins. When the moon is at her full, he issues forth to run his course, to suck the blood of living men by biting deep into their dorsal vein . . . [they] are especially eager to quaff the hot blood of young girls.[30]

The moon and the crossroads are images closely associated with the vampire in Eastern European cultures. In Romania, crossroads represented the *coloana ceriului*, the pillar that linked heaven and earth. Sabbats were held here and ghosts haunted them. Long before ley lines (supposedly psychic pathways) came to dominate magic landscapes, the crossroads was a place of fear, especially after dark.

What was the defence against the vampire? In some Eastern European countries, white garlic (*allium sativum*) had the necessary magical powers. It was strewn around all entrances to buildings, doors, windows and chimneys and even, since night was the real dangertime, around a sleeper's bed. There is a long tradition of this. Pliny the Elder,[31] cavalry commander and admiral, wrote in his monumental thirty-seven books on natural history, that garlic was an antidote to snake bites. Fifteen centuries later, the magician Heinrich Cornelius Agrippa, the German magus, believed it could ward off attacks by panthers![32]

In Romania, as in other parts of Eastern Europe, garlic was placed as a wreath on coffins and cloves often stuffed into the mouth of the deceased to prevent the corpse from turning into a vampire. Elaborate rituals for vampire detection were worked out. A teenage virgin, whether male or female, rode an equally virginal white or black horse around a graveyard. If the animal hesitated or refused to pass a grave, that was deemed to be evidence enough of the existence of a vampire, and the coffin was exhumed.

What followed will be familiar to all watchers of vampire

films. As early as the fourteenth century the English traveller
Sir John Mandeville[33] wrote:

> Therefore hath the whitethorn many virtues, for he that
> beareth a branch on hym thereof, no thunder, ne, no
> manner of tempest may dere him, ne, in the house [that] is
> ynne may non evil ghost enter.[34]

The whitethorn was thus the perfect wood with which to
fashion a stake to be driven through the heart of the resting
vampire. But it had to be a single stroke – more than one
would merely revive the monster. The ritual of death by the
stake was very important and it is a recurrent theme in the
story of Vlad Ţepeş. Known as the 'Great Reparation' in
Transylvania, it has echoes of the symbolic slaying of the
dragon by St George, who, in medieval art forms, is a plate-
armoured knight driving his lance into the monster's heart.
George is an interesting meeting place of Christian and pagan
beliefs. The eve of the saint's day, traditionally 23 April, was a
time in Eastern Europe for precautions to be taken against all
forms of evil. The myth of the dragon will be discussed later,
but it is a familiar symbol of evil, and all that is primitive and
terrifying. Saint George, perhaps an unlikely patron saint of
England, was in fact George of Cappadocia (modern Turkey),
put to death by the Emperor Diocletian at Lydda on 23 April,
AD 303. The dates proposed for his death are conflicting, as
are the reasons for it, but he can be identified with the
*kresniki*, the vampire-killers of Eastern European folklore and
the character of van Helsing in Stoker's novel, who describes
the moment of the vampire's destruction in his 'journal':

> Oh my friend John, but it was butcher work; had I not
> been nerved by thoughts of other dead, and if the living
> over whom hung such a pall of fear, I could not have gone
> on. I tremble and tremble even yet, though till all was over,
> God be thanked, my nerve did stand. Had I not seen the
> repose in the first face and the gladness that stole over it
> just ere the final dissolution came, as realization that the
> soul had been won, I could not have gone further with my

butchery. I could not have endured the horrid screeching as the stake drove home; the plunging of the writhing form, and lips of bloody foam. I should have fled in terror and left my work undone . . . For, friend John, hardly had my knife severed the head of each, before the whole body began to melt away and crumble into its native dust, as though the death that should have come centuries agone had at last assert himself and say at once and loud 'I am here!'[35]

The decapitation which followed staking was performed ritually with a single sweep of a specially consecrated sword or sickle. The victim's mouth was stuffed with garlic and the heart and liver removed from the corpse. In Romania the heart was pierced with long needles, in Serbia it was boiled in vino sacro (communion wine) and replaced in the rib cage.

Why should Voltaire, in his cynical, enlightened eighteenth century, be amazed that people still believed in vampires? We are not talking about literature as the source of such beliefs. After all, Polidori, Rymer and Stoker were as yet unknown. What prompted Voltaire's attack was the outbreak of a series of vampire epidemics that swept Europe in his own time. Such epidemics were not unheard of. The oldest use of the word – upyr – is found in Russian sources between 1047 and 1059. The Serbian *vulkodlak* dates from 1262 and the first official accounts can be found in Silesia (Germany) in 1591, where the revenant of a shoemaker from Breslau returned to plague the town following his suicide.

There are reports of vampirism from Bohemia and Moravia as early as 1618 and Poland six years later. Outbreaks occurred in Istria in 1672, spreading to East Prussia in 1710 and 1721, south to Serbia in 1727 and 1732, Prussia in 1750, Silesia in 1755, Romania in 1756 and Russia in 1772. Surgeons with the army in Austria investigated a case in the village of Mednegna (or Medvedija) near Belgrade in January 1732 in which fourteen corpses were examined. Twelve of these had not decomposed in the usual way. According to the surgeons, they were 'unmistakeably in the vampire condition'.[36] and this accorded with the ritualistic excommunication of the Orthodox Church – 'Your place shall be with the devil and the traitor Judas, and after that do not turn into ashes, but remain as undecayed as stone and iron.'[37] Other surgeons spoke of vampirism spreading 'like a pestilence through Salvia and Wallachia . . . causing numerous deaths and disturbing all the land with fear of the mysterious visitors against which no one felt himself secure'.[38] Farson cites a number of examples from the Belgrade region in the 1730s, including many in which the vampire targeted members of his own family. In one case, in today's Croatia, a vampire killed a brother and three nieces. The investigating party sent by the authorities was closer to the witchfinders of the seventeenth century than van Helsing's little band of heroes. It included a public prosecutor and civil and military officers who visited the vampire's grave and cut off his head with an axe before reburying the body in quicklime.

In another case, reported to the Imperial Council of War in Vienna, a Hungarian soldier, Arnod Paole (the name was probably Pavel), was killed in a cart accident. Dead for thirty days, he returned and took four victims 'in the manner traditionally ascribed to vampires'. When his body was exhumed, according to surgeon Johann Fluckinger, it 'showed all the marks of an arch-vampire. His body was flushed; his hair, nails and beard had grown and his veins were full of liquid blood which splashed all over the winding sheet.'[39] Since Paole had attacked animals and humans in his bloodlust, the epidemic broke out again five years later, with the recurrent contagion associated with the 'subspecies'.

Austrian officialdom in the form of the Catholic Church could offer no help. Whereas Pope Innocent VIII was quite prepared, in the 1480s, to issue orders for the destruction of the anti-Christian elementals, the incubi and succubi, his successor in the mid-eighteenth century, Clement XII, was rather more circumspect, believing that vampirism was a delusion. At the same time, the Vatican hedged its bets by recommending that suspected vampires be exhumed and burned.

Synonymous with the vampirism associated with Count Dracula is the symbolism of the bat, although the vampire bat (*desmodus rotundus*) is a native of Central and South

America, and is found nowhere in Europe. The animal received its name from the Spanish Conquistadors of the sixteenth century, obviously using their own folkloric knowledge. It lives on the blood of mammals, usually grazing cattle, although there are about half a dozen recorded cases each year of human hosts. It was probably one of the animals listed by F. de Oviedo y Valdez in *Sumario de la Natural Historio de las Indias* in 1526. The only reference to Spanish vampirism I have been able to find is the associated *lobombre*, literally wolf-man, from the Pyrenees and Cantabrian Mountains, whose condition was created by drinking magical waters or eating certain flowers. The vampire bat was first catalogued by name by French naturalist Buffon in his *Natural History* in 1749, implying that the animal regularly attacked humans. The vampire tradition in Buffon's native France is connected with the *loup-garou*, the werewolf, but it is interesting that Buffon was writing at the time of the various vampire epidemics in Europe.

What was the cause of these extraordinary epidemics? There are rational explanations, but we are dealing with superstitious, uneducated societies into which the Vienna-based cognoscenti found themselves thrown, where the normal rules of evidence were ignored. A number of contemporaries commented on this situation. Archbishop Giuseppe Davanzati wrote in his *Dissertazione sopra I Vampiri* (1744) that the whole epidemic was a thing of the mind. Contrary to Stoker's elegant, cultured Count of the 1890s, Davanzati noted that vampires were never 'scholar[s], philosopher[s], theologian[s], landowner[s] or bishop[s]', but always 'base-born plebeians'. Those who believed in them were 'the half-witted and the ignorant'.[40]

Voltaire, as always, was even more scathing:

We have never heard tell of Vampires in London, or even in Paris. I do admit that there were in both those cities speculators, brokers and businessmen who sucked the blood of the people in broad daylight, but although corrupted, they were not dead. Those true bloodsuckers lived not in cemeteries, but in the most congenial places.[41]

One obvious thread links vampirism and disease. Two variants in Nigel Jackson's list of eighteen werewolf–vampires found in Eastern Europe refer to specific physical epidemics: the *dschuma* of Romania is linked with cholera and the *nosferat* of the same region is associated with bubonic plague, the Black Death. Because of the narrowly defined limits of medical science, the disapproval of the Church and poor diagnosis, the vampire was thought to be a *cause* of the disease. In fact, the corollary was true: disease, especially fatal epidemics, bred belief in and fear of vampires. This notion may even be present, however subconsciously, in Bram Stoker. In 1832, the great cholera epidemic reached County Sligo in the West of Ireland. Charlotte, the author's mother, lived through this, but her house was attacked by looters driven to desperation by the suddenness and inevitability of the disease. Horror stories about pallid corpses, panic-stricken regions and wild tales of cannibalism were part of young Bram's childhood during the famine of the 1840s.

The prevalence of diseases in Eastern Europe in the seventeenth and eighteenth centuries can be held to explain the vampire outbreaks. Tuberculosis causes weight loss and extreme fatigue, symptoms associated with vampire victims. The coughing up of blood from infected lungs speaks for itself. Cholera causes similar weight loss and dehydration; rabies (with its obvious links with the wolf-coats and lycanthropy) leads to convulsions and breathing problems, with an apparent terror of water (which in some areas vampires were believed to be unable to cross). Rarer diseases and conditions, although not contagious, were still inexplicable and bizarre. Albinos and porphyriacs are sensitive to light, giving rise to the vampiric fear of the sun.[42] In porphyriacs, the body cannot metabolize iron, so taking it in some digestible form, perhaps blood, becomes a craving. Garlic's 'magical' properties break down old blood cells, recovering iron needed by the body. Pernicious anaemia likewise exhibits a blood-craving and causes a shrivelling of the body.

Tony Thorne hypothesizes that some vampiric symptoms

– exhaustion, lethargy, even paralysis – can be the result of the shock of personal loss, the trauma of war or pestilence. He also argues convincingly that there is nothing unique to the eighteenth century about either the cause or the effect of vampire epidemics; it was merely that the period saw a growth in literacy, and perhaps a new-found interest in the occult.

Another phenomenon may explain the vampire outbreak: the ancient problem of premature burial. In 1885, well before Stoker's *Dracula*, the *British Medical Journal* claimed ruefully, 'It is true that hardly any one sign of death, short of putrefaction, can be relied upon as infallible.'[43] Scientists today are still arguing about the concept of brain death. Rather depressingly for those who put their faith in today's science, health expert Jessica Sachs contends that we are actually *further away* from accuracy here than at any time in the past.[44] We are able to keep people 'alive' on machines for years, so the concept of the irrevocable ending of life is still blurred. Edgar Allen Poe capitalized on the fear of premature burial in a number of his short stories in the 1840s, and in 1851 Dr Herbert Mayo, Professor of Anatomy and Physiology at King's College, London, wrote:

> That the bodies which were found in the so-called Vampyr state, instead of being in a new or mystical condition, were simply alive in the common way, or had been so for some time subsequent to their interment; that, in short, they were the bodies of persons who had been buried alive, and whose life, where it yet lingered, was finally extinguished through the ignorance and barbarity of those who disinterred them.[45]

The condition known as catalepsy could easily be confused with death as under such condition the body is immobile and the pulse and heartbeat very difficult to detect. It is thus likely that an unknown number of people were buried while still alive, and in outbreak periods, when large numbers must be interred quickly, there is even more likelihood of this. According to Montague Summers, 'a quarter of a century ago' (i.e. 1900) it was computed that in the United States, an average of not less than one case a week of premature burial was discovered and reported.[46] The mid-nineteenth century in particular became obsessed with fear of premature burial, and stories of such abound all over Europe. In England, Sir Henry Thompson, surgeon to Queen Victoria, argued in February 1874 that the best solution to the problem was cremation, although this filled most of his contemporaries with horror. In Russia in 1901, Count Karnicki invented a device which saved a potential victim from an appalling fate. A tube was inserted into the coffin through a hole drilled through the lid. At the end of the tube was a glass ball, resting on the 'deceased's' chest. Even the slightest movement of the thorax would break the glass, release a spring, and above ground a flag would fly upwards from a box on top of the tube. Simultaneously, a bell would ring and an electric light flash on should the movement take place after dark. In Styria and other parts of Austria a century earlier, a simpler device merely linked a rope inside the coffin to a central churchyard bell. It is not known whether such devices were actually used.

There is, finally, a more prosaic explanation for the vampirism outbreaks, and it is similar to that of the witch fever that gripped Western Europe. The Reformation of the sixteenth century saw upheavals in religion and social structure unparalleled in the West. In the vacuum left by the retreating Catholic Church and the maelstrom created by its counter-attack, devil-worship and similar practice was believed to reign unchecked. So, too, the ongoing struggle between the Catholic and Orthodox Churches resulted in anarchy in areas where both contended for people's souls. The fall of Byzantium in 1453, in some ways commensurate with Martin Luther's attack on Rome,[47] led to the focus of power shifting north, to Moscow. This clash of Christian churches caused confusion, hatred and bigotry; and the buffer zone, torn between the two, was Transylvania.

Here, in the late fifteenth century, Vlad Ţepeş ruled three times. He was probably as superstitious as his people, believing that the hobgoblins haunted his mountains. It would take Bram Stoker to turn the man into the vampire, but by the nineteenth century horror stories of the blood-lusting mass-murderer were well established in Eastern Europe, and especially in Transylvania, 'the land beyond the forests'.

# 5

# DRACULA'S PEOPLE

In a large open space between the Capitol and the Palatine Hill in Rome, the architect Apollodorus built a superb esplanade. Made of red and yellow marble, 375 feet long and 350 feet wide, it was built to contain two vast libraries, one for Greek, the other for Latin books. Between these was a huge column, 110 feet high, a tribute to its architect and monument to the man who commissioned it, the general and emperor Marcus Ulpinius Trajanus, known to us as Trajan.

The monument was unveiled on 15 May, AD 113. Nothing like it had been seen before: spiralling up its 110 feet, the column's carved bas-relief depicted Trajan's campaigns in Dacia, the most northerly of the provinces of the Roman Empire. The designs resemble an infinitely superior Bayeux Tapestry, unrolling on twenty-three drums of Persian marble, extending, if laid end to end, to 600 feet and containing 2,500 'action' figures, originally brightly painted, who are building fortifications on the plains that would become medieval Wallachia, Vlad Ţepeş' principality, crossing the treacherous Danube on a pontoon of war galleys, hurling missiles at Dacian strongholds. The carving is realistic; no two faces are alike, and as a source of information for the military historian of the second century, the column is unparalleled.

Trajan himself was born near Seville about twenty years after the Crucifixion of Christ. Distinguishing himself in wars of conquest in Parthia and Germania, he was made consul in 91 and succeeded his colleague the elected Emperor Marcus Nerva seven years later. He was fifty-four, straight-talking, loyal, kind and tough, and he won the hearts of his people. Ever a man of action, he rowed himself across the Danube and would swim the Euphrates at sixty years old. His object, both in commissioning the column and in undertaking the campaign that was delineated on it, was simply to make Rome the greatest power on earth. To do this, lesser states had to be subdued. The same pattern would occur fourteen centuries later, when the Ottoman Sultan Mehmed II nursed similar ambitions. One of the states was the same too – Roman Dacia became medieval Wallachia; war was the only constant.

The first known inhabitants of what would become Trajan's province were the two tribes of the Getae and the Daciae, both of Thracian origin. The squint-eyed philosopher Strabo, whose seventeen-volume *Geographica* has survived since the time of Christ, claimed that the Getae lived on the Danubian Plain and the Daciae further north in the Transylvanian region of the Carpathian Mountains.

One of the many authorities, several of them now lost to time, from whom Strabo quoted was the Greek historian Herodotus, the 'father of history', who travelled widely to the north of his birthplace in Helicarnassus. He called the Daciae 'the bravest and most law-abiding among the Thracians',[1] though the Thracians 'were a meanly-living and dim-witted folk', and he mentions, too, their god, Zalmoxis, a god of the sky and a god of the dead. The first known ruler of the Daciae, a tribal chieftain like Caractacus in Britannia or Vercingetorix in Gaul, was Burebista, who died some forty years before Christ.

When Trajan set out in 101 to conquer Southern Dacia (Dacia Inferior) before marching north to Dacia Superior, the Roman legions were second to none in military terms throughout Europe. Even so, the Dacian tribesmen, in their wolf-coats and carrying their wolf's-head standards, fought to the bitter end and the campaign lasted five years. In common with the various bands of Celts further west, the Dacians relied on the single, hectic charge in battle, accompanied by as much noise and speed as possible, hoping that the terror of their advance would unsettle the enemy and make them run. Years of training had taught the Romans to hold their lines, locked steady behind their shield walls, and had taught that such steadiness won victories. It is probable that the Dacians, like the Celts, collected enemy heads as trophies, but the severed head may also have had a shamanistic and spiritual significance. Not for nothing were vampires' heads in folklore and reality hacked from their shoulders and not for nothing was the head of Vlad Ţepeş sent to the sultan in Constantinople.

Like many tribal chieftains who faced the disciplined conquest of Rome, the Dacian King Decebal, who ruled from 87 to 106, swallowed poison rather than submit to the humiliation of being dragged in chains through the streets of the empire's capital.

The Roman occupation of Dacia has left its mark for two millennia. Not only does modern Romania take its name from Trajan's legions, the veterans who settled and intermarried in the villages north of the Danube, but its language is still curiously Latin-based, unlike that of the Slavonic states all around it. 'These people', wrote the urbane and widely travelled scholar Eneo Silvio Piccolomini, who would be elected Pope Pius II during Dracula's reign, 'have a Roman language that has changed a great deal so that it is very difficult for someone from Italy to understand it'.[2]

Despite the fact that, rather romantically, some Romanians today make a great play of this lineal descent from the legions, the country could not remain isolated, despite the protection of its mountains, 'the horseshoe of the Carpathians', as Stoker called them, to the north. The anonymous author of *Slavs and Turks; the Borderlands of Islam in Europe*, written in the 1880s,[3] stated:

[The Carpathians] have been the battlefield of nations; on their soil have contended in succession Scyths, Romans, Huns, Bulgarians, Hungarians, Poles and . . . Ottoman Turks.

The draw for these nomadic, warring peoples as the Roman Empire crumbled, apart from the inevitable fact that

Dacia lay on the route to an even richer south, was the richness of its soil. The barbarians who drove the legions out in 271[4] knew that the Carpathians were rich in gold, silver, copper, iron, lead, mercury, bitumen and rocksalt. The forests of oak, beech and pine were prime providers of building materials, firewood and shelter, while the flood plain of the Danube offered superb grazing land for sheep and cattle.

As Dacia ceased to be so named with the fall of Rome, the Vlachs, the Magyars, the Szekely and the Cumans dominated the region. Piccolomini, in *Cosmographia*, has a simplistic, antiquarian explanation of the name:

> A colony of Romans was brought there, who ruled over the Dacians, under the leadership of one known as Fluccus, after whom the land was named Flucchia.[5]

All four tribal groups were nomadic, the Vlachs in particular taking refuge in the northern mountains that the Romans had called *trans silva*, the land beyond the forests. They followed their flocks to the extent that the word Vlach became synonymous with shepherd, though in the harsh Transylvanian winters they came south with an altogether less pastoral intent – to raid the trade caravans on the silk road to the East. These caravans, groaning with expensive brocades from China, rumbled westwards via Constantinople, before that great city began to produce silk of its own. It would eventually be Ottoman raids on the silk and spice roads that led Christóbal Colón (Christopher Columbus) to look for a new way to the East.

Christianity came to Dacia early in the fourth century, the Zalmoxian cult, already probably bastardized by the huge panoply of Roman gods, blending easily with the new faith.[6] According to Herodotus, the Dacians believed that Zalmoxis was originally a man imbued with Greek and Egyptian wisdom, who vanished;

> . . . into a whirlpool chamber, where he lived for three years, the Thracians wishing him back and mourning

him for dead; then in the fourth year, he appeared to the Thracians.

The parallel with Jesus's Resurrection is clear, as is Zalmoxis's hint of Heaven. He:

> taught them that neither he nor [the Thracians] should ever die, but that they should go to a place where they would live for ever and have all good things.

What is most intriguing about Zalmoxis – and utterly unlike his Christian counterpart – is that he was a god who demanded human sacrifice. Every five years, Herodotus tells us, the Dacians chose a man by lot to be a 'messenger' to be sent to Zalmoxis:

> and this is the manner of sending: three lances are held by men thereto appointed; others seize the messenger to Zalmoxis by his hands and feet and hurl him aloft on the spear-point.

A god who vanished beneath the earth? A god for whom his people longed? Are we talking about Vlad Ţepeş, the humanized Zalmoxis of his day? And what was the method of sending the messenger if it was not Dracula's favourite method of execution, impalement?

While the origin and use of impalement as a method of execution is discussed elsewhere, it may seem far-fetched to link the god Zalmoxis with all-too-human Vlad Ţepeş, a thousand years later. The parallels, however, are too much of a coincidence to ignore.

The first visible signs of Christianity in what would become Wallachia was a bishopric at Constanta on the Black Sea, which survived into the time of the Magyar invasions. Under their warrior leader Arpad, a chieftain from the Caucasus, the Magyars migrated west soon after their defeat by a neighbouring tribe, arriving in the late ninth century. Speaking a Turkic language and descended from Altaian nomads, they were related to the Huns who had in the ninth century driven out the Romans and settled in Pannonia, the vast plains to the east of Transylvania. Here they intermarried with the Dacians. In 997, Duke Stefan took the title of king, was crowned by Pope Sylvester II and forced Christianity on his people, organizing the church and endowing monasteries. He was canonized in 1083.

Within fifty years the people known as the Szekely established their settlements on the fringes of the Hungarian kingdom. The name itself means 'beyond the seat' and several anthropologists see them as the direct descendants of Attila's warriors: their broad faces, high cheekbones, sallow skin and black hair are perhaps a physical legacy of that descent. It was possibly a misreading of all this information in the British Museum or a misunderstanding of the history fed to him by Arminius Vambery that led Bram Stoker to claim, in *Dracula*, that the Count was of Szekely descent.

The Cumans' base was the steppe lands of Poland and the Ukraine, but they were of Turkish origin from central Asia and had spread west into the Carpathians and were fully Christian by the late twelfth century. They in turn fell to the Mongols, Khans of the Golden Horde.

These fierce nomadic peoples with their short-legged, fast ponies were the cavalry *par excellence* of the steppes. In 1240 an army of 40,000 Cumans fled west before them to the welcoming arms of Bela IV, King of Hungary. The Mongol leader Batu Khan wrote to Bela:

I have heard that you have taken the Cumans, who are my subjects, under your protection. I command you to send them away, for by taking my people away from me, you have become my enemy.[7]

Bela responded in a way similar to that of Vlad Ţepeş two and a half centuries later: he had Batu's envoys murdered. Hungary would be dissected by the whirlwind attacks of the great general Subedei Bat'atur of the Reindeer people. The Vlach leaders, nominally under the suzerainty of Byzantium, with their hard-riding cavalry and their spell-bound shamans, had no time to run to Pest, the Hungarian capital, for safety.

Village after village fell until Bela's army, stiffened by Cuman cavalry, faced the Mongols at Nady Czeks on the banks of the River Sajo. There, on 10 April 1241, the vastly outnumbered Mongol army won a dazzling victory with their deadly archers and heavy cavalry. The road to Pest was littered with Hungarian and Cuman corpses, according to one source, 'like stones in a quarry'.[8] An estimated 60,000 had died.

As the original inhabitants of the area, the Vlachs had migrated north in the late thirteenth century to the safety of the Carpathians, to settle permanently in Muntenia, the land of the mountains, called today Tara Romanesca, the Romanian land. A second period of migration in the middle of the fourteenth century led to the colonization of Moldavia, the mountainous territory that stretched to the River Moldova, which by Vlad Ţepeş' time would be a separate province.

Victoria Clark, travelling in the area recently, forms an excellent snapshot of this land:

> Naturally bountiful, bucolic, woodsmoke-scented and hemmed in on all sides by a crown of the Carpathian Mountains and the Transylvanian Alps, the province sits like a bright, rough jewel in its mountain setting. A world apart, Transylvania is a Bruegelesque-cum-Grimms'-fairy-tale place, dotted with little villages – some Hungarian, some Romanian and a few Saxon German settlements dating back to the thirteenth century. Its Orthodox churches, fat-bellied and squatter than the taller, sharp-steepled Hungarian Catholic competition or the few, now sadly crumbling, Saxon church-fortresses, embellish the countryside. Silver-roofed and freshly painted, they gleam in the cleavages between rolling green hills.[9]

Wallachia, the land of the Vlachs, came into existence as a state in 1290, although the term requires some qualification. In Western Europe the feudal system, with its vertical structure of lord and vassal, was creating nation states with a definite identity, bound by law, language and culture. It was in the 1290s, for example, that Scotland was flexing its military muscles in a war against the English overlordship of

Edward I, the 'Longshanks' whose reputation would be at least dented by the courage of William Wallace and the dogged perseverance of Robert the Bruce. A similar national identity was forged in France in the thirteenth century under Philip II and his Capetian successors, establishing hereditary monarchy and controlling the unruly aristocracy exactly as Vlad Țepeș would do in Wallachia two centuries later. There was no feudalism as such in Eastern Europe and the notion of a nation state would not emerge until the fifteenth century. According to today's hero-hungry Romania, it was Vlad Țepeș who provided the focus for an independent Wallachia. Wallachia was also very small, at 48,000 square miles only the size of New York State. Its population reached perhaps half a million (giving the lie to the later numbers of victims of Vlad Țepeș), scattered over the 3,000 or so villages between the mountains and the Danube.

The legendary founders of Wallachia were Radu Negru (Rudolf the Black) and his immediate successor, in 1310, Besarab the Great, whose shield carried three blackamoors, black-faced dancers who may symbolize his victory over the 'dog-faced Tartars' (Mongols) at the turn of the fourteenth century. His name has survived in Romanian folklore, but there is virtually no written evidence of him. His name suggests a Turkish origin and it may be that he was of Cuman stock. Thirty years after his death, however, Mircea the Old, often referred to as Mircea the Great or Wise, ruled Wallachia for an unprecedented thirty years. His grandson would become Vlad the Impaler.

Unlike Western Europe, where the concept of primogeniture, the right of the first born, was by now well established, in Wallachia only the ruling family retained hereditary powers. Neither was there an obsession with legitimacy which dominated the West. In France and England, for instance, younger and bastard sons were given titles, lands and armies, but they could not actually rule. In Wallachia, it was the blood of the royal father that was important, not the noble or marital status of his mother. In other words, a prince could inherit even if his mother were merely his father's mistress. There are interesting echoes here of the *nosferat*, defined in folklore as the still-born illegitimate child of two people who are similarly illegitimate. The *voivod* or prince was in fact elected by the boyars or nobility, and this led to a great deal of confusion in later years over Vlad Ţepeş' title. In John Polidori's time Vlad was referred to as 'the Wallachian boyard', thus reducing his status, which may even explain why Bram Stoker gave his eponymous hero/villain the rank of Count. What characterized the rule of medieval Wallachia was the frequent change or bloody removal of *voivodes*. For instance, between 1418 and 1456, no less than seven different *voivodes* reigned. All charges of brutality against Vlad Ţepeş should be measured against this yardstick – 'nobody's virtue was overnice', as the poet Austin Dobson was to write of a much later age.

The term *voivod* is of Slavic origin, and although it dominates the contemporary and neo-contemporary writings on the Impaler, Romanians preferred the term *domnul* (from the Latin *dominus*, lord) whose power varied according to the holder's personality and popularity. The *voivod* effectively was the government, in the way the king of Christian Castile or France, or England was the government. He was the highest judge in the land and alone had the right to mint coinage. He levied taxation and led his armies in time of war. Unlike the rulers of Spain and France, however, the *voivod* owed a particular debt to his boyars in the sense that he was merely *primus inter pares*, first among equals. He did not have to be the eldest son of the previous *voivod* to inherit the Wallachian throne; neither, as we have seen, did he have to be legitimate. But he had to be chosen by the Boyar Council and crowned by the Metropolitan of Ungro-Wallachia and Exarch of the Plains, the senior representative of the Orthodox Church.

The term boyar is associated in the West with Tsarist Russia, the definition in the 2000 edition of the *Penguin English Dictionary* clarifying it still further as 'a member of the pre-imperial Russian aristocracy'.[10] The origin of Wallachian boyars is obscure. They probably began rather as the *hetmen* of the Ukrainian Cossacks to the east, village elders rather than hereditary chivalric commanders of armies in the sense of the French *noblesse* or the Spanish *hidalgos*. There is disagreement among Romanian historians over the origin of the boyars. Some, like Peter Panaitescu, claim that linguistic evidence survives in proof of the fact that these rulers were the Romanized Magyar, Pecheneg and Cuman invaders. Others claim the native tradition as being more likely. In practice, however, they appeared little different from their counterparts in the West. A boyar might own vast estates with dozens of settlements, acquiring these, as did the western nobility, through dynastic marriage, outright cash purchase or as a gift from a paternalistic prince.

Rather as in England, where certain families were developing a reputation for a specific kind of service to the king,[11] boyars were given Byzantine titles and a complex hierarchy of power. Most of this came from the *voivod*, so the odd symbiotic relationship continued: the *voivod* needed the election and at least nominal support of his boyars; they needed the occasional hand-out from him. The senior boyar, or ban, was the governor of the province of Oltenia, through which the River Olt ran. Below him were two supporters, lesser nobility, who governed provinces or commanded castles much as the aristocracy did in England.

Far below the boyars – in every sense – were the peasants. Nominally free, these illiterate, superstitious people, so easily gripped by the night-terrors of the *varcolac* and the *strigoii*, actually lived as serfs on the estates of the boyars or the Orthodox Church. Ironically, as the concept of feudalism, with its freemen and serfs, was disappearing in the West in the rapid onset of a cash economy and mobile capitalism to become bastard feudalism, so the idea was becoming more firmly established in fifteenth-century Wallachia. This was so partly because of the influence of western ideas crossing the region via trade routes to the East, and also because of the increasing threat from the Ottoman Turks to the south-east.

The whole complex problem of Eastern European peasants and their relationship to *voivod* and boyars has been brilliantly researched by historian Kurt Treptow,[12] who begins by redefining what feudalism actually was. Finding the lord–vassal vertical relationship definition too narrow, Treptow believes that the structure has two major elements. First, it contains the 'hegemony of small-scale individual production',[13] and, second, 'the exploitative relationship between landowners and peasants in which the surplus beyond the subsistence [of the peasants] . . . is transformed under coercive sanction to [the landowners]'.[14]

This parasitic economic relationship was hit hard in what one contemporary called the 'hurling time' of the fourteenth century by the death caused by the spread of the plague and the upheavals of serious and prolonged warfare between rival states in Europe. Famine and fear in this most turbulent of centuries led to peasant risings, which had previously been insignificant, intensely localized and easily crushed. Wat Tyler's peasants, by contrast, marching from Blackheath in the summer of 1381, tore down John of Gaunt's palace of the Savoy and held the City of London for four days before a kind of order was restored. In France the *Jacquerie*[15] spread terror in the spring of 1358, leaving perhaps 20,000 dead between the Seine and the Marne. As one chronicler wrote, 'cultivation ceased, commerce ceased, serenity was at an end'. When Vlad Țepeș was six years old, the peasantry of Transylvania rose in revolt against an intolerable burden of boyar exploitation. The rising could only be crushed with help from Hungary. Other risings took place in the Balkan lands to the south of the Danube, especially in Albania, between 1343 and 1405.

The Serbian ruler Stefan Dusan set out his famous laws in 1349 in an attempt to control the peasantry, including Vlachs, who by mid-century had drifted south into his territories in large numbers. In England, the 1351 Statute of Labourers tried to do the same thing and it is likely that both were responses to the crippling economic and demographic effects of the plague, although Dusan was also concerned to establish the Serbian state. On the positive side, Serbian peasants had the right to bypass potentially unjust and avaricious boyars by contacting Dusan's courts direct. On the negative side:

If a serf flee anywhere from his lord's to another land . . .
where his master find him, let him brand him and slit his
nose and assure that he is again his.

Bandits were to be summarily hanged and any village
sheltering them severely punished. Vlad Țepeș would
introduce a similar code over a century later.

There was virtually no middle class in medieval Wallachia.
The three estates of Europe – *pugnare* (the boyars; literally
those who fight); *orare* (the Orthodox Church; literally those
who pray); and *laborare* (the peasants; literally those who
work) were fully represented, but whereas the bustling states
of England, France, Germany, Italy and the Low Countries
all provided native-bred merchants and artisans who bought,
sold and manufactured in the increasingly capitalist pursuit
of profit, the middling sort in Wallachia was almost
exclusively German.

The reason for the (almost totally urban) existence of these
'Saxons' in Transylvania and Wallachia is that they were
imported as colonists by the Hungarians in the twelfth
century. Still trickling in up to fifty years before Vlad Țepeș'
birth, they came from all the myriad German states, not just
Saxony, and some from as far west as the Rhineland and
Luxembourg, bringing with them their different customs,
fashions, language and culture – which may be the origin of
Robert Browning's alien band in his 'Pied Piper' poem.
Officially recognized as a nation, their wealth and Catholic
(as opposed to Orthodox) religion at once set them apart
from native Wallachians, and was the source of continued
friction. In 2000, Victoria Clark wrote:

> The two Christendoms have been rubbing and chafing for
> a thousand years here in Transylvania and there is still no
> disguising the rift between the minority population of
> Catholic . . . Hungarians and the majority of Orthodox
> Romanians.[16]

The Saxon merchants of Wallachia established towns with
German names: Sibiu was formerly Hermannstadt;[17] Bod

was Benkendorf and Braşov was Kronstadt in Burzenland, the richest and most densely populated of all. They even built fortifications to keep the indigenous population out, solid walls with brattices and barbicans, and governed from within rather in the manner of the powerful city states of northern Italy, Venice, Milan and Genoa. They kept in regular touch with their homelands through family and trade, and, as far as was possible under *voivod* overlordship, were a law unto themselves.

These Saxon cities could boast the finest craftsmen in Europe. Goldsmiths, tailors, shoemakers, silk weavers and metalworkers clattered and stitched side by side in the open-fronted workshops that lined the cobbled streets. In Braşov and Sibiu they made bronze cannons, the new and terrible engines of war that would change the world for ever, using the Carpathian ores of copper, gold and silver over which they had been granted a monopoly. Through the mountain passes of Bran and Turnu Roşu they carried on a trade that extended to the Danube delta on the Black Sea and to Constantinople, the ancient heart of Byzantium that would beat until the Turks crushed it in 1453. Bistriţa, on the northern, westward-facing route out of the 'horseshoe of the Carpathians', carried Transylvanian Saxon goods to Danzig and Hamburg, the ports of the Hanse, the most successful European trading venture before the Common Market in the twentieth century. At the Impaler's later capital of Tîrgoviste and the neighbouring Tîrgsor, large fairs were held where goods were displayed and sold to an admiring population. Whether selling internally or externally, the Saxons paid duties to the *voivod*; in 1456, Vlad Ţepeş wrote to the Germans of Braşov describing them as 'honest men, brothers, friends and sincere neighbours'.[18]

By the fifteenth century the Orthodox Church held sway over Wallachia and Transylvania although with less power than in countries nearer to Byzantium's heart, at Constantinople. The population of the Carpathians had nominally been converted to Christianity by missionaries during the ninth century, although incursions by pagan Slavs and marauding Mongols had made this an unsteady and haphazard process. The Metropolitan of Ungro-Wallachia and Exarch of the Plains was the Orthodox Church's leader in Wallachia and Transylvania, acting on behalf of the Patriarch in Constantinople, who had officially recognized the Church in 1359. Based at Curtea de Argeş, the Metropolitan presided over bishops and abbots who ruled estates as large as those of the boyars and whose monasteries, such as those at Tismana, Dealul and Snagov, were large and powerful centres of ecclesiastical wealth. In common with the church in much of Europe, they paid no taxes unless pressed by the emergency of war. Traditionally, *voivod* and boyars alike hid treasure in their fortified vaults; everybody paid the Church lip service because they guarded men's souls and presided over their path to Heaven or Hell. Besarab I was buried at Cîmpulung, like many other medieval rulers in his own foundation.

An underlying concern of the Orthodox Church was the dualist Bogomil heresy which surfaced in the Balkans in the tenth century. Believing that God's first-born was Lucifer, the cult's leader, the priest Bogomil, thought that the fallen angel had seduced Eve and that their son was the killer, Cain. Following on, both Moses and John the Baptist were Lucifer's servants, although he himself was ultimately defeated by Christ's Resurrection. The Bogomils, based largely in Bulgaria south of the Danube, resurfaced as an ascetic cult in the thirteenth century and were crushed by the Ottoman onslaught in the 1390s. They despised marriage and condemned the eating of meat and drinking of wine. To them, the Church's rites of communion and baptism smacked of Satan. In purely religious terms, the heresy spread west to influence the much more serious stand taken by the Cathars and Albigensians.[19] Here, the word 'bugger', derived from the word Bulgaria, where the sect had originated, crept into the French language by the thirteenth century, with as thick a gloss of sexual deviancy as the Catholic Church could muster.

The danger Bogomilism posed for the ruling elites was that, like most heresies, it had its insidious, political dimension. A priest named Cosmas wrote in the tenth century that the Bogomils:

teach their own people not to obey their masters; they blaspheme the wealthy . . . condemn the nobles, regard as vile in the sight of God those who serve the tsar [of Bulgaria] and forbid all slaves to obey their masters.[20]

We do not know how many of the sect lived north of the Danube in the Impaler's principality, but their existence in large numbers south of the river certainly helps to explain why Serbia was destroyed by the Turks at the Field of Blackbirds in 1389. 'It is not our business to defend the king,' one of the Bogomils told Stephen of Bosnia, 'Let the nobles do it.'[21]

Outside the tiny state of Wallachia, with its alien middle class, its avaricious boyars and its discontented peasantry, was a world far more powerful, waiting to swamp it.

In religious terms, what would become the Impaler's principality was still under the control of Byzantium, the Eastern Roman Empire, whose native language was Greek. At the heart of this exotic and ailing white elephant lay Constantinople, the city of the Golden Horn, lying between two worlds. For just over eleven centuries, this place of magic and wonder guarded the approaches to the Black Sea and stood as what it considered itself to be, the rightful successor to ancient Rome.

Constantine the Great[22] chose Byzantium for his capital, which he renamed after himself, the City of Constantine, on 11 May 330. General decline in eastern Roman towns, exacerbated perhaps by Slav, Persian and Arab invasions, led to a shrinkage in which Constantinople stood out as the shining exception, the sun dazzling for ever, it seemed, on the dome of Justinian's Hagia Sophia, the last great Roman basilica ever built.

The sixth-century Byzantine historian Procopius wrote of this church:

Within it is singularly full of light and sunshine; you would declare that the place is not lighted from without, but that the rays are produced within itself, such an abundance of light is poured into it. The gilded ceiling adds glory to its interior, though the light reflected upon the gold from the marble surpasses it in beauty. Who can tell of the splendours of the columns and marbles with which the church is adorned? One would think that one had come upon a meadow full of flowers in bloom . . .[23]

The style of church building born in Byzantium spread throughout the Balkans in the seventh and eighth centuries, although here the churches and monasteries, like the Impaler's Snagov, were rather more compact and modest. Everything about Constantinople was vast and designed to overawe. The Pantokrator monastery, for example, sanctified in 1136, had a leper-house, asylum and hospital. It employed 165 staff, including four permanent grave diggers, and its land yielded nearly 10,400 tons of corn a year. Even today, modern Istanbul has not filled the old city walls.

Constantinople was just as much a fortified, armed camp as it was a religious centre. Its outlying villages provided regiments to defend the city, many of whom would die on the ramparts in May 1453 when the Turkish sultan, the Impaler's enemy Mehmed the Conqueror, ended not only an era, but a way of life. The city also had its own merchant fleet and war galleys, whose powerful oars and lateen sails were the envy of the marauding Turks who quickly copied them.

By 1204 Constantinople had grown even larger, the old walls of Constantine abandoned and the later ramparts of the Emperor Theodosius marking its south-western boundary. The Golden Gate was the industrial quarter, with its overcrowded clutter of potters, tanners, wheelwrights and smiths. Beyond that stood the imperial barracks and parade ground of the men who would die under the Conqueror's guns. The city's water supply was poor and the roads that stretched away across Bulgaria (ancient Thrace) merely dusty tracks.

In that year, Venetian crusaders took Constantinople in the Fourth Crusade and from then on, Byzantium lay awaiting a long and lingering death. The essential difference between East and West was that at Constantinople, the Emperor and the Patriarch of the Orthodox Church cooperated (although the secular power was paramount). In the West, however, the Papacy refused to accept this situation, regarding itself superior to merely secular kings and princes. Even the Holy Roman Emperor was a slightly inferior partner to whom little deference was owed or paid. Between 1204 and 1261 Constantinople was a Latin kingdom under the control of Venice, although it reverted to Greek control after 1261.

When the Emperor Manuel II Palaeologus travelled west to attempt some sort of compromise with Rome, his reception was lukewarm, although the astonishingly successful flank attack by the 'Scythian shepherd' Timur-i-Leng (Christopher Marlowe's Tamburlaine) halted for fifty years Turkish designs on the City of the Golden Horn. The West continued to treat Constantinople as a sideshow at best, and the serious rift between Greek and Roman Christianity left a power vacuum all too willingly filled by the Turks. As the English poet G.K. Chesterton would write 500 years later:

And Christian killeth Christian in a narrow dusty room,
And Christian hateth Christ who has a newer face of doom.[24]

So the Council of Florence, signed in the presence of the Byzantine Emperor John VIII when Vlad Ţepeş was eight years old, was boycotted by the Orthodox bishops of Wallachia and Russia, who could find little common kindred with Rome.

Against this background, it is hardly surprising that the calls for crusade in 1459 by Eneo Silvio Piccolomini, Pius II, against a common threat from the Islamic Ottoman Empire, fell largely on deaf ears in the East.

The kingdom of Hungary to Wallachia's immediate west was to play a vital role in the life of Vlad Ţepeş. By 1301, the Arpad dynasty, which had reigned since the ninth century, had come to an end. In many ways, this was the most enlightened of the medieval kingdoms, with three diets (assemblies) representing aristocracy and gentry a full century before Simon de Montfort, Earl of Leicester, set up what could be considered the first English parliament at Lewes in 1264. Its monarchy was also elective, because primogeniture was not established here and, under Louis the Great, a first step towards emancipation of the serfs was taken in the Golden Bull of 1351. Louis' successor was his daughter, Mary, but only on the condition that she maintain Salic law by styling herself 'King Mary'. Salic law was originally a Turkish code of the fifth century, and its best-known feature was its banning of females from inheritance; for example, under its provisions, Queen Victoria could not inherit the Electorship of Hanover on the death of her uncle William IV in 1837.

Further west still lay the scattered lands and widely differing cultures that called themselves the Holy Roman Empire. Voltaire, who had firm views on the vampire epidemics sweeping Europe in his eighteenth century, famously commented that it was 'neither Holy, nor Roman', and Napoleon Bonaparte took the concept further forty years later by destroying its very existence as an empire. Some sixty years after the death of Vlad Ţepeş, the Emperor Charles V was allegedly to sum up the problems of ruling his vast dominions in the words, 'Je parle espagnol à Dieu, italien aux femmes, français aux hommes et allemand à mon cheval.' ('I speak Spanish to God, Italian to women, French to men and German to my horse.') The 'Germanies' (the single country was not welded together until 1871) comprised over 300 tiny states, with their own rulers, laws, customs, commerce, armies and dialects. As in Hungary, the Emperor was elected by three archbishops and four archdukes – the Electors – whose normal ploy was to choose an idiot whom they could control. One bad choice, from their point of view, was Sigismund, son of Charles IV, who was crowned in 1411. Sigismund had married 'King Mary' in 1387 and assumed the role of king of Hungary too. When his half-brother Wenceslas died in 1419, the Emperor also became king of Bohemia.

To the north of Wallachia, the most powerful state in the East was Poland. The modern world has tended to treat this kingdom like a political football, wedged as it was between the twentieth-century 'superstates' of Germany and Russia. The country had been badly ravaged by the Mongols in 1241, as part of the campaign which had destroyed Bela of Hungary's army, but Poland survived, only to become a battleground between the Teutonic knights of the Cross, one of the most formidable of the medieval orders of chivalry, and the pagan Prussians further east.

Under King Casimir the Great, Poland became a united and important state, Casimir's laws of 1347 being the first complete legal code anywhere in Europe. He founded a university at Kraków in 1364 and, almost uniquely among Christian rulers, welcomed Jews into that city, and others, to develop trade and banking.[25] His nephew, Louis, was also king of Hungary, and his daughter, the ten-year-old Jadwiga, married the pagan Duke Jagiello, who was baptized at the wedding and adopted the Christian name of Ladislas II. His son, in turn, would die in battle with the Turks, fighting alongside the elder brother of Vlad Ţepeş.

To Wallachia's north-east lay the duchy of Muscovy. Eighteen years after Vlad the Impaler's death, its ruler, Ivan III, described himself as 'Tsar of all the Russias', yet two centuries earlier, Muscovy was only one tiny city state along with the duchies of Tver, Riazan, Novgorod and Pskov. Easily defended and on the busy river network which made trade easy, the duchy grew inexorably in its defence against the Mongols, whose own internal divisions had led to weakness. In 1380 the Muscovite Duke Dmitri Donskoy smashed the Golden Horde at Kulikovo Polje, and despite a reversal two years later, the victory proved that the legendary Mongols could be beaten. In a series of dynastic marriages and open military attacks, the highly capable Ivan incorporated both Riazan and Tver into his duchy and then subdued Novgorod, its famous cathedral bell dragged to Moscow as a symbol of the defeated city's collapse.

Like Casimir in Poland, Ivan codified a *sudebnik*, a list of laws to govern his expanding territory. As we have seen, he sent envoys such as Fedor Kuritsyn to the West to learn their secrets in an age of rapid change, inviting the best Italian architects to work at his palace-fortress of the Kremlin some time before the Impaler's death. In November 1472, he married Zoë, the niece of the last Byzantine Emperor. It was from the Roman legacy of Byzantium that Ivan chose the double eagle as his soon-to-be imperial standard, and from the old Roman title of Caesar that he took the term Tsar.

Although geographically as far from Ţepeş' Wallachia as was Muscovy, the bustling city state of Venice had, by the fifteenth century, made a profound mark on the late medieval world. It faced the Balkans across a twenty-mile strip of the Adriatic and, in the opposite direction, its arch trading rival, Genoa. It had outposts for commerce along the Black Sea coasts, the Crimea and Constantinople itself. Ragusa (today's Dubrovnik, Croatia) was Venice's principal outpost in the Balkans, until it was won back from Venice by Louis of Hungary in the mid-fourteenth century.

Venice was an island, sheltered by a series of lagoons and protected by an army of grim-faced *condottieri* (mercenaries, literally contractors). It reached the height of its commercial success in the years immediately preceding Vlad Ţepeş' birth. Some city merchants sailed on the armed merchant galleys themselves, supervising the arrival of silks and spices from the East, gold from Africa, jewels from Arabia and glass from Syria, dealing in wine, grain, dyes and alum, all in the name of profit. By the year of the Impaler's death, Venice had its own arsenal employing over 2,000 people, along with foundries, magazines, shipyards, chandlers and an army of sailors. The rest of Europe envied this city state and its rival Genoa. Its very name was synonymous with luxury and wealth. Not for nothing did Shakespeare, a century later, set one of the most tragic of his 'comedies' there. Officially, Jews like Shylock had to wear yellow hats as a mark of their race, and were only allowed to engage in those most despicable of professions, medicine and usury. But over the whole city presided the Doge, an elected official who had assumed the status of a prince, sailing out on the lagoons each Ascension Day to bless the waters and give thanks to God for the bounty of the money-bearing sea.

Further south, central Italy was the province of the Holy Father, the pope, with the Holy See of Rome at the heart of the Papal States. In the year of Vlad Ţepeş' birth, a great council of the Western Church was called at Basle to heal, once and for all, it was hoped, the great schism which had split the Catholic Church in the previous century. It was then, in 1381, that Clement VII had retired to Avignon in Southern France, while his rival, Urban VI, had remained in Rome. Inevitably, because the pope was an Italian princeling, a political as much as a religious figure, the kingdoms of Europe took sides. France, Spain and Scotland supported Clement; England, the Italian states, the Holy Roman Empire and Hungary backed Urban, even when the latter began torturing recalcitrant cardinals to death. A series of councils, from Pisa in 1409 to Constance in 1414, was held to resolve the split in the College of Cardinals, from among whom popes were elected. Between 1415 and 1418 no less than forty-five assemblies were held with dozens of committee meetings and no doubt hundreds of cloister-side chats. Scholars descended from all over Europe, including representatives from the Orthodox Church, which had in theory been separated from Rome since 1054. One pope was at last elected in 1417, but by the time of the Basle conference, other issues had arisen and exposed the papacy once again. The new pope, Eugenius IV, clashed with his cardinals, and both sent envoys to Constantinople to effect some sort of reunion with the Eastern Church. The whole process collapsed under a welter of bickering and animosity and by the end of the '30s there was even a schism of councils – one at Basle, one at Ferrara, and finally one at Florence.

Even so, it was this papacy, petty and small-minded, that alone had the power to call for a crusade. And alone of the rulers of Europe in 1462, it was Vlad the Impaler who actually took it up.

The Europe of Vlad Ţepeş was a changing world. The Renaissance was already under way. Essentially an attempt to recreate the 'glory that was Greece and the grandeur that was Rome',[26] the movement in fact took men forward to an age of humanism, technology and science.

Leonardo da Vinci was ten years old when Ţepeş attacked the Turks along the Danube; he was eighteen and apprenticed to the sculptor–painter Verrocchio by the time the Impaler was a prisoner of Hungarian King Matthias Corvinus. Verrocchio himself was already working with the goldsmith partner whose surname he adopted by the time Țepeş took the throne of Wallachia for the first time. Donato di Niccolo di Betto Bardi (Donatello) was already carving his fame in marble in both Florence and Padua before Țepeş was born, and the future *voivod* was still a prisoner of the Turks and perhaps witnessing impalement at first hand when the artist cast the first life-size horse ever to be made in bronze, the mounted figure of the Venetian *condottiere*, Erasmo da Narni, known as Gattamelata, the Honey Cat; it might have been a statue of the Impaler. Paolo di Dono Uccello, the Florentine goldsmith, was working with Ghiberti on the magnificent doors of the baptistry when Vlad was still a boy in Sighişoara. The lumbering horses and dazzling heraldry of his *Rout of San Romano* resembles a painted snapshot of one of the Impaler's battles against the Turks.

Filippo Brunelleschi, the great architect, fascinated by straight lines and mathematical symmetry, had already established vanishing point perspective by the time Vlad was a boy, and by the decade of his death, the Italian explorer-adventurer Christóbal Colón knew that the earth was round. All he needed was the money, ships and men to prove it.

Wherever there were artists, sculptors and painters, there were patrons, powerful men who collected works of art and kept their makers busy with the designing of tombs to impress God and the weapons of war to kill His enemies. The Sforzas in Milan and the Medici in Florence vied with each other for the accolade of the most influential scions of the arts, although the honour should probably go to the Impaler's contemporary Lorenzo the Magnificent, who encouraged archaeological digs and archive-sifting as well as aspiring geniuses.

How much this Renaissance world travelled East in Vlad Țepeş' time is difficult to gauge. Nicolas Copernicus studied at the University of Kraków, but not in the Impaler's lifetime, and the Copernican 'heresy' of the heliocentric universe belongs to another generation. Matthias Corvinus was certainly a patron in the mould of the Medicis, and while Țepeş was under house arrest at Visegrád, Benedetto da Maiano, Giovanni Dalmata and Chimenti Camicia were all present in Buda, working on the king's castles and palaces. Visegrád itself was described by the ambassador of Pope Sixtus IV as a 'terrestrial paradise', and the extraordinary alabaster relief of Corvinus made by Giancristoforo Romano thirteen years after the Impaler's death is a wonderful example of Renaissance artistic skill.

But south of the River Danube, teeming with its rainbow trout, grayling, dace, sturgeon and Grecian carp, lay Bulgaria and the dangerous, creeping armed camp that was the Ottoman Empire of the Turks, the greatest military force on the edge of Europe. Here was a very different civilization, at once fatalistic and aggressive, poetic and barbarous. And against it stood the tiny mountain state of Wallachia, with its *voivod*, Vlad Ţepeş, and his people.

# 6

# 'A WILD
# BLOODTHIRSTY MAN . . .'

In May 1484, a Silesian knight, Nicolas von Popplau, met King Richard III of England at the castle of Pontefract in Yorkshire. Von Popplau, emissary of the Holy Roman Emperor, Frederick III, was a giant of a man, known equally for his skills in the tilt as for his classical learning and diplomacy. 'I wish that my kingdom', the king told von Popplau, who later recorded the words in his diary, 'lay upon the confines of Turkey; with my own people alone and without the help of other princes I should like to drive away not only the Turks, but all my foes.'[1]

The Silesian does not record what prompted the comment, but in all probability, Richard III was talking about a man of his own stamp, a warrior-king whose reputation was destroyed by subsequent generations – Vlad Țepeș, the Impaler.

Vlad ruled as *voivod* and prince of Wallachia three times. The first reign, lasting barely two months in 1448, was perhaps too brief to be worthy of anecdote and legend, but the second, between 1456 and 1462, produced scores of tales on which the man's reputation rests. He inherited a throne that was usually won and lost on the battlefield and came to rule a people whose ruling hierarchy was fickle and untrustworthy. Intent on centralizing and consolidating his power, as so many of his contemporaries were doing, Țepeș was prepared to use harsh measures to achieve his ends.

Above all, he took a principality under threat – from the ever-pushy Hungarians to the west and the terrifying advance of the Ottoman Turks to the south. It is against this background that the stories of this 'wild bloodthirsty man' must be set and against this background that he should be judged.

Apart from the official documentation from his court, which will be discussed later, there are three broad sources of information on Vlad Ţepeş the man. The first, made possible partly by the Renaissance achievement of the printing press, comes from the 'Saxon' community living in Wallachia, but more especially Transylvania itself.

Europe did not invent printing. The earliest examples of printed texts come from Korea in the eighth century, and the first example of movable type using individual letters is again Korean, and dates from 1409. In the West, however, it was Johann Gutenberg's great Bible of forty-two lines per page that lays claim to being the first printed book. Gutenberg called his printed Gothic letters 'artificial writing', nearly three million of them making up the 1,282 pages. He made perhaps 200 copies, when Vlad Ţepeş was in his twenties, of which a staggering thirty-eight survive today.

The printing press caught on. By 1500, 250 towns had presses, employing in each case dozens of specialist craftsmen to boil and wash linen rags to make paper or prepare vellum (calf-skin), to pour molten metal into tiny moulds and to file off rough 'flash'. The compositors laid out the letters to form the lines and paragraphs; the printers used ink made from lampblack or charcoal mixed with linseed oil. Mainz had been the first town to perfect this technique, possibly as early as 1455, but the technology spread to Leipzig, Stuttgart, Nuremberg and Augsburg within fifteen years. Kraków in Poland and Buda in Hungary had their own presses five years before William Caxton set his up at the sign of the red Pale in Westminster Abbey in the year that Vlad Ţepeş died.

Inevitably, many of the earliest books, like Gutenberg's, were Bibles, psalters or other religious works. But by 1463 the world saw one of its first political pamphlets, printed in Vienna, the Austrian capital, on the subject of Vlad Ţepeş, *voivod* of Wallachia. Entitled *The Story of a Bloodthirsty*

*Madman Called Dracula of Wallachia*, it was probably based on a poem penned the previous year by Michel Beheim, the court poet of the Holy Roman Emperor, Frederick III. Beheim was the son of a Bohemian weaver, born in Sulzbach, Württemberg in September 1416. He tried his hand at travel and the bloody trade of war before studying music and theology. Beheim's first patron was Count Ulrich Cilli (who was later assassinated). By 1457 Beheim was court poet to Ladislas V Habsburg and should correctly be regarded as a *minnesinger*, a court minstrel in the mould of the thirteenth-century troubadours; some books describe him as a *meistersinger*, but technically such performers were attached to the powerful guilds that dominated European towns. Both *meistersinger*s and *minnesinger*s were balladeers who took folk tales and even actual events, embellishing and changing them for particular audiences' tastes. At the close of the 1450s, Beheim was flitting among patrons in Bohemia and Hungary, and it was by chance that he met the itinerant preacher, Brother Jacob, at Wiener Neustadt, thirty miles south of Vienna, near Jacob's monastery of Melk. Jacob seems to have been the sole source for *The Story of a Bloodthirsty Madman Called Dracula of Wallachia*, which was probably completed in four months.

The 1,070-line work found its way in published form to the University of Heidelberg, while Matthias Corvinus's scribes probably made an even more defamatory version for propaganda purposes late in 1463. The poem quickly became a favourite with the Emperor Frederick, who for the next two years insisted that Beheim recite it to important guests at banquets. There is no equivalent of *minnesinger* or *meistersinger* today. Known in Wallachia as guslars, schools for such singers, where the apprenticeship was long and arduous, were set up throughout the Holy Roman Empire, but the earliest was probably at Mainz, followed by Augsburg in 1450. Whether Beheim ever set his Dracula poem to music is unknown, but, given the bias of Brother Jacob, who was Beheim's source, we cannot rely on the poem as history. It is as warped and dramatized as Shakespeare's version of the reign of Richard III, and for the same reasons. Beheim's poems about the Impaler were the direct forerunners of the works of Polidori, Stoker and the celluloid fictions that followed.

The German stories were often accompanied by woodcuts of a particularly grisly kind. Some were mere representations of the Impaler, as in the frontispiece of *Dracole Waida*, printed at Nuremberg about twelve years after his death. The text begins, 'In the year of our Lord, 1456 Dracula did many dreadful and curious things.' The best known, printed by Ambrosius Huber, again at Nuremberg, in 1499, shows the famous blood feast. The text above the ghastly scene, in effect a sort of caption, reads:

Here begins a very cruel frightening story about a wild bloodthirsty man, Dracula the *voivod*. How he impaled people and roasted them and hacked them into pieces like a head of cabbage. He also roasted the children of mothers and they had to eat their children themselves. And many other horrible things are written in this tract and also in which land he ruled.[2]

The woodcut shows Țepeș, a benign-looking Renaissance prince with full beard and civilian clothes, sitting at an open-air table with food and goblets in front of him. Feet from him an underling is hacking the limbs off corpses with an axe, and behind the table, near-naked men and women are writhing in their deaththroes, impaled on spikes. The event depicted refers to Țepeș' attack on the 'Saxon' city of Brașov, called by the Germans Kronstadt,[3] in April 1459. The pamphlet reads:

And he led away all those whom he had captured within the city . . . near the chapel of St Jacob. And at that time Dracula . . . had the entire suburb burned. Also . . . all those whom he had taken captive, men and women, young and old, children, he had impaled on the hill by the chapel and all around the hill and under them he proceeded to eat at table and enjoyed himself in that way.[4]

Most of the German stories found their way into the monastery of St Gallen in Switzerland or the cathedral at Lambach near Salzburg, where Adolf Hitler, five centuries later, would sing in the choir. The Lambach Papers, like Ţepeş' body and grave furniture, have disappeared. Today, St Gallen is a canton, named after a seventh-century saint. The abbot of the monastery presided over the area until the nineteenth century. The fact that the paper trail of the German stories of Ţepeş leads to Lambach and St Gallen is important and explains a great deal about their bias. According to historical fact, the Impaler launched a series of raids against 'Saxon' towns and churches in Transylvania between 1457 and 1460. The German Catholic monks fled to the West, taking their horror stories with them, rather as did the aristocratic émigrés fleeing the Terror in Paris in the 1790s. The Benedictines told their stories while anonymous scribes copied them down. One name in particular emerges, however: Brother Jacob, the probable source of the epic poem written by Michel Beheim.

St Gallen houses the bulk of the 'Saxon' stories, thirty-two tales of terror written in *Plattdeutsch*, the low German dialect, and can only have been intended for consumption by the monks themselves. Rather than translating, as most authorities do, all the stories, this book attempts to categorize them according to type. Of the thirty-two, a possible ten can be verified by historical sources, which, while not unimpeachable, at least have an air of authority. The first of these, numbered one in MSS No. 806 in the St Gallen Library, refers to the murder of Vlad's father, Dracul, and his brother, Mircea, by 'the former governor'. This must be János Hunyadi, the 'white knight' whose name was legendary among the crusaders of the late medieval period. His influence on Ţepeş and the effects of the murders are crucial to an understanding of the Impaler, and will be discussed elsewhere.

The second tale relates Ţepeş' killing of Ladislaus Voda, the Vladislav II who was his rival and who ruled Wallachia for the eight years before his execution in 1456, the year in which, the St Gallen tales remind us, 'this Dracula did and threatened to do terrible things in Wallachia, as well as in Hungary'.

The third describes Ţepeş' invasion of Transylvania, destroying castles, villages and towns, including Beckendorf, which was either Bod or Benesti near Braşov, and the monasteries of Holtznundorff and Holtznetya. Prisoners and refugees from these raids were impaled, irrespective of age or sex. 'He had a big family uprooted,' reads one translation of tale number seven,[5] 'from the smallest to the largest, children, friends, brothers, sisters and he had them all impaled.'

This family has been identified with that of the powerful boyar Albu cel Mare (Albert the Great), himself no stranger to rape and pillage, who had defected to Prince Dan III, another of the Impaler's rivals.

Dan himself came to a suitably sticky end for crossing Ţepeş, as tale nine relates:

He [Ţepeş] also captured the young Darin [Dan]. Later on he allowed him to go through his priestly function and when he had completed it all, then he had him make a grave according to the custom of the Christians and he had his body slaughtered by the grave.

Other sources give us Dan's execution date in April or May 1460, probably at Tîrgsor.

Tale ten is typically repetitious and involves the imprisonment of emissaries sent by Matthias Corvinus, King of Hungary, who appear to have turned up with 'Saxon' delegates from the various Transylvanian towns. He held them for five weeks, mentally torturing them by setting up stakes in view of their cells as though for their impalement. He launched his attack on Transylvania, burning the fields around Kranstatt (Braşov) and rounding up the populace 'near the chapel called St Jacob'. This was the infamous occasion when the Impaler reputedly sat down to dine al fresco within sight of his dying, twitching victims.

Tale number fourteen is a similar, if less gruesome recital:

there [in the towns of the seven fortresses at Siebenburgen and Talmetz] he had men hacked up like cabbage and he had those whom he took back . . . as captives cruelly and in various ways impaled.

In the story that Peter Painitescu describes as 'additions to the St Gallen manuscript',[6] Ţepeş' attack on the village of Amlaş is told with particular relish:[7]

In the year 1460, on St Bartholomew's Day [August 24] in the morning, Dracula crossed the forest with his servants and looked for all the Saxons, of both sexes, around the village of Amlaş and all those that he could gather together he ordered to be thrown, one on top of the other, like a hill and to slaughter them like cabbage, with swords and knives. And their chaplain and the others who he did not kill immediately, he took back to his country and there had them hanged. And he ordered that the village and everything in it, including the people, who numbered more than 30,000, to be burned.

And then, from all the lands which are called Figaras, he took the people and brought them to Wallachia, men, women and children and he ordered that all of them be impaled.

And then, he ordered that more of his boyars be decapitated and he took their heads and he used them to grow cabbage. After this, he invited their friends to his house and he gave them the cabbage to eat. And he said to them: 'Now you eat the heads of your friends.' After this he ordered that all of them be impaled.

And then he ordered that some of his people be buried naked to the navel. After this he ordered that they be shot. He also had many roasted and the skin peeled off others.

In some translations, the final paragraph appears as a separate story, and it is one of a possible eleven which seem to have no purpose other than to nauseate the reader and blacken Ţepeş' reputation. Tale number six, which has echoes throughout history – including a notorious mass execution of British troops by SS General Wilhelm Monck in 1943 – concerns the murder, which seems to have no motive, of 'young boys and others from many lands' who were sent to Wallachia ostensibly 'to learn the language and other things'. Ţepeş 'brought them together and betrayed them. There were four hundred in the room.' Story number thirty is very similar. In this, the victims are 200 paupers lured to a feast provided by the Impaler.

As if bored by incessant impalement, Dracula experimented with other forms of torture. In story number thirteen:

> he had a great pot made with two handles and over it a staging device with planks and through it he had holes made, so that men's heads would fall through them. Then he had a great fire made underneath it and had water poured into the pot and had men boiled in this way.

Tale number seventeen takes up this theme, perhaps with a hint of the ethnic cleansing that has become a Balkan way of life in our own time. A gypsy was caught stealing and the Impaler gave his own people the chance to hang him. When they said 'That is not our custom', Ţepeş had the gypsy boiled in a pot and when he was cooked, he forced them to eat him, flesh and bone.

To see Vlad's singling out of a gypsy as well as his targeting of 'Saxons' as examples of racism or xenophobia is to misunderstand the temper of the times. Wallachia was not yet a nation state but the fact that the gypsy was branded a thief has echoes throughout Europe, where it was widely believed that the nomadic travellers stole children. Legend has it that Vlad Dracul, the Impaler's father, brought thousands of gypsies (*tiganes* in Romanian) as slaves to his principality, but in fact, they were indigenous to the area long before reaching northern Europe by the end of the fourteenth century.

Tale number fifteen is particularly repellent:

> Once he had thought up terrifying and frightening and unspeakable tortures, so he had mothers impaled and nursing children, and he had one- and two-year-old children impaled. He had children taken away from their mothers' breasts, the mothers separated from their children.

He also had the mothers' breasts cut out and the children's heads pushed through the holes in their mothers' bodies and then he impaled them. And he caused many other sufferings and such great pain and tortures as all the bloodthirsty persecutors of Christendom, such as Herod, Nero, Diocletian and other pagans,[8] had never thought up or made such martyrs as did this bloodthirsty berserker.[9]

Tale number eighteen has a moralizing tone which is found in other 'Saxon' stories relating to Țepeș and echoed in the other translations concerning him (see below). A surreal scene is conjured up in which the *voivod* and a boyar are strolling under rotting, impaled corpses 'as many as a great forest'. Țepeș asks the nobleman if the smell offends him and when the answer is yes, 'Dracula immediately had him impaled and hoisted up high in the air, that he would not smell the stench.'

Among these quite random and repetitive stories of atrocities, there is a clear obsession with cannibalism. This aspect of the character of Vlad Țepeș will be analysed later, but the constant reference to cabbages and relatives being forced to eat each other might tell us more about the clerical compiler of the tales than about their subject. So, in number twenty-nine, 300 gypsies were forced to 'eat the others until there are none left'. In tale thirty-one, Țepeș 'had very young children roasted and forced their mothers to eat them. He cut the breasts off women and forced their husbands to eat them; after that', the tale continues with a certain inevitability, 'he had them impaled'.

Two stories in particular stand out and point perhaps to Țepeș' real character. Tale number twenty-one describes not the usual summary ordering of execution, but a hands-on murder directly committed by him. It provides, if true, a rare glimpse of a warped human being behind the mask of terror he showed to the world:

He had a mistress who announced that she was pregnant, so he had her looked at [examined] by another woman, who could not comprehend how she could be pregnant. So he took the mistress and cut her up from under to her breast and said 'Let the world see where I have been and where my fruit lay.' He also had similar things cut or pierced and did other inhuman things which are said about him.

Tale sixteen takes us further into the dark soul of a madman:

He had people impaled, usually indiscriminately, young and old, women and men. People tried to defend themselves with hands and feet and they twisted around and twitched like frogs. After that he had them impaled and spoke often in this language: 'Oh, what gracefulness they exhibit!' And they were pagans, Jews, Christians, heretics and Wallachians.

The point about the list of groups of victims is to show the Impaler's lack of discrimination. It is unlikely that the refugee monks fleeing to St Gallen would be unduly perturbed by anything Vlad Țepeș chose to do to pagans, heretics and Jews, who were all fair game in their denial of God and Christ.[10] But to kill Christians, and Wallachian Christians at that, was truly unforgivable.

We know the names of some of those monks whose memories, reportage and embellishments form the crux of the thirty-two 'Saxon' stories. The three referred to by Michel Beheim in his epic poem of 1463 are Brother Jacob, Brother Michel and Brother Hans the Porter, who may be based on, or actually be, real characters described to the minnesinger by the one, Jacob, who was undoubtedly a flesh and blood priest. The records of St Gallen also mention Blasius, who came from Bistrița, one of the Impaler's target towns with its sawmills and tanneries, and Johannes de Septum Castis (John of the Seven Fortresses, i.e. Siebenburgen, Transylvania).

It is the 'Saxon' stories, with their obvious bias, distortion and repetition, that formed the written kernel of the legend of the Impaler used by the Hungarian King Matthias Corvinus' when it suited his political purpose, as propaganda against the *voivod*. The lurid nature of the tales quickly made stationers (publishers) realize that here was a money-spinning spine-tingler that would run and run. Historians McNally and Florescu suggest the reasonable hypothesis that Țepeș was the first non-religious best-seller and that probably only the Bible outsold him in the late fifteenth century. In 1488, three Dracula tales were printed at Nuremberg, and one at Lübeck. The stationer Hans Spörer produced another in Bamberg in 1491 and a fourth rolled off the presses of Martin Landsberg at Leipzig two years later. As the new century dawned, the stories travelled westwards. Matthias Hupfuff published the tale in Strasbourg in 1500; Des Iegher produced a variant in Hamburg two years later. And they were still appearing in Nuremberg as late as 1521.

It was in these years, when the Ottoman Turks destroyed the flower of Hungarian chivalry at Mohácz (1526) and Martin Luther unleashed his torrent of protest against the Catholic Church, that Vlad Țepeș appeared in works of fiction far removed from the effects of Polidori, Rymer and Stoker. He appeared in the satirical poem 'Flöhaz, Weiber Traz' by Johann Fischart in 1573. Thirteen years earlier, he is referred to in another poem, this time by the Hungarian priest Matthias Nagybanki. And the use of Țepeș as a tyrant synonymous with pure evil extends through German and Hungarian literature well into Stoker's time.

The second set of sources for our knowledge of Vlad Dracula comes from the Russian narratives preserved in the Kirillov-Belozersky monastery collection in the Saltykov-Schredin Public Library in St Petersburg. We have already noted the 'sinner' monk Efrosin who probably wrote the manuscript, and Fedor Kuritsyn, the envoy of Muscovy, who met the Impaler's family at the Hungarian court and collected stories about him. Whereas the 'Saxon' stories blacken the Impaler's reputation because he came down hard on them as foreigners and avaricious capitalists bleeding his own people, the Russian tales seem much more ready to accept that such violence was normal for the time and justified by what contemporary Englishmen called 'good governaunce'. There is a sense in which Vlad Țepeș became a blueprint for later Russian governments, rather as Cesare Borgia, born in the year of the Impaler's death, was the model for Niccolò Machiavelli's *The Prince*, written in 1515.

There are nineteen Russian tales from the Kirillov-Belozersky monastery compiled about the year 1490, sixteen years after the Impaler's death:

There lived in the Wallachian lands a Christian prince of the Greek [Orthodox] faith who was called Dracula in the Wallachian language, which means devil in our language, for he was as cruelly clever as was his name and so was his life.

Using the same criteria for categorization as in the 'Saxon' stories, a different pattern emerges. Six are historical and can be verified, not only by reference to 'Saxon' and Romanian versions, but also by independent documentary evidence. Of these, three refer to the Impaler's crusades against the Turks and will be dealt with elsewhere.

Three stories, however, exhibit a streak of morality totally missing from the Saxon tales. The first, number four, reads like a story from the Arabian nights:

Dracula so hated evil in his land that if someone committed a misdeed such as theft, robbery, lying or some injustice, he had no chance of staying alive. Whether he was a nobleman or a priest or a monk or a common man, or even if he had great wealth, he could not escape death. And he was so feared that in a certain place he had a source of water and a fountain where many travellers came from many lands and many of these people came to drink at the fountain and the source, because the water was cool and sweet. Dracula had put near this fountain in a deserted place a great cup wonderfully wrought in gold; and whoever wished to drink the water could use this cup and put it back in its place. And as long as this cup was there, no-one dared steal it.

There are strange echoes here of Prester John, the semi-mythical Christian king who lived, according to various commentators, in either Cathay (China) or Ethiopia. John had a magic mirror that enabled him to see all corners of his kingdom to eradicate crime. The fabled king, however, predates Țepeș. The 'English' knight John Mandeville discusses him in 1366, and his name first appears in written texts as early as 1145.

Tale number six concerns two Hungarian monks who visited Wallachia. Dracula shows one of them his victims, 'countless people on stakes and spokes of wheels'. 'Have I done well?' the *voivod* asks the monk. 'No, lord,' comes the reply. 'You have done badly. You punish without mercy.' The second monk, however, has a very different perspective. 'You have been assigned by God as sovereign to punish those who do evil and to reward those who do good. Certainly they have done evil and have received what they deserved.' This cleric is given fifty gold ducats and safe conduct by carriage to the Hungarian border. The first is quizzed by Țepeș as to why he has left his cell and wandered abroad when clearly he is so stupid. 'And he ordered that he be impaled from the bottom up.'

The next story in the sequence describes the arrival in Tîrgoviste of a Hungarian merchant who leaves his gold-laden carriage in the street outside the Impaler's palace. In the night someone steals 160 ducats from the vehicle and, not unreasonably, the merchant complains to the *voivod*. The Impaler orders a search for the thief, threatening destruction of the city if he is not found. In the meantime, Țepeș has the carriage loaded with 161 ducats and waits for morning. The merchant counts his money, extremely impressed and reports to the *voivod* that there is one extra coin. The thief is caught with the original haul and Țepeș delivers the moral of the tale himself: 'Go in peace. If you had not told me about the additional coin, I was ready to impale you, together with the thief.'[11]

Seven of the Russian stories are variations of the 'Saxon' tales. In place of the Wuetzerland merchants whose headgear was nailed to their heads because they refused to uncover before the *voivod*, we have the much more likely Turks:

When they entered his palace and bowed to him, as was their custom, they did not take their caps [turbans] from their heads and Dracula asked them 'Why have you acted so? You ambassadors have come to a great sovereign and you have shamed me.' The ambassadors announced 'Such is the custom of our land and our sovereign.' And Dracula told them, 'Well, I want to strengthen you in your custom. Behave bravely.' And he ordered that their caps be nailed to their heads with small iron nails. . . . 'Go relate this to your sovereign, for he is accustomed to accepting such shame from you, but we are not.'

Tale number two follows on to suggest that this insult to his ambassadors stung the Sultan, Mehmed II, into an invasion of Wallachia, rather as Henry V is supposed to have sailed for Harfleur after the slight of the gift of tennis balls from his rival, the king of France. The truth, as always, is far more complicated.

A variant on this appears in story number twelve. Any ambassador who appears before Ţepeş improperly dressed or unable to answer a question to the *voivod*'s liking is likely to die, the blame for this lying squarely with the monarch who sent him. '"I am not guilty of your death, but your own sovereign."' Alternatively, it could be the fault of the emissary himself – '"because you are slow-witted and . . . not properly versed . . . then you yourself have committed suicide."'

Only two of the Russian stories appear to be examples of cruelty for its own sake, and the first of these is widely found in folklore throughout the world, so perhaps can be dismissed entirely. Ţepeş orders workmen to fill iron-hooped barrels with gold and bury them in a river-bed. He then has the men killed 'so that no one would know the crime committed by Dracula except for the devil whose name he bore'. The only glimmer of veracity here is the *voivod* propensity for stashing valuables in monastic and church vaults. Could the lake at Snagov be one such hiding place?[12]

The other is a decidedly odd narrative concerning the Impaler's time under house arrest in Pest, across the river from Buda, where he had been placed by King Matthias Corvinus some time in the mid-1470s. There is a hue and cry in the city, the felon hurtling through Ţepeş' courtyard in his desperation to flee the mob. Grabbed by the prefect (constable of the watch), the criminal suddenly finds himself free because Ţepeş has decapitated the officer with his sword. Taken to task by Corvinus's magistrates, the Impaler's reply is unabashed:

> I did not commit a crime. He committed suicide. Anyone will perish in this way should he thievingly invade the house of a great sovereign.

Corvinus is impressed with the *voivod*'s courage, and laughs the incident off.

There is little doubt that Ţepeş' tales of terror struck a chord not only with Fedor Kuritsyn but the Russian psyche generally. And it manifested itself most obviously in the reign of Ivan III's grandson, the Terrible. The Russian version of his nickname is actually *groznyi*, which means awe-inspiring. The first of the Muscovite grand dukes to adopt the title Tsar, Ivan carried out a grim regime which might almost be taken as a blueprint from Vlad Ţepeş. Like the Tudors in England, he reduced the power of his nobility, elevating humbler men whom he could trust. After poisoning his wife, Anastasia Romanova, in 1558, he turned on opponents with increasing cruelty. He punished unruly ambassadors who failed to show him respect by nailing their caps to their heads. (Interestingly, as recently as 1917, Tsarist officers who refused to submit to Bolshevik power by removing their epaulettes had them nailed to their shoulders.) Ivan also used impalement as a slow and excruciating form of execution, which had rarely if ever been used in Russia before his time. Many authorities, including Dracula experts, dismiss Ivan IV as insane, but are loath to draw the same conclusion about the Impaler. The exhumation of Ivan the Terrible from his tomb in St Petersburg revealed that the impaler–tsar suffered from osteoarthritis, an incurable condition that would have caused him almost constant pain and may explain at least some of his eccentric and vicious behaviour.

The final strand of information on Vlad Ţepeş comes from

the mangled memories of his own people, the Romanian folktales. Of the eight usually listed in modern translations, seven also occur in the Russian texts and six in the 'Saxon' versions. What is interesting is that several of them have two or three variations, reflecting their folkloric origin. So, for instance, the story of the merchant whose carriage is robbed in Tîrgoviste of 160 golden ducats has two more variants. In the first, the merchant calls to passers-by at crossroads for help; the cash is in lei, Romanian currency. A local, described as 'a Christian' and 'a God-fearing man, as were the Romanians at the time of Prince Vlad the Impaler', finds the money bag, but it is short by 100 *lei*. The merchant takes the peasant to court, accusing him of helping himself to the money as a reward. Țepeș presides and decides that the merchant is the dishonest one, declaring, 'Master merchant, at my court people do not know what a lie is.' In the third variant, 'there reigned in Wallachia a Prince Dracula, also known as the Impaler. This prince was very severe, but also just. He would not tolerate thieves, liars and lazy people.' The travelling merchant is specifically from Florence and he goes to ask Țepeș for safe conduct through his land. Instead the *voivod* orders the merchant to leave his money in the square overnight, insisting it will be safe until morning. And, in the usual pattern of morality tales and fairy stories, this is true.

In the story of the man with the short shirt, whose wife had clearly neglected him, Țepeș orders her to be impaled despite her husband's protestations – 'She never leaves home and she is honest' – and provides him with another wife, whose sole duty is to work for the peasant. Tellingly, in this, as in other Romanian folktales, the story looks back nostalgically to a 'golden age' in which life was much more pleasant:

It is just as well that Dracula does not rule our country today, for he would have had to expend many stakes, which might have eliminated from our land the innumerable drones who wither the very grass on which they sit.

The burning of the poor story, which occurs as 'Saxon' tale number thirty and Russian number five, is treated as a cautionary tale of the type made popular throughout Europe in a later period.[13] The emphasis here is on the shiftlessness of Wallachian beggars, a view shared by the authorities of all European states concerning their own poor. The English Poor Law of 1601 was introduced as an attempt to control the 'sturdy beggars', gangs of armed and potentially dangerous ruffians who threatened law and order. As the Romanian tale says of such people, 'I am looking for a master, but God grant that I don't find one.' Țepeș' policy was to eradicate the poverty problem rather more ruthlessly than Elizabeth's government. He invites the poor to a feast in Tîrgoviste, the tables groaning with wine and fine food. When they are more than merry, the *voivod* orders the doors to be locked and the fire lit:

> The blaze rose high like inflamed dragons. Shouts, shrieks and moans rose from the lips of all the poor enclosed there. But why should a fire be moved by the entreaties of men? They fell upon each other. They embraced each other. They sought help, but there was no human ear left to listen to them. They began to twist in the torments of the fire that was destroying them. The fire finally abated, there was no trace of any living soul.

The teller of the tale ruefully admits that Țepeș' fire did not solve the problem, as 'Beggars will cease to exist only with the end of the world.'

A tale in the Romanian collection found nowhere else relates to the *voivod*'s attack on his boyars. In language reminiscent of his handling of the poor, he invites them to a banquet at his capital and in the course of the evening, asks each of them, 'How many reigns have you, my loyal subjects, personally experienced in your lifetime?' There is a variety of answers, but one that probably annoys the Impaler most is, 'Since your grandfather, my liege, there have been no less than twenty princes. I have survived them all.' This is precisely the point. The answer is, in fact, wrong, but the moral is the issue. Such was the anarchy in Wallachia when Țepeș assumed the throne in 1456 that he was faced with an oligarchy of self-servers prepared to condone and even commit murder to survive and to protect the status quo; any number of princes could come and go as long as the boyars continued to hold power. According to the tale, 500 boyars, their families and hangers-on are impaled on the spot.

Further stories continue their saga. According to other variants Țepeș ambushed the boyars as they attended the Easter service with its famous words *Hristos o-nviat* ('Christ is risen') and the response *Adevărat c-o-nviat* ('Truly, He is risen'), and the most recent research tends to confirm that this is historically possible, even probable.

Oral history is an infuriatingly vague field, and when translated from a foreign language can sound a little naïve. The problem with Țepeș stories in Romanian culture is that the language itself was not written until the sixteenth century. Church Slavonic was the language of the Impaler's own court and we have no way of knowing whether the Impaler himself understood the various dialects of his principality or could even make himself understood without an interpreter.[14] The story of the building of Țepeș' castle at Poenari was first written down from Romanian folklore by a writer called Constantine Cantacuzino in the seventeenth century:

> He sent his retainers who, striking on Easter Day, apprehended the husbands and their wives, their sons and daughters in their gaudy clothes and took them to the castle of Poenari, where they toiled until their clothes fell off their backs.

The folktales began to appear in print by stages after this time, the castle-building saga being written up by the Metropolitan Neofit in 1747, at a time when the Enlightenment was taking root in Europe and vampire epidemics were on the increase. The printer Petre Ispirescu published the tales in Bucharest over fifty years after Neofit, but he was no folklorist and much seems to have been lost in translation. The teacher C. Radulescu-Codin did a better job more recently, and more recently still the Institute of Folklore under Mihai Pop has carried out invaluable research on the tales. Much of this is still going on and the need is pressing. Under the Conducator, there was a marked drift to the cities in search of work because of the destruction of village life in order to modernize. This led to a breakdown of old cultures, and the folkloric tradition can be said to be under threat.

Vlad Țepeș emerged hesitantly in Romanian literature as a folk hero along the lines of Spain's El Cid, Switzerland's William Tell or England's Robin Hood. Whole books have been written about these characters, at once men and legends, in an attempt to find the truth. In the nineteenth century, the age of nationalism, Romania was still under the rigid influences of the ailing Ottoman Empire on the one hand, and the aggressive Russian Empire on the other. In 1848, the Year of Revolutions, Țepeș assumed an Arthurian quality in Romania, a hero asleep and waiting for the trumpet call to waken him. The poet Mihai Eminescu imagined him sorting out the idiots who dominated the state:

> You must come, O dread Impaler, confound them to your care.
> Spilt them in two partitions, here the fools, the rascals there.[15]

The 'Saxons' saw Țepeș as a monster because he brought their rapacious capitalism to heel; the Russians, perhaps looking to echo the Impaler's centralized state, saw him as cruel, but just; the Romanians saw him as a hero on a white horse, at once delivering them from the corruption of the boyars and the Turkish onslaught on their borders. Where, in all this, lies the *real* Vlad Țepeș?

# 7

# THE SIGN OF THE DRAGON

From the eighth to the seventeenth centuries the West experienced many attacks by Muslim forces: no coincidence, surely, that this period was the high plateau of the Devil's career in Christendom. Bearded, swarthy, impulsive, violent, deceitful and oversexed.[1]

We have only one signature known to be that of Vlad the Impaler. In a letter to the citizens (mostly German) of Braşov dated 4 August 1475, he signs 'Wladislaus Dragwlya', Vlad, son of the Dragon. In the as yet unwritten Wallachian language, however, Dracul meant devil as well as dragon and in this double sense it can be found elsewhere in Europe. A century after Vlad Dracula, the English seaman and pirate Francis Drake was called El Dracque by his Spanish enemies, as a pun on his name, on the fact that 'draco' means dragon in Latin and that with the success of his raids on Spanish silver convoys and Cadiz, he must, indeed, be the devil.

Peter Dickinson, in his *The Flight of Dragons*, gives three possible views on the beasts: they are legendary; they are second-hand sightings of real, exotic animals like crocodiles or boa constrictors; they were once real. In the medieval mind, they were associated with fierce courage: in Britain, Arthur's battle standard was traditionally the dragon:

The voice of the dragon is thunder, the trembling of the earthquakes his footfall, forest and heath fires are the heat of his breath . . .[2]

The dragon is a destructive and dangerous power, hoarding gold and striking terror into its enemies. The Celtic tradition of the dragon as a symbol of sovereignty probably explains the Arthur connection. The dragon was also associated with the serpent, who seduced Eve in the Garden of Eden:

> Now the serpent was more subtil than any beast of the field . . . And he said unto the woman, Yea, hath God said Ye shall not eat of every tree of the garden?

Eve, tempted by the fruit of the forbidden tree, relented. God's vengeance was swift:

> And the Lord God said unto the serpent Because thou hast done this, thou art cursed above all cattle and above every beast of the field; upon thy belly shalt thou go and dust shalt thou eat all the days of thy life.[3]

Artistically, there was little to distinguish the dragon from the snake in medieval art. Heraldically, the dragon was a common device; the snake rare. The heraldic serpent was a symbol of evil – a result of the Fall. Often found at the feet of medieval saints, the serpent crushed by a cross was a typical Byzantine motif. So the terms serpent and dragon were interchangeable and, probably because of the biblical curse, the dragon came to be associated with terrible events. For instance, the *Anglo-Saxon Chronicle* of 793 records:

> Here dire warnings were come over the land of the Northumbrians and sadly terrified the people. There were tremendous lightnings and fiery dragons were seen flying through the air.[4]

These were the ominous signs of the Viking raids on Lindisfarne and along the coast of north-east England. The imagery of the devil is associated with these marauders too – berserkers chewing their shields in their battle-madness, horns protruding through their headgear – and the myth of the Viking horned helmet has survived until recent times.

According to Dickinson:[5]

> The Devil, in Christianized art, became *the* dragon. We are so used to the identification that it is hard for us to see that it is not a very logical piece of symbolism, if everybody knew in their hearts that dragons were mythic monsters. Elsewhere, Christian symbols are very concrete, following the limitations of the parables of Christ. The souls of men are sheep; the Holy Ghost is a dove; sinners are goats; the enemies of the Church are wolves . . .'

Dragons are part of the folklore and mythology of many cultures world-wide, but in Europe they took a certain shape and are almost always associated with fire.[6] In the third century, the Greek philosopher Flavius Philostratus wrote knowledgeably about the dragons of the mountains which:

> had yellow scales the colour of gold and [were] longer than the dragon of the plains, with a beard like the bristles of the swine and very heavy eyelids and brows, giving a horrible appearance. When the dragon climbed and dragged itself across the land the scales on its stomach resounded like metal. And it would seem that these reddish creatures gave off sparks of fire.

In biblical references, which would have been known by Catholic and Orthodox priests alike, a dragon is equated with the primordial monster referred to in the Books of Job, Isaiah and Amos:

> . . . And the great dragon was cast out . . . which deceiveth the whole world: he was cast out into the earth . . .[7]

The Apocalypse compares the dragon directly with the serpent of Eden and whenever dragons are found in pseudo-histories, the heroes who vanquish them are listed too: in Egyptian mythology Anubis; in Greek, Apollo, Perseus, Hercules and Jason; in Christian, George, Michael and Margaret. In the last cases, typified by St George as an armoured knight piercing the dragon with a lance (an excellent example is the painting by Paolo Uccello completed during Vlad Țepeș' lifetime), the representation is of good destroying evil. Impalement with the lance has fascinating echoes, as we have seen, both of Zalmoxian sacrifice in ancient Dacia and of the execution methods of Vlad Țepeș. The Order of the Dragon gained a new member, the Impaler's father, probably in the year of Vlad's birth; but among its many scions, only the rulers of Wallachia seem to have adopted the word as a sort of nickname, no doubt to drive terror into the hearts of their enemies.

Vlad Țepeș' grandfather was Mircea the 'Great', a nickname sometimes translated as the Wise or even the Old. Lord of Wallachia from 1386 to 1418, he ruled a country as large as modern Romania, with the Black Sea to the east and the Danube to the south. It included most of what is today Transylvania, with a line of marcher castles to keep out the ever-pushy Hungarians to the west and an Island fortress at Giurgiu on the Danube, watching over events to the south.

The river was important, not just as a source of trade, but for defence. At 1,780 miles the longest river in Europe, it rises in the Black Forest and was navigable by the ocean-going ships of the Middle Ages as far inland as Ulm. To facilitate the Dacian campaign Trajan built a stone bridge across it, the ruins of which still survive. In Țepeș' time there was no bridge, but a determined army could cross in rafts or boats, hence the strategic importance of Mircea's castle at Giurgiu. Brother Jacob's Benedictine monastery of Melk still frowns down from its 200-foot perch above the river, and at Belgrade, where the Impaler's mentor and nemesis János Hunyadi died of the plague in 1465, it extends a mile across and forty feet deep. Further south, at Kazan, the Danube narrows to 480 feet with a depth of 150 feet. As it glides past the Wallachian plain, it approaches Orsova, where rocks – the Iron Gates – block the river bed and make the crossing easier. At its eastern end, the river flows into the Black Sea via channels, the Kilia, Tulcea, Suchia and St George, forming a delta teeming with its 110 species of fish, despite oozing with its post-Ceaușescu pollution.

In 1389 Mircea took this area, Dobriya, and also built a delta stronghold at Chilia. He gave himself the rather grand title of 'God's anointed and Christ's loving autocrat Ioan Mircea, Great *Voivod* and Prince, with God's help ruler over Ungro-Wallachia and parts of the country beyond the mountains, the Tartar lands, the duchies of Amlaş and Fagaras, ruler of the Banat of Severin and of both banks of the Danube up to the Black Sea.'[8]

The reason for Mircea's obsession with the Danube is that beyond it lay Serbia, a land increasingly at the mercy of the Ottoman Turks pushing to gain territory from the south-east. This astonishing expansion, which terrified central and Western Europe by its speed and success, will be evaluated fully in the next chapter, but between 1320 and 1390, the Turks had crossed the Dardanelles into Europe and were on the southern banks of the Danube. As historian Jason Goodwin says:[9]

They moved so fast and so suddenly that they swerved beneath the eye of chroniclers and no single battle can be dated with precision before 15 June 1389, when they shattered the Serbs at Kosovo, on the Blackbird Field.

In all probability, there were Wallachians sent by Mircea to fight at Kosovo, a battle still remembered today by the Serbs as a black day in their history. It was there that Sultan Murad I was killed, according to legend, in his tent. He was stabbed by a Serb assassin, Milosh Obravitch, who, in turn, was hacked to death before he could reach his horse to escape. Typical of a rising nation which had neither the time nor patience to cope with the contending rule of two sons, Murad's elder boy, Bayezid, known as Yilderim, the 'Thunderbolt', had his brother executed either on the field or days later, and assumed the throne. Jason Goodwin sums up the man who was to be an implacable enemy of the Christians:

He dressed like a Greek, practised buggery like one, drank wine . . . he seems to have enjoyed having enemies. 'For this was I born – to bear arms and to conquer whatever is before me.'

The concept of bearing arms and conquering was part of the creed of the Ottoman Turks. The Koran, on its first page, points the way:

As to those who reject faith, it is the same to them whether thou warn them or do not warn them; they will not believe. Allah hath set a seal on their hearts and on their hearing and on their eyes is a great veil; great is the penalty they incur.[10]

Since the Arab conquests of the seventh century, European Christendom had good reason to fear the Muslim world. In the 1460s the songs of the guslars bemoaned:

The Wallachian land is split apart, the people run to the mountains, to the valleys, away from the cruel Turks . . . The old men, cut down, they enslave the young ones, they rape the girls, they capture the youth and enlist them in their armies . . . wherever they pass, they burn the villages.[11]

Two years after the death of the prophet Mohammed, Abu Bakr and his followers had conquered the Arabian peninsula. Driving their cavalry hard into the deserts of Egypt, Syria and Mesopotamia, they had besieged Constantinople by 669 and again between 673 and 678. The astonishing speed of their success can be attributed to much the same malaise in their opponents that existed in Vlad Țepeș' time and explains the ultimate failure of the crusading ideal. Both the Byzantine and Persian empires were riven by internal feuds, and in an age before the coming of the nation state, nationalist loyalty and its corollary, xenophobia, was not yet a sufficiently potent force to act as a rallying cry for anything approximating collective security.

On their part, the Muslims used their faith like a weapon. Surprisingly tolerant of other faiths among the peoples they conquered – they did not insist on conversion to Islam – the prophet promised paradise to Muslim warriors who died for

Allah.[12] By the eighth century, they had spread west into southern France before being defeated by Charles the Hammer and his Franks at Poitiers in 732, and as far east as the Punjab beyond the mountains of the Hindu Kush.

The concept of the Muslim holy war, jihad, was echoed in the West by the crusade. Under the battle cry *Deus Io Volt* (God Wills It) the crusaders first assembled under the banner of Pope Urban II in 1095, marching to the Holy Land with its shrines and Christian legacy, to free the holy places from the Infidel (a name for unbelievers used by both sides). The crusade was the approximate ideological equivalent of the Cold War of the twentieth century, only at this time the eastern versus western philosophies centred on God rather than politics. The important difference was that the crusades were 'hot' wars, with bitter campaigns, pitched battles and wholesale slaughter. Neither did they live up to the chivalric ideal of the medieval knight epitomized in the Victorian view of Richard the Lionheart, who led the Third Crusade in 1189. It is possible to see Richard today as a psychopathic killer with a homosexual streak, a far cry from the fictionalized view of him in, for example, the Robin Hood stories. Ninety years earlier, Godfrey de Bouillon's Frenchmen had massacred men, women and children in Jerusalem, wading, according to one chronicler, up to their spurs in blood.

But it is important to see this in context, as we must the life of Vlad Ţepeş. The crusades were extraordinarily difficult, long-range military operations involving relatively small, sometimes multi-national armies travelling the length of Europe and beyond, by land and sea. After the First Crusade, which took Jerusalem in 1099, later crusades achieved less success, partly because of the disunity of the crusaders themselves. Godfrey de Bouillon's army was depleted seriously in numbers because his commanders, Baldwin of Boulogne, Raymond of Toulouse and Bohemond of Taranto, broke off to establish their own fiefdoms at Edessa and Antioch. In the Third Crusade, fierce bickering broke out between Richard of England, his cousin Philip Augustus of France and Duke Leopold V of Austria. According to legend, which, even if apocryphal, makes the point well enough, when Richard saw Leopold's eagle flag flapping over the captured city of Acre, he ordered it to be hauled down and used as a dishcloth.

Many histories of the crusades assert that the movement ended in 1291, when the last Christian outpost fell in Palestine. The idea survived, however, depending on one's definition of crusade, and, with the appearance of the Ottoman threat in the fifteenth century, it revived with renewed urgency.

Bayezid's advance was clearly not going to stop at Kosovo. If Serbia fell, Bulgaria would be next and Bulgaria was only across the Danube from Mircea's principality of Wallachia. For safety's sake, the *voivod* looked to friends in the West, most notably Sigismund of Luxembourg and Bohemia, the Margrave of Brandenburg, who by virtue of his marriage to Maria, daughter of Louis the Great, had by now been elected king of Hungary. Like George the elector of Hanover who three centuries later would become king of England, Sigismund did not love his new Magyar lands, but became grudgingly fonder of them as his reign continued. Shown in contemporary manuscripts as a wise man with a magnificent forked beard falling over his ermine robes and fine plate armour, Sigismund realized that he would need to check the Ottoman advance if the Turkish threat to the south were to be averted. The Balkan states were like a set of dominoes: if one fell, there was a risk to them all.

Accordingly, because it was mutually beneficial to them, Sigismund and Mircea signed an alliance some time in 1395; but there must have been an element of mistrust because Mircea had to send one of his sons, Vlad, as a hostage to ensure the Wallachian ruler's continued support.

We do not know the date of Vlad's birth, but it is likely that he was under ten when he was taken, as a political prisoner, to the court of Sigismund at Buda on the Danube. The notion of political hostages and noble sons growing up in other noble or even royal households is not as alien as it seems. Mircea would have wanted the boy to have the best education available, and, as Sigismund's court, in keeping with that of most European royalty, was endlessly peripatetic, the boy would have visited Prague, Nuremberg and Rome as well as the Hungarian and Transylvanian towns nearer to home. It is likely that Vlad would have learned Hungarian, Greek, Latin, Italian and perhaps French, because Sigismund's wife, Maria, was the daughter of a French prince.

Vlad's mother is unknown. Mircea's first wife was Maria, of the Hungarian house of Tolmay, and the couple's only surviving son was Mihail, who would co-rule with his father for the ten years after 1408. Vlad was the result of a liaison with an unknown mistress, but his claim to the throne of Wallachia was as strong as Mihail's under contemporary law.

There are differing dates for the foundation of the Order of the Dragon with which Vlad and his son the Impaler would both be invested. It was possibly December 1387, the year in which Sigismund was elected to the throne of Hungary and it is likely that his wife Barbara (Barbola) was co-founder. It was not actually a knightly order, unlike the earlier crusader examples of the Templars and Hospitallers, but it served much the same purpose. The Order of the Dragon is an obscure organization and it is possible, according to D'Arcy Boulton of the University of Notre Dame, that it was founded before 1381. It makes no mention in its statutes, reaffirmed in 1431, the year of Vlad Ţepeş' birth, of knighthood being a prerequisite of membership.

The reason for the Order's creation is also shrouded in mystery, but it is likely that Sigismund intended it to be all things to all men and a source of feudal power whose support he could count on in time of need. His election to the throne of Hungary was not as peaceful as it appeared at first sight. Sigismund had been betrothed to Maria, Louis the Great's daughter, as was the custom of the time, when she was eleven and he ten. On Louis' death, however, Maria's mother ignored her late husband's will and married Maria to the younger brother of the French king, Louis of Valois-Orleans. In August 1385, the seventeen-year-old Sigismund kidnapped the girl and forced her to marry him. Only after the removal of a rival, Carlo 'di Durazzo', in February 1386 and a carefully worded agreement among the electors which Sigismund had to sign, was he allowed to co-rule with Maria.

The king's reign, however, was to be as troubled as the Impaler's. A rival clique of Hungarian nobility centring on the house of Horvathy backed the claims to the throne of Carlo's son, Ladislas, and Maria's death in the year of the treaty with Mircea left Sigismund with a weak claim to the throne.[13] It was now that young Vlad was probably sent to Buda, but at an inauspicious time.

Bayezid the Thunderbolt laid siege to the city of Constantinople in 1396, but news of Sigismund's crusade against him persuaded him to lift it and march north-west to meet his enemy. A besieging army attacked by a relieving force would be trapped, and Bayezid was too wily an opponent to be caught that way. The crusade of 1396 began with an army of 6,000 French and Burgundians marching to free Constantinople. The capital of Byzantium had been besieged many times before, but there was a sense now that the city was vulnerable, and if it fell, a way of life would be destroyed for ever. In Buda, they joined forces with Sigismund's army of Teutonic and Hungarian knights, who, together with their peasant billmen and archers, probably numbered about 20,000. It must have been a colourful sight, the banners of Sigismund, Jean de Nevers, Frederick of Hohenzollern and, according to some sources, Henry Bolingbroke, Duke of Lancaster, the future King Henry IV of England, dancing at the head of the host.

The crusader army was caught napping on the hills overlooking the fortress of Nicopolis on the Danube on 25 September. There are conflicting explanations as to what happened, but the weakness, as ever, seems to be lack of cohesion among the crusaders. A rational explanation is that Bayezid sent out a feint, a weak force of *spahi*, heavy cavalry, knowing that the Christian tactic was the shock charge of armoured knights. In European battles at this time, only English knights fought dismounted, relying on the superiority of their archers' longbows. Sigismund, perhaps advised by the more cautious Mircea, who knew Turkish tactics well, advanced slowly with his Hungarian infantry. Someone, probably Jean de Nevers, son of the Duke of Burgundy, ordered the charge of his 6,000 knights. These men were riding 'ham to knee' up a hill (as Oliver Cromwell later described in his own cavalry charges), never a sensible ploy for cavalry, the *spahi* breaking before them as pre-arranged. The destriers (war-horses) of the fourteenth century, weighing a ton and with a maximum speed of ten miles an hour, forged their way past the slogging footsoldiers and reached the ridge, but found themselves cut off and facing a force of Turkish janissaries (infantry) about ten times their strength.

In a scene redolent of Vlad the Impaler and the English tactics at Agincourt nineteen years later, the Turkish horse-archers parted to reveal a row of sharpened wooden stakes angled into the ground, into which the terrified, rearing animals of the crusaders ran, skewering themselves on the points. In the frantic hand-to-hand combat that followed, the janissaries closed in and hacked down those who still had fight in them. Were the Hungarians too cautious? Were the French, notorious for their dash and fire, too impetuous? It looked to some as though Mircea had abandoned Sigismund to his fate, but he may simply have judged the battle lost and his troops melted away to the sheltering Carpathians forests.

On the field, the Thunderbolt ordered the execution of all but twenty-four of the best-armoured knights and a handful of baggage boys who would be trained as janissaries, as was the Thunderbolt's custom. An estimated 10,000 died before dusk on that September night, although the exact method of their despatch is not recorded. A column of cavalry followed Mircea into Wallachia to carry out punitive raids on his villages; others struck west into Styria, taking thousands of prisoners. Back in Paris, it was forbidden to utter the name Nicopolis at court, and the stragglers of the French army returning over the coming months were threatened with the rope if they told what they knew.

The effects of Nicopolis could have been worse, but Sigismund was forced into exile for five years, having been toppled by his rivals, and he spent his days until 1408 contending with those rivals to win back his throne. In that year, to thank those who had stayed loyal to him, the Garai and Cilli families in particular, and to secure their continued support, he reinstated the Order of the Dragon. Its statutes, written on 13 December 1408, simply call it in Latin *Societas*, its members to be recognized by the *signum draconis*, the sign of the dragon; but it is called elsewhere *fraternatis draconem*, the dragon brotherhood. The statutes took the form of an agreement between Sigismund and Barbola and twenty-one *barones* (nobility):

> . . . in company with the prelates, barons and magnates of our kingdom, whom we invite to participate with us in this party, by reason of the sign and effigy of our pure inclination and intention to crush the pernicious deeds of: the same perfidious enemy, and of the followers of the ancient Dragon; and . . . of the pagan knights, schismatics and other nations of the Orthodox faith; and those envious of the Cross of Christ and of our kingdoms and of his holy and saving religion of faith.

The *signum draconis* was clearly described:

> the sign or effigy of the Dragon incurved into the form of a circle, its tail winding around its neck, divided through the middle of its back along its length from the top of its head right to the tip of its tail with blood [forming] a red cross, flowing out into the interior of the cleft by a white crack untouched by blood, just as and in the same way that those who fight under the banner of the glorious martyr St George are accustomed to bear a red cross on a white field . . .[14]

Members of the order swore fealty to Sigismund and his wife and to their heirs as yet unborn, and to defend them and their realm from attack or plot against them. They also swore to protect each other, coming to each other's aid and support wherever the need arose. In accordance with the feudal obligations on the wane in the West, but only now strengthening in the East, Sigismund and Barbola promised to defend the Order's members, their families and property. Each member was to attend the funeral of a fellow member or, if that was not possible, to have thirty masses said for his soul, to dress in the black of mourning every Friday, to have five masses said for the five wounds of Christ and to wear the dragon.

In this respect, the Order of the Dragon was superficially similar to earlier monarchical orders of knighthood. But it was also different: there was no patron, despite references to St George; there was no headquarters or regular meetings; and lastly, since no mention was made of knighthood, it may be that this was purely a political organization, the elements of which were essentially secret. True to his word, Sigismund granted lands and titles to his Draconists and they passed these among themselves, adding to their power so that in effect the Order, not the king, was the real power in Hungary by the time of Sigismund's death in 1437. Four years earlier, Sigismund, King of the Romans from 1410 and King of Bohemia by 1419, had the Dragon Order's statutes confirmed by Pope Eugenius IV when he was crowned Holy Roman Emperor in 1433.

Official documentation survives referring to the fact that the Order of the Dragon was not merely Hungarian, but international. Ernst 'the iron' of Austria was invested in 1409, the Marquis of Ancona (from northern Italy) in 1413, Vitautis, Grand Prince of Lithuania in 1429 and, in either January or February 1431, Vlad, son of Mircea, soon to be Prince Vlad II of Wallachia.

Since about 1395, Vlad had been with Sigismund's court wherever he went, some at least of that time out of his kingdom because of the years of political intrigue. Florescu and McNally conjecture that the boy became profoundly unhappy as he grew to manhood surrounded by the infighting and intrigue of an alien court. This is highly likely, but the truth is we know almost nothing of Vlad's early life.

In these years Mircea's vulnerable principality was saved from Bayezid's continued advance by the timely arrival of another conqueror from the East, Timur-i-Leng. Born about 1346 near Samarkand, this Turkic Muslim hurtled westward with a huge army, bent on destruction of anything in their path. A bronze bust made from the man's exhumed skull shows a fierce-looking warrior with high cheekbones, a full mouth and hard eyes; but since these features reflect the artist's imagination rather than the facts of bone formation, we cannot be sure that this is an accurate portrayal of the lame 'Scythian shepherd'.[15] While Timur's protégé Toktamish swept north into Russia, burning Moscow in 1381 and slaughtering thousands of its inhabitants, Timur himself turned due west.

Here, in the spring of 1398, he was met by an extraordinary delegation. Ambassadors from Constantinople, emirs from Anatolia, emissaries of the merchant states of Venice and Genoa and from the king of France all called on the warrior to take on the Ottoman Empire. By this time, the territory of the unpopular Bayezid stretched to an incredible 267,000 square miles. There was a sense that the Thunderbolt had overreached himself.

Although Timur refused the Christian offer, it was perhaps inevitable that the Muslim–Tartar clash would happen anyway. He took the town of Sivas, executing Bayezid's son and burning alive 3,000 soldiers. With a fighting force twice the size of the enemy's he met the Thunderbolt's army at Ankara on 28 July 1402. But it was now Bayezid's turn to be wrong-footed. Unaccountably setting out on a long hunt with six thousand retainers when he should have been scouting the hills for the enemy, he returned to find his camp and the only water supply for miles in the hands of Timur. Deserted by his Anatolian emirs, Bayezid was outnumbered and outmanoeuvred by the Mongol cavalry on their sturdy little ponies. Timur even had elephants with him, which must have struck terror into the Thunderbolt's janissaries, on foot as they were. By nightfall it was all over, Bayezid, one of the 'pampered jades of Asia', as the English playwright Christopher Marlowe wrongly called him two centuries later in his play *Tamburlaine,* chained in a cage and dragged in the dust behind Timur's conquering army. His wife was made to serve naked at Timur's table, to the jeers of his troop commanders. Humiliated, the Thunderbolt smashed his brains out on the bars of his cage.

Everyone in Europe breathed a sigh of relief. But the slaughter went on. Timur captured Izmir in Anatolia and made a ghastly pyramid from the heads of those he executed.

In Ephesus, where the apostle Paul had wandered 1,400 years earlier, the children came out to greet Timur, singing and offering flowers. 'What is this noise?' he is reputed to have asked – and then rode them down with his cavalry. Luckily for Europe, he turned eastwards to China, and his own death.

Since 1408, Mircea had ruled in Wallachia with his only legitimate son, Mihail, but even before the death of the old man ten years later and of Mihail two years after that, old rivalries emerged in the principality rather as they had in Hungary. Dan, Mihail's nephew (Vlad's cousin), threw his hat into the ring to establish a feud that had echoes in just about every state in Europe. Vlad now began a throw of his own. Leaving Sigismund's court at Buda in the spring of 1423, he was apparently on his way north to the kingdom of Poland to seek support from Ladislas II of the Jagiellon family, a rival of Sigismund. Vlad's plan was discovered, however, and such treachery was rewarded by Sigismund confirming Dan as the second prince of that name of Wallachia. An odd relationship now existed between Vlad and the Emperor which would be continued into the next generation. Vlad had been caught intriguing, his mission foiled, and he was for a while under observation by Sigismund's courtiers. On the other hand, he was entrusted as a diplomat for the Emperor in the ongoing negotiations between the Eastern and Western Churches. Specifically, Vlad travelled east to Constantinople to the court of the Emperor John Palaeologus, the representative of one of the two families who had ruled Byzantium for years. 'In those days,' recorded the Greek chronicler Michael Ducas, 'there appeared one of the many bastard sons of Mircea, the profligate *voivod* of Wallachia'.[16]

It may be that Vlad had ambitions of his own, perhaps to gain Byzantine support for his struggle in the complexities of Wallachian politics, perhaps to cement this with marriage to a Byzantine princess. But if this was in his mind, at some point Vlad abandoned the plan and stayed loyal to Sigismund.

Throughout the 1420s, the decade before Vlad Ţepeş' birth, Wallachia was in turmoil. After Nicopolis, Mircea had not licked his wounds for long before involving himself in the internecine struggle going on between the sons of Bayezid, the

Thunderbolt. It was his bad luck perhaps that he backed Musa when the eventual survivor would be Mehmed, who, every inch the warrior his father was, captured Wallachian strongholds and exacted an annual tribute from the 'profligate *voivod*' of 3,000 ducats. This was not the capitulation it seems on paper. A few thousand ducats was a small price for freedom of action, and Mehmed was content to leave Mircea and his principality alone. The old king died and was buried at his monastery at Cozia on 4 February 1418.

His co-ruler and successor, his son Mihail, had none of his father's sense of balance and *realpolitik* and refused to pay Mehmed his tribute. He even joined Sigismund's army in raids on the Turks along the Danube in the late summer of 1419. Mehmed was occupied extending his empire elsewhere but he swung north for long enough to take Mircea's old castle of Giurgiu and demand back-payment of his tribute. In a move that would be grimly re-enacted in the next generation, he took Mihail's sons Mikhail and Radu as hostages.

Dan's challenge for the throne of Wallachia dates from 1420, when he engaged the help of the Turks. This action appalled Christendom and it certainly weakened Wallachia's future chances of keeping out of Turkish clutches. Inviting in a powerful foreign power, no matter what the pretext, is never a good idea. During these clashes Mihail was killed and Dan took the Wallachian throne as Prince Dan II. As Mihail had his rival, so too did Dan, in the form of his cousin, Radu Praznaglava. Dan had the backing of the Turks, Radu of the Hungarians under Sigismund, setting the scene for Wallachian politics for the rest of the century. Another ally whom Radu enlisted was Alexander the Good, Prince of Moldavia to the east of the Carpathians, but despite this Radu was killed along with his sons in 1427, while Dan held on to the throne.

By 1431, the likely year of Vlad Țepeș' birth, there were two rivals for Dan's throne, the future Impaler's father and Alexandru Aldea, another of old Mircea's bastard sons. Also in that year, at Nuremberg on 8 February, Vlad senior was invested in the Order of the Dragon and from that day he styled himself 'Dracul', the Dragon. Meanwhile, the Order had been busy.

Jan of Husinetz, known as Hus, was born near Prachatitz in Bohemia probably in 1369, the son of a peasant. Even with this unlikely background, the brilliant young man took a master's degree at the university of Prague in 1396 – the year of the debacle at Nicopolis – and had come under the influence of the philosophy of Englishman John Wycliffe. Six years later Hus was rector of the university, but by 1408 was no longer allowed to officiate as a priest and the following year an Inquisitorial investigation into his preachings led to a bull from Pope Alexander V ordering all his writings and those of Wycliffe to be burned. Hus himself was banned from preaching. His philosophy was deceptively simple: it emphasized purity and piety and stressed the importance of scripture. Everything else he considered to be a veneer, and counselled that the doctrines of popes, cardinals and bishops, which ran counter to the Bible, could and should be ignored. Pilgrimages and false relics were so much 'hocus-pocus'. It was essentially this attitude that Martin Luther would take a century later, commenting at his trial at Worms in 1521, 'Here I stand. I can do no other.' But whereas Luther was allowed to leave the church and live out his life throwing ink-pots at the devil in castles along the Rhine, Hus was not so lucky.

He continued to preach after the ban and was excommunicated in 1411. Now a popular hero, there were riots on his behalf in the streets of Prague, but the Bohemian King, Wenceslas, suggested he leave the city for his own safety. Stating his case at the Council of Constance in November 1414, he talked himself into a public execution. Despite the safe conduct guaranteed to him by Sigismund, this was carried out after a rigged trial on 6 July 1416. Controversy still rages over to what extent Hus was a heretic.

Important to the Order of the Dragon were the Hussite Wars that followed in his name. Just as Martin Luther's stand led to the Peasant Wars in Germany in the 1520s, there were many peasants and members of the nobility ready to use Hus' proto-Protestantism to strike a blow against the all-powerful Catholic Church, and, in the case of Bohemia, to begin what many historians have seen as the birth pangs of Czech nationalism. The Hussites had a formidable general in Jan

Žižka, a nobleman from Trocznov, brought up as a page in the court of King Wenceslas. A commander of vast experience, he had fought for the Teutonic Order against the Poles, for Sigismund's Austrians against the Turks and even for the English against the French at Agincourt. Losing an eye at Tannenberg in 1410 fighting for Wenceslas, he became an ally of the Hussites at the king's court, orchestrating an outbreak of violence in Prague on 30 July 1419. Against him, Sigismund sent an army which included members of the *societas draconem*, but the wily Žižka defeated them in a series of battles that culminated in his building a fortress at Tabor, from which his followers came to be known as Taborites.

By this time, Žižka had lost the sight in his other eye, but his victories continued, largely due to Hussite zeal and his innovative use of the *wagenburg*, literally wagon fortresses, loaded with men, crossbows and (perhaps for the first time in southern Germany) firearms. Žižka used these rather as Napoleon would operate his highly mobile *corps d'armée* four centuries later, driving the horses to vital points on the field and disgorging men and firepower where they were most needed rather than allowing them to be locked into traditional battlefield formations. In a defensive circle, these wagons were virtually invincible. Mehmed II, the Impaler's enemy, would adopt their use to protect his camp while on the march. For the last three years of his life, Žižka invaded Hungary and south Germany before succumbing to that dread of all late medieval armies, the plague.

The Hussite rebellion continued, however. Under 'Holy' Andrew Prokop, the priest-general who succeeded Žižka, the Hussites twice defeated Sigismund at Tachov and Domazlice. By 1429, the 'great raids' had reached as far north as Dresden before snaking south to Leipzig. At Nuremberg in 1430, Prokop insisted that Hus's famous Four Articles of Faith be read out in the town square. It was only the internal breakdown of discipline that led to the collapse of the movement and gave Sigismund and his Dragon Order a chance to relax once more, Prokop himself dying in battle with them at Lipan in 1433.

We do not know what, if any, part Vlad Dracul played in

the wars against the Hussites. They were an embarrassment for Sigismund, and, for European tactical warfare, an important turning point. For the context of this book, however, they establish an even more important point: if the Order of the Dragon took up arms against heretics, in accordance with its statutes, which spoke of the Orthodox Church as its enemy, then Vlad's 'education' at the peripatetic court of Sigismund must have meant that he was a Catholic: indeed, to be invited to join the Order, this must have been the case. If his son Vlad Ţepeş was despised by the Orthodox Church for his alleged lapse of faith, and if this is why he was not buried near the altar at the monastery of Snagov, then this seems harsh in the extreme. The boy was merely continuing his father's faith.

McNally and Florescu, perhaps a little overanxious to prove the veracity of the yellow- and red-robed corpse in the Snagov grave, paint a vivid picture of Vlad wearing the colours of the Order and its curling dragon in gold and white. They picture him receiving the crown of Wallachia from Sigismund, swearing allegiance to him and clashing in the lists in the guttering flames of bonfires with bells ringing and crowds cheering. In reality, we know nothing of these entertainments, and D'Arcy Boulton in his monumental work on medieval orders mentions no colours at all in connection with the robes of the Dragon. The civic sword of York, a broadsword of cruciform pattern, was given to the city by Sigismund (father of Anne of Bohemia, the wife of the English King Richard II). Along its plush crimson covered scabbard are six metal dragons, each with its tail curled into a ring and each with a cross on its back. It is a fascinating example of the Dragon Order which has survived to our own time.

By 1431 a treaty came to an end between Sigismund's Hungarians and the Ottoman Turks. The Sultan now was Murad II, who had taken the throne only after the usual destruction of rivals, who included his uncle and brother. The set-back at the hands of Timur-i-Leng had almost been redressed, and the Ottoman Empire was once again straining at the leash to march north.

In the same year a baby was born in a house with thick ochre walls, high gables and small windows that still stands today in the Wallachian town of Sighişoara. We do not know who the boy's mother was, but he was christened Vlad after his father, Dracul, the dragon, the devil.

# 8

# THE CRESCENT ASCENDING

The Ottomans were frontier peoples, ever nomadic, ever expanding territorially, born, as Bayezid had said, to bear arms. Expert horsemen, brilliant innovators, clever assimilators of ideas, they posed a threat to Christian Europe that would not be finally eclipsed until 1683, when a long decline set in that, by the nineteenth century, would see the empire become the 'sick man of Europe', bullied by Russia and bolstered, a little reluctantly, by Britain.

The founder of this empire was Osman, the son of a border chief, born in Bithynia. His tiny state centred on Bursa, near the Sea of Marmara, and historian Jason Goodwin paints a rugged portrait of the ragtail army that flocked to his early successes and saw him lord of much of Asia Minor by 1299. They were 'hard-bitten pastoralists, shepherds-in-arms, adventurers, Sufis [holy men], misfits, landless peasants, runaways'.[1] But, under Osman, they forged themselves into an army, and a formidable one at that.

The eminent Ottoman expert Halil Inalcik[2] refers to the chieftain's son as Osman *Gazi*, and *gaza* is the equivalent of jihad, or holy war. The concept of holy war was not unlike Leon Trotsky's concept of international socialism in the twentieth century. Islam, like the Marxist revolution, aimed at world domination – *darulislam* (the Islamic kingdom) would eclipse *darulharb* (the lands of the infidel) not by destruction, but by absorption. Faced with this military reality, the West posited another view. In the 1880s, when the fire of the

Ottoman faith had gone out and their conquests were no more, the British could write:

> It is not in wild frenzy that the Turk destroys, but in calm blood and in strict accord with his habits and laws and creed. The tendency of his rule is to corrupt, torment, destroy. There are those who tell us that Turkish cruelty and injustice are foreign to Islamism and to Islamic law. But this is quite the reverse of true . . .[3]

The author was reacting no doubt to the Bulgarian atrocities of 1876 in which 12,000 Christians were butchered while the Sublime Porte looked on. The incident, so redolent of medieval slaughter in Tepeş' day, divided Britain. William Gladstone, leader of the Liberal opposition, came like a latter-day thunderbolt out of retirement, demanding that the Prime Minister, Benjamin Disraeli, kick the Turks out of Europe 'bag and baggage'. Disraeli, more concerned to check Russian aggression from the North, continued to support Turkey despite the massacres.

In the early fourteenth century, Osman's followers spread westwards, settling in villages and small towns like Milas, Izmir and Manisa, creating mini-sultanates in what was in fact Byzantine territory. Osman's son Orhan inherited this expanding kingdom on his father's death in 1326. The following year he had silver coins minted (always the mark of a stable and permanent state) at Bursa. Six years later, an Arab traveller, Ibu Battuti, found the place 'a great city with fine bazaars and broad streets'.[4]

Perhaps the most disastrous of the *gazi* advances – from the Christian viewpoint – saw Ottomans crossing the Dardanelles, the narrow straits that separated Asia from Europe. Even more disquieting was the fact that Bulgarian ferrymen were only too ready, for the usual haggled fee, to help them. The Dardanelles were called the Hellespont by the ancient Greeks, and were guarded by a Christian fortress at Gallipoli which acted as an outpost of Constantinople itself. In the early hours of 4 March 1356, the hand of Allah struck, for Orhan's followers and an earthquake brought the castle crashing down. Similar rumblings would echo through the Balkans for the next two centuries.

The story of the early fifteenth century is as much one of Byzantine decline as it is of Ottoman ascendancy. On Christmas Day, 1400, King Henry IV of England, who, according to some sources, had fought, as Duke of Lancaster, at Nicopolis four years earlier, entertained the Emperor Manuel II Palaeologus. One of the guests, a lawyer named Adam of Usk, sat at a lower table from the Emperor and his king:

> I reflected how grievous it was that this great Christian prince should be driven by the Saracens from the furthest East to the furthest Western islands to seek aid against them. O God, what dost thou now, ancient glory of Rome?[5]

Manuel had come cap in hand to England because allies nearer to home were falling away. As early as the twelfth century, the advance of Islam had robbed Byzantium of its Anatolian cornfields and the traditional recruiting grounds for its armies. In earlier centuries, every male under forty had been conscripted into the Byzantine army, which had once been 120,000 strong. Successive emperors, however, had to spend a fortune paying mercenaries to patrol their southern borders and became old and grey before their time attempting to cooperate with Islam and to play down any new wave of crusading zeal from the West. After the crusader attack on Constantinople in 1204, it seemed as if there might be a recovery under Michael Palaeologus, but the moment of greatness had gone.

Opposition to Byzantium did not just come from Islam, but also from the Christian West. *Voivodes* in Wallachia and princes in Serbia and Bulgaria flexed their muscles, paying only nominal regard to Constantinople via the Orthodox Church. The Greek islands were heavily populated by Venetians, Genoese and even French merchants. Pera, across the Golden Horn's Sea of Marmara was in Italian hands. As Jason Goodwin puts it, 'the nap had long gone on the velvet glove and there was no mailed fist underneath'.[6]

And in Constantinople, as in the moving capitals of the successors of Osman and in Wallachia, internecine squabbles added to the chaos. John Palaeologus (1341–91) was removed from the throne three times, on each occasion by members of his own family. And the spread of bubonic plague, the Black Death, creeping westwards from China, took its toll on Byzantine towns and villages too.

In 1346 Orhan formed an alliance with Palaeologus' rival, the Emperor's former chief minister John Cantacuzenos, cementing it with marriage to Palaeologus' daughter, Theodora. Orhan's son, Suleyman, ostensibly working for Cantacuzenos against the Serbs and Bulgars, occupied fortresses on the European side of the Dardenelles and refused to hand them back. Suleyman's death in 1357 barely slowed the advance as Murad, his younger brother, cut off the Byzantine supply lines and captured the Greek city of Adrianople, which now took its Turkish name, Edirne. What delayed the ultimate destruction of Constantinople itself was the arrival of Timur-i-Leng, but if Bayezid the Thunderbolt were stopped, there were plenty who would follow. By 1431, the year of Vlad Țepeș' birth, the Ottoman Empire was as powerful and greedy as ever; and Byzantium was still in its death throes.

Vlad Țepeș was already a young man when a child was born hundreds of miles away in Fotheringhay Castle, Northamptonshire, who would one day become King Richard III of England. There are dark similarities, as we have already noted, between the two men, but the jury of history is still out on whether they were princes 'more sinned against than sinning'. For the first seven years of the English boy's life there is only one cryptic comment about him: 'Richard liveth yet.'[7] We do not even have a single line about the infant Vlad.

The house where the future Impaler was born in his father's fortress town of Sighişoara was typical of the impressive merchants' houses that flanked it. The town itself was powerfully defended, with thick stone walls, 3,000 feet long, supporting fourteen huge towers, each one built at the expense of a town guild. It was a wealthy town, trading goods west into the Germanies, east to Constantinople and north into Poland. Travel writer Georgina Harding talks romantically of:

> the mystery of its stones and the gateways opening on to some other and secret place, on to an unexpected side of things. The slender, pointed iron banners which surmount the towers are silhouetted clearly against the sky, intrepid in the wind, fearless knights in the arena, waiting for the tourney and an unknown destiny.[8]

The house was probably new when Ţepeş was born, a solid, stone and timber construction of three storeys, large enough to house servants and a small body of armed retainers.

Sigismund may have made Vlad Dracul Prince of Wallachia, but it was politically in that intriguer's interests to maintain his relationship with Dracul's half-brother Alexandru Aldea and his ally Alexander the Good, Prince of Moldavia. Sigismund's common enemy in this particular piece of *realpolitik* was, Dragon brother notwithstanding, King Ladislas of Poland. For the moment, Dracul was merely *voivod* or governor of Transylvania, briefed to keep an eye on the Turks, trickling across the Danube now and again with the apparent blessing of Aldea, following, as did a number of local warlords, what was in effect a policy of appeasement.

We do not know if Vlad Dracul was present at the birth of his son because we do not know precisely when the future Impaler was born. Some historians posit a date as early as 1428,[9] others the autumn, 'under the sign of the scorpion', of 1431. We do not know the name of the boy's mother because of the low status in which Wallachian and Transylvanian women were held. It is possible that Dracul had married Cneajna, the eldest daughter of Alexander cel Bun (the Good) and that this ceremony took place about 1425. It would make dynastic sense were this to be the case and the legitimate result of the union was Mircea, born in 1428. Once the prince had been given the Order of the Dragon, all his sons – Mircea, Vlad and the youngest, Radu cel Frumos (the Handsome), born in 1435 – took the 'surname' Dracula.

It is equally likely that Vlad Ţepeş' mother was one of the

many mistresses the prince collected in his lifetime. One, who later became a nun with the holy name Mother Eupraxia, was the daughter of a boyar from Transylvania and was called Căltuna before she took the veil. Her son was Vlad Caligarul, the Monk. In Wallachia, unlike Western Europe, there was no barrier to inheritance by a bastard son, so we may assume that Vlad Dracul would not ignore any of his sons born to mistresses.[10]

The sources are not clear as to how Vlad Dracul's household was ordered. He would have had a steward to organize the servants, order the food and the wine, and regulate the day. Numerous skivvies would be employed to cook, clean and sew. The male children would have learned to give orders and adopt the airs and graces expected of men who would one day rule an entire country, however small by modern standards. Today, we bemoan the fact that our children grow up too quickly. In the late Middle Ages children of this class barely had a childhood at all.

Historians Florescu and McNally ponder the excitement that little Vlad would have known before the reality of his father's world was borne in on him:

> There were . . . the usual distractions that followed the feast days: puppet theatres . . . ambulant artists, acrobats, minnesingers . . . In summer there were ball games, running and jumping contests and games on quadrilateral swings made of red cloth and fastened in the form of a pyramid. In the winter, they hunted eagles with slingshots, slid down the Sighişoara slopes on primitive double-runner sleds, trapped hares . . .[11]

In summer were the harvest fairs, preceded in May by the festival of the Measurement of the Milk and countless Orthodox and Catholic saints' feasts.

When Ţepeş was still a small boy, his father received orders from Sigismund to do what was necessary to prepare for a potential Turkish advance. The Ottomans had defeated the Venetians at Salonika in 1430 and conquered southern Albania by 1432. In 1434 Dracul called up troops from the neighbouring fiefdoms of Fagaras and Amlaş and paid the craftsmen of Sibiu for their elaborate and deadly cannon. The bronze cup given by the *voivod* to cannon-founder Master Leonardus is still in the church at Sibiu today. What Dracul probably did not know is that other German gunsmiths were selling their wares to the Turks too.

Alexandru Aldea died of unknown, but natural, causes in the summer of 1436. It is difficult to empathize with this man and his lieutenant the boyar Albu. Treading what was undoubtedly a difficult path between the Christian West and the Muslim East, Alexandru seems to have gone too far down the reconciliation road, paying a tribute to the Sultan, Murad II, agreeing to back him militarily and sending political hostages to Edirne, now the *gazi* capital on the Ottoman fringes.

Dracul tried to take advantage of Aldea's duplicity before the man died, but found himself outnumbered by Albu and his Turkish allies before Sigismund decided to authorize Dracul to take what he needed from the towns of Transylvania. With this backing, the weapons of his gunsmiths and the billmen and archers of Amlaş, Dracul reached Tîrgoviste, Aldea's capital, in December. His sons Mircea, Vlad and Radu joined him later.

Now, in the gigantic palace built by Mircea the Old, Vlad Ţepeş' apprenticeship to knighthood began. If it followed the western pattern, and bearing in mind his father's recent acceptance into the Dragon Order it probably did, then training would have begun for the boy when he was seven. He would have learned to ride, not perhaps as he already had on a pony at Sighişoara, but on a palfrey, a saddle-horse used in campaigning and perhaps of the Hutul breed. Ultimately, by the time he was about fourteen, he would need to manage a destrier, the sixteen-hand war-horses bred for battle. He would need to ride in the saddle with legs straight, to balance sword and shield and he would practise for war at the tilt. No doubt, as with most squires, he would ride at the ring or quintain, an ingenious device which swung on a pivot. If the tilter were too slow in galloping past and striking the dummy's shield with his blunted lance, a mace, with chain and ball, would swing round and crunch into his back. No doubt Vlad received his share of bruises from this training device. He would learn to buckle on another knight's plate armour before he was given a suit of his own, probably of excellent German manufacture from Augsburg, in Sigismund's Austrian provinces. He would learn to run errands, hold horses, carve meat and serve wine at his father's table; the essence of medieval chivalry was the notion of service, as well as *hauteur*. In that strange geographical hinterland between East and West in which Țepeș lived and that strange cusp of time between the medieval and modern worlds, we cannot know how purely this code was taught.

It is likely that all the boys would have been taught together, perhaps by a tutor, probably a boyar who had fought at Nicopolis. From him he would have learned Latin, some Greek, Hungarian, French and Italian. He would also have been taught Church Slavonic and Cyrillic as the formal languages of his father's court.

In the meantime, while the education of a future *voivod* was in hand, events moved swiftly. Sigismund died in 1437, and whether latterly *actual* power had slipped to the Dragon Order or not, effectively Dracul's patron had gone. In that year, too, the peasant rising in Transylvania, brought on by the pressures of war, famine, plague and the much less tangible feudal crisis, was the most serious for years and could only be put down by a combination of Magyars, Szeklers from Transylvania and 'Saxons'. With his new principality fragile, and bereft of friends, Dracul found himself in the same position as his predecessor, Alexandru Aldea, had been only two years earlier. And he had to deal with the crescent's ascending star, Murad II.

The sultan dressed so soberly that at his mother's funeral he had to be pointed out to guests who did not know him. According to the Greek chronicler Michael Ducas, he treated his slaves as brothers. The Burgundian traveller Bertrandon de la Brocquière had seen him in his palace at Edirne: 'He sat on this [a raised dais] in the manner of tailors when they are at work.'[12]

Seven years later, Murad would build a magnificent stone bridge, nearly 400 yards long and with 174 arches over the River Ergene near this palace, with a cool resting place for travellers, a mosque for the good of their souls and a university for their intellects. During his reign some of the finest minds in Islamic history were making names for themselves, usually far ahead of Christian scholars in their sophistication. Mullah Husrev wrote textbooks used extensively in Ottoman universities. Ali al-Fanari, a Koranic law expert, taught in Persia and Egypt. Samarkand became the centre of mathematical excellence in Murad's empire. His attitude to potential rebellion compares favourably with the West: while the Council of Constance burned Jan Hus and Sigismund did his best to wipe out his followers, Murad met a dervish peasant called Hacci Bayram, whose fanatical religious movement had neo-socialist undertones, and not only pardoned him, but exempted his followers from taxation. Unlike most Western rulers, who frowned on any kind of apostasy, Murad was fascinated by the Meulevis, the whirling dervishes, and founded a lodge specially for them at Edirne.

It is perhaps no credit to Vlad Dracul, but very much a sign of the times, that the August of 1438 saw him campaigning with Murad against the Transylvanians. The Sultan crossed the Danube at Vidin and raided as far as Albu Iulia and Ţepeş' birthplace of Sighişoara. He besieged Sibiu for eight days before pulling back and re-crossing the Danube at Nicopolis. Dracul was now in a dilemma. As a Catholic, a Christian and a member of the Dragon Order, he had a clear duty to defend fellow-Christians; yet here he was allying with the infidel, the enemy. The town of Sebeş surrendered to Murad on the condition that its people should not become Ottoman slaves. The chronicler, 'brother George', styling himself a 'student of Sebeş', recorded that a great deal of loot and perhaps as many as 70,000 prisoners were taken.

The first written mention of Vlad Ţepeş can be found in a deed dated 20 January 1437 in which Dracul mentions his 'first born sons, Mircea and Vlad'. He appears again in August of the same year and by 2 August 1439, Radu is added to the list.[13]

The death of Sigismund saw the collapse of the powerful empire he had created largely by crafty politics and skilful determination. His son-in-law, Albert of Habsburg, Archduke of Austria, probably intended to become emperor, but died of dysentery in 1439, leaving his son Ladislas Posthumous (he was born after his father's death) as his infant heir. Into the breach – the advent of the boy-king inevitably spelling disaster in kingdoms held together largely by force of personality – stepped the man whom Albert had created governor of Transylvania, the 'white knight',[14] János Hunyadi.

Like Skanderbeg (see below) and Vlad Ţepeş himself, Hunyadi has assumed legendary qualities over the centuries. Ottoman mothers hushed their children into an uneasy sleep with the whisper of his name. Born about 1387 in Wallachia or Transylvania, the man with the distinctive high forehead and powerful build was a self-made businessman, warrior and a highly skilful dancer. Despite a lack of formal education he spoke Serb, Croat, Italian, Hungarian and Romanian, and made himself indispensable to Sigismund by lending him money. At first a page to Sigismund in Nuremberg, Hunyadi was sent, as was the custom of the day, to learn the art of war from a professional, in his case the *condottiere* Filippo Visconti. In 1409, Hunyadi had been knighted and given the castle of Hunedoara in Transylvania.

To the Wallachians, Hunyadi was Iancu de Hunedoara, and the great, brooding Gothic castle the most powerful in Transylvania. Simon Marsden visited it in 1993, crossing on a wooden bridge held up by 'precariously tall' stone pillars:

> I passed through the towering gates to find myself within a vast and intimidating courtyard, off which led a maze of galleries, spiral stairways, Gothic vaults, deep dungeons and dark halls . . . Everywhere pollution had added its ghastly stench and a layer of dust to the castle's aura of death.[15]

The well in the courtyard was dug by Turkish prisoners with their bare hands to a depth of sixty feet. It took them nine years, and when they had finished, rather than receiving the freedom Hunyadi had promised, they were thrown from the castellations to drown in the 100-foot-deep moat. Their names are still carved in the rock along with the inscription 'You have water, but no soul.'[16]

More prosaically, the late Professor Allen Brown[17] points up Hunedoara's imposing position over its city and notes the same Teutonic influences in its architecture as in castles in Poland and Russia. But it is difficult to be prosaic about Hunyadi's power base. Its walls are immense, rising out of solid rock, with a combination of circular and square towers, fringed with an elaborate Gothic canopy under the pointed eaves that date from the reign of Hunyadi's son, Matthias Corvinus. Skeletons have been found in its recesses, including that of a woman whose skull had been split in two by a spike (found in 1873).

Murad II may have dressed soberly, he may have been tolerant of the wilder religions in his Sultanate, but he was a shrewd warrior. Informed by his formidable spy network of Hunyadi's appointment in Transylvania, he struck first, taking the fortress of Smederevo from the Serbian overlord George Branković in August 1439. The incestuousness of this border warfare and the ease with which Christian and Muslim could cooperate for political purposes is shown by the fact that one of Murad's many wives in his harem was Mara, Branković's daughter. Her sons Gregor and Stefan were taken hostage by their new uncle.

In Wallachia, Vlad Dracul continued to play both ends against the middle. Creeping around the Hungarians after his role in Murad's raid into Transylvania, he welcomed Hunyadi on a state visit to Tîrgoviste some time in 1441. By now, because Ladislas Posthumous, the 'miracle child', was rumoured to be the bastard resulting from his mother's flirtation with a courtier, the electors had chosen Ladislas III of Poland as king of Hungary. The boy was only sixteen, but he looked a better bet than the infant Posthumous and, for the time at least, had the support of men of ability and courage like Hunyadi. The white knight and the prince of Wallachia had met at Nuremberg, probably in 1408–9, but there was no love lost between them. Apart from other considerations, Hunyadi would never compromise with Turks, whom he detested, and Dracul had just finished raiding his homeland. It must have been an uneasy meeting.

Perhaps because of guilt, perhaps because of Hunyadi's persuasiveness, Dracul did not join the next Ottoman raid into Wallachia in March 1442. The raid, led by Murad's general Sihabeddin, Bey (Lord) of Rumelia, was allowed to reach the Carpathians before Hunyadi destroyed it.

Murad summoned Vlad Dracul, nominally his vassal, to meet him in the spring at his quarters in Gallipoli. He also summoned George Branković, but the Serb pulled up the drawbridges of his fortified city of Belgrade and refused to move. It is difficult to understand Dracul's trust that spring, for although he had fought alongside Murad against his own people, his current leanings towards the always dangerous Hunyadi cannot have been missed by Murad, who was known to be a shrewd judge of men and to have spies everywhere. Perhaps in order to maintain a brave front, perhaps because he thought they were old enough to appear publicly, his sons Vlad and Radu went with him. Serbian chronicles mention that Dracul put about a false rumour that Mircea, his eldest son, had been killed, so that he could not be sent as a hostage.

At Gallipoli the hostages were shackled like slaves, the boys being taken to Anatolia, to the fortress of the 'crooked eyes' at Egrigöz in the principality of Caraman, the fiefdom of Ibrahim Bey, Murad's brother-in-law. Dracul was Murad's 'guest' at Edirne for nearly a year, before being released on certain conditions. In an act reminiscent of the Bayeux Tapestry's account of Harold Godwinson as 'guest' of William of Normandy in 1065, Dracul took an oath on the Bible and in his case, the Koran, not to take up arms against the Ottomans. He also promised an annual tribute of 10,000 gold ducats (inflation and having the whip hand had taken their toll since Old Mircea's day) and the *devsirme* was a new demand. This levy of boys was in some ways a renewal of the slave prisoners the Turks had been taking since the days of Osman. From each village in Wallachia, Dracul was to provide a certain number (figures vary from 1,000 to 3,000) of boys between the ages of eight and twenty. Urban children were exempt and in the case of an only child, the boy was not taken. The Turks' purpose was to train them as janissaries, the core of the Ottoman army.[18]

Vlad Ţepeş was probably twelve when he was snatched from his father's cohort and taken to Egrigöz. His handsome brother Radu was seven, 'no taller than a bouquet of flowers'.[19] We know nothing of the boys' time in this isolated town. It stands 1,000 feet above the sea, in the Taslidag Mountains and is as heavily forested today as it probably was then, with beech and oak and pine. Vlad and Radu did not speak the Turkish language and, quite possibly, for all their father's double dealing, had never seen a Turk before. According to Constantin Rezachevici, Ţepeş was an 'intermittent' prisoner of the Turks between 1443 and 1448, but this gives a false impression. It is unlikely that he was actually confined to a cell (any more than he was later during his much longer captivity by Matthias Corvinus) but he could certainly not return home. 'Please understand,' wrote Vlad Dracul to the citizens of Braşov, 'that I have allowed my children to be butchered for the sake of the Christian peace, in order that both I and my country might continue to be vassals of the Holy Roman Emperor.'[20]

It is unlikely that Dracul's motives were as noble as this, but hostage-taking was a way of life in the fifteenth century; and Vlad Dracul was certainly not above risking the boys' lives to play the great game of *realpolitik*. After all, he had not taken Mircea, his eldest son, with him to Gallipoli and the boy ruled Wallachia in his father's year-long absence, despite being only fifteen or sixteen years old.

From the Turks' viewpoint hostage-taking served a double purpose. The sophistication and allure of the Ottoman court created a mindset that some found difficult to shake off. In twentieth-century terms it was the rough equivalent of 'turning' enemy agents by seducing them into the ways of either capitalism or Marxism. Accordingly, if the boys behaved, all well and good. If not, they might share the fate of the sons of George Branković, who, suspected of plotting to escape, had red hot irons jabbed into their eyeballs on 8 May 1441 – and they were the Sultan's nephews by marriage!

How long Vlad and Radu remained at Egrigöz is unknown, but they were taken next to Tokat, a far more civilized city on the trade routes to the East. In Vlad Ţepeş' day, the Roman tombs were still standing to mark the legions' furthest reach eastwards and the boys were probably kept in the Byzantine castle that dominated the market square, with its leatherworkers and coppersmiths. From there, following the Sultan's travelling court via Manisa and Bursa, they came to Edirne.

The Greek city of Adrianople had fallen to the Turks in 1362. The city of Hadrian had an ancient history. Originally Uskudama, it was fortified by the Romans in the early second century and remained an important Byzantine city until it was lost to Orhan's *gazi* warriors. Under the Turks it thrived as never before, huge bazaars filling the cluttered tangle of streets, selling wine, opium, attar of roses, dyestuffs, leather, cotton, woollens and tapestries. Until the fall of Constantinople, Edirne was the Ottoman capital, and here Murad built his palace.

Vlad and Radu were the sons of a prince and they were to be treated as such at Edirne, exposed to the full allure of the Muslim way of life. One of the keys to Ottoman success was the way in which they *used* their enemies. They did not insist on conversion to Islam by the sword, knowing that force would only harden resistance and breed resentment. But the boys taken in the *devsirme* became some of the most fanatical and professional fighters for Islam, indoctrinated by the Koranic code and the sensual pleasures of the East. With the sons of Dracul, the idea was clearly to win them over, if not to full Islam, then at least to make them true scions of the Ottoman Empire should the time ever come for either of them to rule Wallachia. They had a role model in someone whose name, like Ţepeş', has survived in the chronicles of Balkan heroism – George Kastrioti, Skanderbeg.

Kastrioti, the son of an Albanian prince, was born between 1403 and 1405, and, like Dracul's boys, was taken as a hostage (by Bayezid) when he was seven. Brought up under

Murad as a Muslim, Kastrioti would be given a generalship in the Ottoman army and named Iskender Bey (Lord Alexander), a name given by Murad, who, like all medieval rulers in the East, was imbued with the folk-memory of Alexander the Great, who had conquered a third of the world by the time he was thirty.[21] Skanderbeg's helmet, with its crest of the head of a mountain goat and its wreath of silver-gilt roses, is in the Kunsthistorisches Museum in Vienna.

The education Skanderbeg received was given to Dracul's sons too, to the extent that the rumour persisted that one or both of them actually converted to Islam during their years of captivity. It was the notion of shifting faiths which has helped to damn the Impaler in the eyes of posterity: a boy who was raised probably as a Catholic, who converted to Islam, reconverted to the Orthodox Church and finally to Catholicism again, was seen to be taking *realpolitik* a little too far, even by fifteenth-century standards. The boys were exposed to the finest tutors the Ottoman court could provide: Iyas, a Serb convert, priests like Hamiduddin and Sinan, the Kurdish philosopher Ahmed Gurani. They learned logic, the Koran, the Ottoman language, spoken and written, and to become proficient with the light, curved swords and the short-bows, fired with such deadly accuracy from the saddle of swift, sure-footed Arab horses. The training, Murad hoped, would be invaluable for future allies – it had worked, after all, with Skanderbeg. It would work with Radu; but not with his brother Vlad.

In the Inner Palace at Edirne, a smaller version of the one that Mehmed the Conqueror would build later in Constantinople, Murad II would spend his leisure hours with his viziers, his scholars, and his army of loyal slaves. It was a complex and highly structured regime which would reach its pinnacle under Suleiman the Magnificent a hundred years later and make the structure of even the grandest Western court look quite primitive. The *Kapi Agasi*, the chief white eunuch, ran the palace like clockwork, hiring and firing, supervising the vast number of pages, administering punishments which could include death if the need arose. These eunuchs had been castrated as children so that backstairs liaisons with the sultan's harem (see below) would not be an issue.

Under him four chambers operated. The *Has Oda* (Privy Chamber) was responsible for Murad's clothes and weapons. The pages here stood guard at his door each night or by the fly of his tent when he was on the march. A whole hierarchy of officers carried the sultan's sword, held his stirrup as he mounted, and wrote his letters. The chief of the chamber never left the sultan's side. Other chambers were the *Hazine*, the Treasury, which handled the expenses and accounts; the *Kiler*, the Larder, whose officers arranged Murad's food; and the *Seferli Oda*, the Campaign Office, a reminder that the Ottoman dynasty was essentially a mobile war machine.

The officer known as the *mir alem* was responsible for Murad's regimental marches, and carried the horse-tail standard that, along with the crescent, was his symbol of authority. Under him a small army erected the sultan's tent at the centre of the vast circle camped under the stars on campaign. The *kapici basi* was the gate-keeper, responsible for the palace guard, safety and discipline. The *mirahur* looked after the sultan's horses, making sure their coats were glossy and their tails dyed red, as was the custom. Even within the palace the sultan was carried on litters maintained by this department. The chief falconers, the *cakirci basi*, kept the royal birds in their mews, and Murad's team, in the outlying provinces of the Empire, were exempt from taxation in exchange for training birds. Love of the hunt had wrecked the Thunderbolt's chances of victory against Timur in 1402, so seriously did Ottoman sultans take their hunting. The *casnigir basi*, the chief taster, had a vast team of cooks to provide meals for the Imperial Council and were watchful of any poison that might find its way into Murad's food.

We do not have accurate figures for the size of Murad II's court. In the decade of Dracula's death, when Mehmed was sultan and based at Constantinople, the janissary corps of the army had 10,000 men. There were 100 gunners, 800 stable-boys, at least 120 cooks with twenty tasters, 200 tailors, 200 tent-pitchers, 100 falconers. There were perhaps 400 doorkeepers, 100 standard-bearers and an unknown number making artillery for the cannoneers.[22]

The harem, which in 1476 numbered 650, was intensely private and access to it forbidden to strangers. Virtually all its members were slaves who underwent a rigorous training to make them skilled in music, dancing, sewing and embroidery, puppetry and story-telling. Sultans only took four legal wives under Shari'a law. Unlike the mysogynism becoming rampant in Christian society,[23] women were seen as equals in the Koran and in the eyes of Allah, as far as religious observance went. One *hadith* (an Islamic tradition) says:

> When a man looks upon his wife and she upon him, God looks mercifully upon them; when they join hands together their sins disappear in the interstices of their fingers. When he makes love with her the angels encircle the earth.[24]

The Burgundian Bertrandon de la Brocquière visited Murad's palace twenty years before Vlad Ţepeş' time there. He remarked:

> We passed through the first gate. The door opened inwards and was guarded by about thirty slaves, all armed with staves. Should any person wish to enter without permission, they warn him at once to withdraw; if he persists, they turn him back with their staves.[25]

The Greek chronicler Laonic (Nicolas) Chalkondyles, who was to write a vivid account of the fall of Constantinople and Ţepeş' war against Mehmed, hints that young Radu fell prey not only to the blandishments of Murad's court, but to the advances of Mehmed himself. Islamic tradition and law do not approve of homosexuality, although, paradoxically, sodomy among the Turks was widespread. Whether this was inherited from the Greeks and the Byzantine Empire they had overthrown or whether it was already established as a native custom is difficult to say. Centuries of racial mistrust and slurs have blurred the truth, especially in the West, where the concept of 'buggery' was associated with Turkish Bulgaria and the Bogomil heresy. Dark doings were hinted at by Colonel T.E. Lawrence, after his capture by Turks at Akabar in 1916.[26] According to Chalkondyles, Radu's beauty seduced Mehmed Celebi, the sultan's son, who was a year younger than Ţepeş. While at first resisting, Radu eventually became a minion of Mehmed and did not leave Ottoman clutches until 1462 when the sultan established him as a puppet on the throne of Wallachia.

If Radu fell victim to the physical seduction of Mehmed and the cultural seduction of Murad's court and the Islamic way of life, Vlad almost certainly reacted differently. Because we know nothing of the boy's temperament, we cannot be sure of the effect this way of life had on him. Did it explain, perhaps even create, a streak of cold cruelty which would come to the fore in his adult years? Did the tension in which he lived and the sense of betrayal from his father's actions at Gallipoli and the treachery of his little brother turn and harden a mind already warped? Above all, in the practical sense, did he witness the impaling and other tortures of Murad's enemies which gave him a blueprint for his own future?

Sources are surprisingly silent on these issues. Legend credits Sir John Tiptoff, the English Earl of Worcester, with using impalement as a means of execution, and Florescu and McNally claim this practice was learned from the Turks and that he was executed 'for his crimes'.[27] Tiptoff was in fact the most renowned English scholar of his day, having studied at Rome, Venice, Florence and Padua in the decade of Dracula's birth. He was also a hard man and a staunch Yorkist. Given the post of Constable of England, his job was to execute enemies of the state, which he did assiduously during the 1460s. His execution was the result, not of others' horror at his unnatural cruelty, but of the vagaries of fortune in the Wars of the Roses. He quietly asked the headsman in 1470 to use three strokes to remove his head 'in honour of the Trinity'.[28]

Writing with varying degrees of bias, J.A. MacGraham, the *Daily News* correspondent, reached Batik in Bulgaria in August 1876. He was reporting on the massacre of 12,000 Christians by the Turkish irregular cavalry, the *bashi-bazouks*:

The number of children killed in these massacres is something enormous. They were often spitted on bayonets and we have several stories from eye-witnesses who saw little babies carried about the streets . . . on the point of bayonets. The reason is simple. When a Mahametan has killed a certain number of infidels, he is sure of Paradise, no matter what his sins may be . . . Here . . . the *bashi-bazouks*, in order to swell the count, ripped open pregnant women and killed the unborn infants.[29]

When Charles Meryon, a surgeon, travelled in the entourage of the eccentric Lady Hester Stanhope to Latakia, Syria in July 1813, he witnessed a ghastly sight:

I was walking out of one of the gates of the town, about eight in the morning, when I came suddenly on a man who had been impaled an hour or two before, and was now dead, but still transfixed by the stake, which, as I saw on approaching him, came out about the sixth rib on the right side . . . the stake was planted upright, seemed scarcely to be sharp and was somewhat thicker than a hop-pole. I was told that it was forced up the body by repeated blows of a mallet, the malefactor having been bound on his face to a heavy pack-saddle and an incision being made with a razor to facilitate the entrance of the stake. The body, yet alive, was set upright in a rude manner, for the Turks preserve no decorum in executions . . . Jewish, Christian, Druze and Ansary criminals are alone subjected to this horrible punishment; Turks are beheaded.[30]

Meanwhile, the world had changed. In 1440 Pope Eugenius IV had called for a crusade against the Ottoman Turks, perhaps in an attempt to conclude the flimsy reconciliation he had set up at the Council of Florence between the Eastern and Western Churches. The crusaders were anxious not to repeat the disaster of Nicopolis, and it was not until 1442 that an army numbering 20,000–25,000 marched east under the command of Ladislas III of Poland. Under him were the warlords János Hunyadi and George

Branković, the latter no doubt distraught at Murad's blinding of his sons. The pope was represented by Cardinal Guiliano Cesarini. And with them, a little half-heartedly perhaps, bearing in mind his brothers' predicament, was Mircea, the eldest son of Dracul. There were other Wallachians too, from Banat and Maramureş, but fighting under other banners. The cosmopolitan army of Germans, Austrians, Poles, Serbs and Wallachians did well, defeating the Turks at Niš in November 1443, recapturing Sofia in Bulgaria in December and driving the Ottomans back. A medieval army was always at the mercy of the weather, and by Christmas particularly heavy snows saw the crusaders falling back to Branković's Belgrade on the Danube. Their food had all but run out and the provision carts were chopped up for firewood. Most of the horses had died.

Murad sued for peace. Cynically, it gave him time to concentrate on a crusade of his own, to be fought in the Morea. Branković's blind children were returned and, as things turned out, he was the only signatory of the treaty with Murad – the Peace of Seghedin – to keep his word. In the autumn of 1444, before any arrangements could be made to release Vlad and Radu Dracula, Ladislas launched another campaign season. This time the target was Varna on the Black Sea and would entail an ambitious amphibious operation involving Venice's renowned fleet.

Hunyadi summoned Vlad Dracul to join the *chevauchée*[31] at Nicopolis, but the Wallachian was unimpressed by Hunyadi's muster of less than 20,000 men, which the German soldier of fortune Hans Mägest estimated at no more than 14,000, and may well have been warned by a soothsayer of the fruitlessness of the expedition. For all his Catholic leanings, Vlad Dracul was probably as superstitious as most Wallachians. Above all, his sons were still at Edirne and he knew the risk he was taking. In the event, he sent Mircea again with 4,000 cavalry, no doubt with instructions to keep his father's dragon banner discreetly folded.

The Varna campaign was as great a disaster as Nicopolis had been for the previous generation. It had begun well, with George Kastrioti, Skanderbeg, now on the side of the

Portrait of Vlad Dracula the Impaler, a sixteenth-century copy of an original in Ambraş Castle, Austria. (© Bridgeman Art Library)

The house of Vlad Dracul in Sighişoara. The Impaler was born here, probably in 1431. (© Corbis)

The ruins of Vlad the Impaler's palace in his capital of Tîrgoviste. Five hundred boyars and their families were reported to have been impaled in the courtyard. (© Corbis)

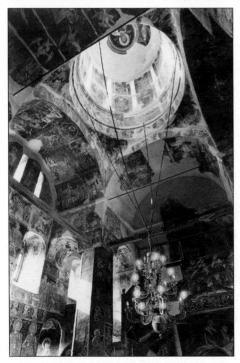

The restored chapel at Tîrgoviste, typical of the iconic embellishments of the Orthodox Church. (© Simon Marsden)

The restored church in the monastery of Snagov, alleged resting place of Vlad the Impaler. (© Corbis)

The interior of Snagov Church, showing the main altar. The slab beneath the carpet and portrait was removed in the 1930s, but only pottery shards and animal bones were found. (© Simon Marsden)

Mehmed II painted by the Florentine artist Gentile Bellini, *c.* 1515. The Ottoman sultan was both the Impaler's captor and nemesis in their frontier wars. (Reproduced by kind permission of the National Gallery, London)

Matthias Hunyadi, called Corvinus, the crow. The calculating ruler of Hungary kept the Impaler prisoner for fourteen years. (© Szépművészeti Múseum, Budapest)

Janos Hunyadi, a nineteenth-century statue of the 'white knight' who defended Christendom against the Ottoman advance. (© Corbis)

The Black Church at Sibiu, a landmark of the 'Saxon' city in the Impaler's time. It is likely that letters leading to the Impaler's arrest by Corvinus were forged here. (© Corbis)

'The Feast of the Impaler', a woodcut by Matthias Hupnuff of Strasbourg, 1500: an illustration for one of the early polemics against the Impaler promoted by an increasingly prurient European readership. (© Mary Evans Picture Library)

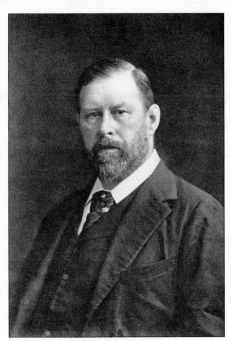

Bram Stoker, the civil servant turned novelist whose creation *Dracula* has stood the test of time as the inspiration for an entire industry – the dead undead of the vampire. (Reproduced by kind permission of the Mander and Mitchenson Theatre Collection, London)

The sword of Sigismund, Emperor of Austria, showing the curled dragon motif of the Order of the Dragon of which both Vlad Dracul and his son the Impaler were members. Now the civic sword of the City of York. (Reproduced by kind permission of the City of York)

Bela Lugosi, the definitive Dracula in the 1931 Universal Studios version. Patriotic Romanians were outraged that 'their' hero should be played by a Hungarian, the old enemy. (© Corbis)

Christians and wreaking havoc among the Turks in northern Albania. Internal problems in the Ottoman Empire saw a rival to Murad's throne and, to cap it all, a fire at Edirne destroyed thousands of homes. The Venetian war galleys effectively closed the narrows of the Dardanelles and the 'white knight' was on his way to exact vengeance. Mircea seems to have swung away from the main army, taking the town of Petretz and using cannon for the first time in Wallachian history. With him was the German mercenary Hans Mägest, whose reminiscences would later provide the *minnesinger* Martin Beheim with the source of new songs.

Petretz was well defended with water-filled moats, and Mircea's first instinct, to use siege ladders, failed. How many guns he had with him we do not know, but he breached the walls with these and found the exit to an underground tunnel escape route that the terrified Turks were using. He had them cut down as they emerged. The fortress itself, in the heart of the city, was stronger, but most of the garrison surrendered and Mircea found himself with hundreds of Turkish prisoners claiming to be Christian. Those soldiers who had not surrendered were thrown into the moat.

All over Bulgaria as Hunyadi and Ladislas advanced, the population flocked to them, rejoicing in being liberated. This was, of course, nothing more than peasants hedging their bets (they welcomed any army in this way), but Turks as far away as Edirne and Gallipoli panicked and fled east.

Varna was a powerful port in an inlet of the Black Sea, specializing in the trade of leather goods, grain, cattle, wine and cloth. The city was defended by an Ottoman army perhaps three times the size of that of Hunyadi. The Venetian galleys may have been blocking the Dardanelles, but they had not rowed further north beyond the Golden Horn and were of no use to the crusaders on land. Murad himself led his cavalry into battle, with the broken treaty document impaled on his lance. In the melée that followed, Ladislas of Poland was thrown from his horse by the crush of *spahis*. Before Hunyadi could reach him, he was hacked to death and his head impaled on a Turkish spear, hideously jiggled up and down in front of the demoralized Christians. Slowly and bitterly, the crusaders fell back, scattering to their homelands as Murad's vengeful cavalry pursued them. It was not until the next campaign season that Mircea and, this time, Dracul, would come upon the mutilated corpse of Cardinal Cesarini, the papal legate, torn to pieces and naked in the hills near Varna, his eyes pecked out by crows. The body of Ladislas was never found but stories claiming sightings of him or his ghost spread through Europe for many years.

On that morning of 10 November, Mircea, who still cannot have been more than sixteen, is believed to have been in command of his Wallachians to the right of the centre. Hunyadi, whose thunderous counter-attack nearly worked, was on his right. Ladislas led the reserve, and, perhaps carried away by his youth or a belief in the invulnerability of his cavalry, charged through the centre, leaving both wings isolated.

The conduct of the Wallachians in battle was criticized at the time by the few observers who lived to tell the tale. The papal legate, Andreas de Palatio, said that they ran in all directions, yet it was they who actually saved his life. A local poet, Zofikos, claims that the Wallachians' only interest was grabbing what booty they could from Murad's coffer-tent. But since, on his own admission, he was hiding in a forest at the time, quaking with fear, *nothing* he says can be trusted.

As with Nicopolis, the Varna debacle left the crusaders in disarray, and, as so often after such defeats, the losers turned to bickering among themselves. As Hunyadi made his way home across Wallachia, he found himself facing the halberds of Dracul's guard. The prince was furious that the Varna crusade had collapsed when he had expressly advised the Transylvanian *voivod* against it. In a charged meeting, probably at Tîrgoviste, each accused the other of treason and Dracul had his sword point at Hunyadi's throat when wiser counsel intervened and pulled the men apart. The white knight was forced to pay 'a substantial ransom' for his freedom.

The 1445 campaign was better conceived than that of the previous year and was probably simply an attempt to find the body of Ladislas. The original protagonists seem to have been Dracul, Mircea and Jean de Wavrin, Lord of

Forestel in Burgundy, whose galleys were to row up the Danube with Wallachian troops (later augmented by Hunyadi's Hungarians) while Mircea followed on the north bank with his cavalry.

The fleet sailed from Brâila under the shadow of the cathedral of St Michael, past the warehouses with their grain, the workshops of the candle-makers and rope manufacturers, and on to Nicopolis. They took Turtucaia, raiding its grain stores and burning it down, Wavrin receiving a wound for his pains and having to relinquish command to Renault de Confide. The attack to recapture Mircea the Old's castle at Giurgiu was far more important and was achieved in Hussite fashion, using war wagons to withstand the Turkish assault. The garrison surrendered, but Mircea Dracula had the prisoners hacked to death.

Either before the taking of Giurgiu or shortly after it, Dracul arrived. Bulgarians now threw in their lot with him in vast numbers, an endless column of refugees with bullock carts and dogs, throwing themselves on the prince's mercy. Five days from the difficult river crossing at Ruscgiuk, the army reached Nicopolis, the scene of the disaster of 1396. Dracul appears to have left them by this time, perhaps anxious to try to safeguard Vlad and Radu, still at Edirne. After a siege of several days and the loss of several Burgundian galleys, the garrison surrendered, much to the crusaders' delight. Their fathers had been avenged.

Winter closed in again. With dwindling food supplies, few friendly ports and the risk of the Danube icing over, Hunyadi and de Wavrin had no choice but to pull back to Constantinople and wait for spring.

Dracul signed a new treaty with Murad in the summer of 1447, but at a price: he had to abandon the recently taken fortress of Giurgiu on the Danube and to promise the return of the thousands of Bulgarians who had drifted north into his safe keeping after the fall of Nicopolis. In exchange, Wallachia was to remain independent and his sons would be saved. As was so often the case in the past, the word of a Muslim carried more weight than that of a Christian. János Hunyadi was doubly suspicious of Dracul. He had refused to fight with him at Varna and was clearly playing a double game. Dracul and Mircea, on the other hand, still blamed Hunyadi for the Varna disaster in that he had not taken the Wallachian prince's advice.

In November 1447 Hunyadi launched an attack on Wallachia, with the intention of placing Vladislav of the Dâneşti family on the throne at Tîrgoviste in place of Dracul. Faced with an attacking army, there seems to have been a boyar revolt in the capital and Mircea was captured trying to flee the city. He was tortured, blinded with red-hot iron stakes and in a murder that would echo through vampire folklore and through Bram Stoker and beyond, he was buried alive.

Dracul escaped, galloping east to the only ally he had left, the Turks. Somewhere in the Balteni marshes near Bucharest, the Dâneşti rebels caught and killed him, decapitating him with an axe. Legend has it that his body was buried in a wooden chapel where the monastery of Dealul now stands, but it has never been found. There is another legend that his body was taken to Snagov and buried there. If that is true, was this the headless corpse with the Dragon robes that Rosetti and Florescu found there in 1931? Dracul was a 'righteous and unconquerable hero', wrote Antonio Bonfini, the Hungarian court chronicler, 'the mightiest and bravest in battle'. Jean de Wavrin, who had known him in the thick of the fight said that he was 'very famous for his bravery and for his wisdom'.[32]

But the righteous warlord, who had betrayed the West by allying with the Turks, who had betrayed his own sons by leaving them to the mercies of the Ottoman court, had at last been conquered. He left to Vlad Ţepeş, his eldest surviving son, his Toledo sword and his insignia of the Order of the Dragon. What he could not leave him, because at the time of his death he had lost it, was the principality of Wallachia.

# 9

# VLAD VOIVOD

Vlad Ţepeş ruled Wallachia three times. Most of the stories attributed to him in the 'Saxon', Russian and Romanian tales belong to the central period that lasted from 1456 to 1462. But in 1447 he was still a prisoner of Murad II and the Turks.

News of his father's and brother's deaths reached him by the end of the year: according to one tradition, these facts were broken to him by Mehmed, already by this time, more than his father's heir apparent. Another possibility is that the news was brought by a galloper, the boyar Cazan who had been Vlad Dracul's chancellor, and that it was he who brought the boy his father's sword and dragon device. There is no doubt that in the complex, parasitical and rather 'big brother' relationship between the Ottoman Empire and Wallachia, the future Impaler's position now changed dramatically. He was heir to Wallachia, no longer simply a *voivod* (a warlord governing for someone else) but a prince with the full hereditary status that that entailed. He was officially freed from his position as hostage and given a rank in the Turkish army, although exactly what is unclear. Given that Skanderbeg had held a similar place earlier and that the janissary corps were made up of 'foreigners', this made perfect sense.

The vacuum created by Vlad Dracul's death had already been filled. On 3 December 1447, János Hunyadi declared himself prince of Wallachia, but this was merely to gain time to establish his protégé Vladislav II, son of Dan, in Dracul's place. The intense rivalry between the Draculeşti and Dâneşti families in this period has an almost exact parallel in England. As Vlad Ţepeş began his second reign in the Carpathians, the houses of York and Lancaster began a thirty-year feud that threatened to annihilate the aristocracy and would pave the way for a new dynasty and a new style of kingship – all of which happened despite the existence of the law of primogeniture. In Wallachia such a law did not exist, so that contention for the throne was even more a free-for-all. Ţepeş, now seventeen and tired of being an exile in an alien land, waited for the opportunity to snatch back the throne.

The chance came in September 1448 when the 'white knight' crossed the Danube and marched through Turkish-held Serbia, to join forces with Skanderbeg to the south. With him slogged perhaps 9,000 Wallachians under Vladislav, the whole army looting and rioting in true crusader fashion among the villages they found. In an eerie repetition of history, Hunyadi's army met the Turks at Kosovo Polje, the field of blackbirds, the scene of the crusaders' defeat by Bayezid the Thunderbolt in 1389. The chronicler Chalkondyles wrote:

> On the left wing there was Dan [Vladislav II] who was [Hunyadi's] great friend whom he had brought to the throne of the land of the Dacians because of his animosity for Dracula . . .[1]

Unusually the second Kosovo extended for three days (a medieval battle normally lasted only hours), although it must have been in reality a series of engagements. Between 17 and 19 October, Christian and Muslim harried each other. Estimates of numbers vary, but it is likely that Hunyadi commanded a little over 20,000 men. Even so he was seriously outnumbered by Murad's 40,000. His German handgunners held the centre well but Hunyadi had not waited for Skanderbeg's forces as was the plan, and one account says that the Wallachians deserted. The probable reason for the second defeat on the 'field of blackbirds' was sheer numbers, and only Skanderbeg's timely arrival to fight a brilliant rearguard action saved Hunyadi's life. In an event similar to

Richard the Lionheart's return from the ill-fated Third Crusade in 1191, the 'white knight' was taken prisoner by the Serbs under George Branković, who held him to account for his army's atrocities on the march south. For a while he languished in the fortress of Smederevo.

The capture of Vladislav and Hunyadi was a golden opportunity for Țepeș. With the backing of the Turks in the form of cavalry and infantry from Varna and Nicopolis, the son of the Dragon invaded his own territory and took Tîrgoviste unopposed. Virtually no evidence exists for these momentous weeks. The chronicler Chalkondyles implies that the Impaler only held the throne until Vladislav's return from Kosovo. This may have been as little as two months. Țepeș had not seen his father's capital for five years. And the boy had returned a man with vengeance on his mind.

It is from this period that the Impaler's first period of rule as prince of Wallachia dates. On the one hand, it was a plain, old-fashioned military coup. Because of the presence of Turkish troops, who had crossed the Danube despite repeated promises to the contrary, it could be interpreted as an act of open warfare – though hardly a surprising one considering that Vladislav and his Wallachians were currently fighting Murad in Serbia. To Țepeș, it was a simple act to claim his rightful inheritance. Vlad Dracul and Mircea Dracula were dead – and Wallachia was his.

From the 'Saxon' city of Brașov in Transylvania, Nicolae of Ocna, the area's vice-governor, voiced an inevitable concern and demanded an explanation for Țepeș' actions. The prince's reply is the first documentation we have from the man who has gone down in history as a monster:

We give you the news that Mr Nicolae from Ocna of Sibiu writes to us [the royal we?] and asks us to be so kind as to come to him until John [Hunyadi] the Royal Governor of Hungary returns from the war. We are unable to do this because an emissary from Nicopolis came to us this past Tuesday [29 October] and said with great certainty that Murad, the Turkish sultan, made war for three days against [Hunyadi] the Governor and that on the last day [Hunyadi] formed a circle with his caravan [the Hussite-style war-wagons]. Then the sultan himself went down among the janissaries . . . broke through the lines and defeated and killed them. If we come now to him, the Turks could come and kill both you and us. Therefore we ask you to have patience until we see what has happened to [Hunyadi]. We don't even know if he is alive. If he returns from the war, we will meet him and we will make peace with him. But if you will be our enemies now, and if something happens, you will have sinned and you will have to answer for it before God. Written at Tîrgoviste the day before All Saint's Day in the year of our Lord 1448.

The reply was signed 'Vlad, *voivod* of Wallachia, your brother in all' and addressed to 'the officials of Braşov, our most loved brothers and friends'.[2]

No doubt vampire-lovers will see something sinister in the fact that the Impaler's first known letter was written on Hallowe'en, but it is important because it gives us an insight into his psyche. It sounds a little naïve in places, perhaps because the boy was only seventeen, perhaps because the Latin or Church Slavonic of the original loses something in translation, but Ţepeş' position was difficult and he had to be careful. He was describing a battle that had happened a fortnight earlier in enough detail to make us believe that he had talked to survivors, or at least received good intelligence, which may have come from Christian or Turkish sources (the emissary from Nicopolis). He was in Tîrgoviste with the support of Turkish troops, owed the sultan his freedom and could not, yet, afford to offend them. We do not know how much he knew of the circumstances of his father's and brother's deaths, but he must have known of the boyar revolt and perhaps suspected the involvement of Vladislav and Hunyadi. If both those men had died at Kosovo Polje, of course, he would already be avenged. On the other hand, he shows a shrewd grasp of political reality when he expresses a wish to make peace with Hunyadi. Towards the end of the letter, despite referring to the Braşov people as his 'brothers and friends', he threatens them with God's wrath if they refuse to accept him as prince of Wallachia. On the one hand, this is typical of medieval thought, the natural belief of ruler and ruled alike that God was the ultimate judge of sin. On the other hand, perhaps Vlad Ţepeş really believed that the hand of God guided all his actions.

What the Impaler may not have known is that Murad had not followed up his victory at Kosovo. Perhaps because of heavy casualties, perhaps because he had lost the heart for slaughter,[3] he ordered a three-day rest to bury the dead. This gave Vladislav the chance not only to escape, but to return to Wallachia to overthrow the young Ţepeş.

Eight years later, the son of the Devil would simply have knocked the pretender aside. As it was, he was inexperienced and lacked support among either the boyars or the peasantry. By Christmas 1448 his troops were outnumbered by Vladislav's forces, backed as they were by Petru II Bogdan, Prince of Moldavia, and he abandoned Tîrgoviste to run east, to the life he had known most recently, at Murad's court at Edirne. We have no exact date for his leaving but in all probability he had ruled Wallachia for only two months.

The years between Ţepeş' first and second reigns were spent in the wilderness and for part of that time at least, he was a fugitive. There is nothing like having to look over a shoulder to make a man vengeful, distrustful and morose. From December 1449 until October 1451, he lived at the court of his uncle, Bogdan II of Moldavia, at his capital Suceava. Here, he spent time and perhaps completed his education, with his cousin Stefan, who would become one of the most celebrated rulers in Eastern Europe as Stefan cel Mare, the Great. Of an age, the princes became friends, pledging to support each other in time of need. Stefan's odd and uncharacteristic treachery against Ţepeş in 1462 does not square with this oath; it probably only added to the already well-established sense of betrayal and mistrust that the prince felt throughout his life.

Moldavian, like Wallachian, politics was often brutal, nasty and the lives of its rulers short. Bogdan was murdered by a rival, Petru Aaron, his own brother, in October 1451, driving Ţepeş and Stefan to escape to Wallachia through the Borgo

Pass made famous four centuries later by Bram Stoker. They knew that by this time János Hunyadi had long since returned from his defeat at Kosovo. Stripped of his titles of governor of Transylvania and Hungary by the newly elected King Ladislas Posthumous of Hungary, he still held Hunedoara and other strongholds. By February 1452 Ţepeş was in Braşov, relying on the tentative links he had made with the powerful city fathers four years earlier. He was still there in September despite Hunyadi's stern orders that the fugitive was to be handed over. Under pressure of some kind and perhaps fearing for his safety, Ţepeş ran to Sibiu.

During 1451 and the following year, Hunyadi's relationship with Vladislav changed. There can be no doubt that the 'white knight' was ambitious and little doubt that Vladislav was very much the junior partner. Even so, Hunyadi's seizure of Amlaş and Fagaras probably prompted the prince to open relations with Mehmed II, now sultan once again in place of Murad who had died of a stroke on 3 February. In one sense, of course, Vladislav was simply carrying on the dangerous tightrope balance that his two predecessors had done. Vladislav's rather grand title on a deed of 28 March reads, 'Prince over all of Wallachia'. Weeks earlier, a document from Tîrgoviste had included 'and of the areas across the mountains on our borders, the duchies of Amlaş and Fagaras'.[4] Obviously Vladislav was furious that Hunyadi had grabbed territory from him. A document from 1453 makes clear the extent of the rift:

> I, my boyars and my country have spilled our blood for the Holy Crown, for Hungary and for Christianity. No matter how much we have sworn, our father, [Hunyadi] *voivod*, does not care and he was not pleased with my work . . . he acted badly towards me; and you can see that he broke the oaths and promises he made . . .[5]

At some point during 1452 a reconciliation was effected between Hunyadi and Ţepeş in a meeting at Hunedoara. We have no record of its substance or how sincerely Ţepeş promised to serve the 'white knight'. We do know, however, that he attended the meeting of the Hungarian diet with Hunyadi and was present at Posthumous's coronation as king of Hungary the following year, at Buda, a city he would come to know all too well in the future. In a deal struck here, Țepeș was given the role of defender of Transylvania, with his headquarters at Sibiu. The long-awaited fall of Constantinople meant that an all-out Turkish attack north of the Danube was now more likely than ever. As Pope Nicholas V lamented in distant Rome, 'The light of Christianity has suddenly gone out.'[6]

The Bishop of Sibiu, where Vlad Țepeș watched the borders, wrote to Oswald Wengel, the town's mayor:

> The Turks will subdue all of Christianity if God will allow it . . . They will next conquer the lands of the despot George Branković of Serbia . . . They also say that the city of Sibiu, which lies in their path, must be destroyed.[7]

While János Hunyadi prepared to defend Branković's strategic city of Belgrade on the Danube, Țepeș mobilized his own forces against his rival Vladislav, now in open union with Mehmed's Turks. In the middle of June 1456, he led his army through the Carpathians past the castle at Bran and caught Vladislav's army somewhere near Tîrgoviste. That month, a strange sight appeared in the night sky – 'as long as half the sky with two tails, one pointing west and the other east, coloured gold and looking like a flame in the distant horizon', wrote the chronicler Antonio Bonfini. He was describing the comet that had appeared in another June, in the year 1066, when Harold Godwinson had gone down fighting with his housecarls on Senlac Hill near Hastings. To some, the comet presaged victory and joy; to others death.

At the end of July, Vladislav II, Prince of Wallachia, was hacked to death in hand-to-hand combat – according to legend – with Vlad Țepeș. By 22 August, the Impaler was at Tîrgoviste, prince once more. One of the first things he did was to have a Brașov goldsmith strike a coin, the only one found from his reign. On the obverse was the Wallachian eagle displayed in all its heraldic glory; on the reverse, a crescent and a star with trailing wake.

We have already heard the account of Niccolò Modrussa, the pope's legate to Buda, written about 1466, but it bears repetition:

> He was not very tall, but very stocky and strong, with a cold and terrible appearance, a strong and aquiline nose, swollen nostrils, a thin and reddish face in which very long eyelashes framed large wide-open green eyes; the bushy black eyebrows made them appear threatening. His face and chin were shaven, but for a moustache. The swollen temples increased the bulk of his head. A bull's neck connected his head from which black curly locks hung on his wide-shouldered person.[8]

A number of portraits of Vlad Țepeș exist, most of them showing a mature man of between twenty-five and fifty.[9] The woodcut from the 1488 Nuremberg edition of *Dracole Waida* is typical. It shows the long dark hair that Modrussa saw, and the moustache swept up and outwards at each end, typical of the time; portraits of János Hunyadi show a similar style. The eyes in the woodcut are hard, focused, the mouth grim and intense. There is a remarkable consistency in most of the Impaler portraits in the headgear. They virtually all show a variant on the 'cap of estate' worn throughout Europe, decorated above the rim with a cluster of pearls around a central precious stone. The Leipzig edition, *An Extraordinary and Shocking History of a Great Berserker called Prince Dracula* from 1493, is far wider of the mark. The curly hair is short, the eyes rather more melancholy than intense and the cleft chin very pronounced. The Strasbourg edition of 1500 shows the famous banquet scene including a bearded Țepeș with long, flowing locks gazing up with a mildly interested look at his victims on their stakes.

There is a further interesting painting which may show Vlad Țepeș. It was discovered by accident in 1970 and was previously known to hang in the Belvedere Palace in Vienna. It is a fifteenth-century oil painting showing the martyrdom of St Andrew, whose mummified head was one of the few relics to survive the fall of Constantinople. Legend has it that the saint, one of the fishermen disciples of Christ, was crucified on a saltire cross at Patra about AD 70. A number of his relics, including the cross on which he died, was taken to Constantinople and supposedly to Scotland by the eighth century. He was the patron saint of the 'Saxons' from Transylvania, which accounts for the presence of Ţepeş, hovering at the left of the canvas and supervising the lashing of Andrew in place on the cross.

Another likeness was discovered even more recently, in 1989, by Dr Virgil Candea, and is now on display in the library of Württemberg, in Stuttgart. On a circular plaque with the legend 'Vladislaus Dracula, Wallachiae Weywoden', it shows a slightly portly *voivod* with high gilt-encrusted collar and fur-edged robes. The eyes are small and mean, but the nose and hair are exactly as Modrussa described them.

It is likely that all three portraits and possibly others now lost are copies of the version that hangs in Ambras Castle near Innsbruck in the Tyrol. This portrait is on display in a bizarre gallery once owned by Ferdinand II, Archduke of the Tyrol in the sixteenth century, who specialized in collecting artefacts of the macabre. Many of the portraits are taken from life, such as the Munich wolf-man, Petrus Gonsalvus (Pedro Gonzalez), whose painting, along with those of his children, is a reminder of the past's fascination for freaks.[10] There, too, is a likeness of poor Gregor Baxi, who suffered the same fate as Henri II of France in having his head pierced by a lance. The portrait shows him with the lance-tip protruding from his eye socket, months before the wound's infection killed him.

And next to Baxi is the famous portrait of Vlad the Impaler. This one is a sixteenth-century copy from an original probably painted at either Buda or Visegrád during Dracula's imprisonment by Matthias Corvinus. Various reproductions distort the colour of the Ambras version and add sinister lights to what is actually a standard fifteenth-century portrait. The eyes *are* very large and the famous crimson velvet cap is augmented with rows of pearls, a gold star and an upright ostrich-feather plume. The hair, hanging in heavy curls, is very long, well below the shoulders. How much of this is artistic licence by the anonymous artist is impossible to say.

The Chinese believe that the shape of the face and its prominent features tell us a great deal about personality. They call it *Siang Mien*. If we are to evaluate the man and to separate him from the monster and the legend, this is worth pursuing. We cannot see the Impaler's forehead in the Ambras portrait because of the heavy brim of his cap, although Modrussa makes the strange reference to his 'swollen' temples. His eyebrows conform to the Chinese ideal, although the spacing between brows and eyes is difficult to analyse because of problems of scale. Fascinatingly, his eye-shape fits that of the dragon, to the Chinese the symbol of power used by their emperors over the centuries. Dragon eyes are always large, with vast areas of white on each side of the iris; traditionally, their owners are innovative and risk-taking, and they are brave and good company. The nose, described by Modrussa as aquiline, is actually thin and narrow and his 'swollen' nostrils lost in the luxuriant moustache. To the Chinese, owners of thin noses have to work harder than most to make their marriages work (we have already seen that Vlad Țepeș reputedly ripped open one of his mistresses to test her pregnancy claims and his wife supposedly committed suicide). The Impaler's mouth presents a major problem. Only the lower lip is visible under the moustache and it is unusually thick, prompting historian Ion Bogdan in 1896 to assume that he had some sort of nervous tic. This seems highly unlikely. No court artist would paint in such an affliction, especially a man of the Impaler's reputation, whether he was a prisoner of Corvinus at the time or not. The portrait appears to be second-rate art and this more than anything else explains the lips – they are simply badly painted. Assuming that Țepeș' upper lip is thin (there is little space between his nose and mouth) this pattern to the Chinese indicates deviousness and that its owner has difficulty in inspiring trust. The Impaler's cheeks are high and the broadest part of his face. Such people, say the Chinese, get things done and they do not have close friends. The combination of those cheekbones and a strong jaw is commonly found in successful military men.

Vlad Țepeș was twenty-five years old when he took the throne of Wallachia for the second time. He inherited a political structure that comprised a council, the *Sfatul Domnesc*, which increasingly was made up of the leading boyars and which doubled as a civil service. The structure was essentially Byzantine although it had its parallels in the Ottoman sultan's court and the Curia Regis (household) of Western kings. Among the documents relating to the Impaler's time as prince, the word *Jupan* refers to any lord who was a member of the Council. There were two *vornici* at the Impaler's capital of Tîrgoviste, one more senior than the other, whose responsibility was the judiciary. The *logofat* headed Țepeș' chancellery, charged with correspondence and retention of court papers. Every surviving document from Țepeș would have been handwritten by a clerk at this court. The *spatar* was a military commander, usually, because of its knightly linkage, of cavalry. He was not technically commander-in-chief of the army, in that the prince himself assumed this role. The *stolnic*, first mentioned in a document in 1392, was the prince's food taster and responsible for the court victuals, while the *paharnic* was responsible for its wine. The prince's horses were the particular remit of the *comis* who also saw to the payment of the cash tribute and the boy levy to the Turks. The *vistiers* kept the prince's wardrobe as well as being his treasurer, keeping records of the taxes paid by the 222 villages and towns in Wallachia. The *stratornic*, also called *postelnic*, was in charge of the prince's private quarters.[11]

Țepeș had been crowned 'Prince Vlad, son of Vlad the Great, sovereign and ruler of Ungro-Wallachia and of the duchies of Amlaș and Fagaras' in the Biserica Domnesca, the great cathedral at Tîrgoviste, probably in September 1456. How far he had planned his domestic and foreign policy and how far he was merely reacting to events is difficult to gauge, but in the six years of his reign there does seem to be a consistency and a new dynamism altogether missing from the rule of his father, grandfather and their Dănești rivals.

In domestic policy, the paramount problem was that of the boyars. Some of these men had openly taken up arms on behalf of Vladislav II (often referred to as Dan, his family name, in contemporary literature) and had been responsible, probably with Hunyadi's backing, for both the beheading of Vlad Dracul and the burial alive of Mircea. The Impaler's treatment of the boyars should be seen in this context. The boyars as a class pre-dated the principality of Wallachia and had been used to garnering wealth and power for some time. The situation was not dissimilar to that in England under Prince John or Henry VI: in the first instance an absent king (John's brother Richard), in the second a weak one (Henry himself) led to the nobility building castles and assuming unlawful powers. Temporarily conciliating the two 'super-powers' on his western and southern frontiers, the Hungarians and the Turks, Ţepeş began a systematic purge of his boyars with Stalinesque efficiency. The famous coup against them probably took place in the first Easter of his reign (arguably on Sunday 17 April 1457). The horror stories attributed to Ţepeş described in Chapter Six of this book can now be seen against the historical framework. The boyars were feasting in the hall of the prince's palace at Tîrgoviste – still, for many modern visitors, a place of death. The Easter rituals in the chapel of the Holy Spirit were over and Ţepeş asked the nobles how many princes had ruled Wallachia in their lifetime. Whatever they told him was the wrong answer. By this time, he had already found Mircea's grave and the tell-tale clawmarks on the coffin lid where his desperate brother had fought for air in his dying agony. According to some accounts, 500 boyars and their families were impaled in the palace courtyard. In reality, the whole party cannot have included more than 200 and the place of execution, the ruins of which still stand today, is only large enough to house about forty. Tîrgoviste today is an isolated cluster of low walls and cellars. Only the chapel and the Impaler's Chindia watch tower, restored in the nineteenth century, show any shadow of their former glory.

The survivors who were not impaled were shackled together and dragged north for two days up the River Argeş, fifty miles away. Here they worked as a chain gang restoring the castle at Poenari – the original of Bram Stoker's Castle Dracula – as a mountain stronghold for the prince. It is debatable how much use these captives could have been in the rebuilding programme. The children, women and old men would have been too weak to last long and the stories say that they worked on the stone-carrying until their fine clothes fell off their backs. As a lesson in humiliation and the power of a prince, the building of Poenari by a previously exalted and privileged elite probably has no parallel in European history.

Poenari, now a dramatic, ivy-clad ruin high above the Argeş, once had five cylindrical towers with platforms for cannon and angles for crossfire. Its walls, double-reinforced with stone and brick, were built to withstand a possible Turkish bombardment. A well provided the castle with its own water supply and there was possibly an underground tunnel that led to the river for escape and the smuggling in of supplies. A series of earthquakes, rather than Turkish or Hungarian guns, eventually destroyed it.

How complete was Dracula's destruction of the boyar class? It may have been decimated. Kurt Treptow has analysed the names of the Council between 16 April 1457 (the day before the palace coup) and 10 February 1461. At Easter 1457, Marea Udriste heads the list, but he has gone by March 1458 and Dragomir Tacal is in his place. Only one *vornic* (Chief Justice) is listed. This is Codrea and his name too is missing by the following March. It would be tedious to recite them all and we cannot know the specific reasons for their removal in each case. Suffice it to say that out of thirteen 'departments' of the council, only two remain unchanged over the five-year period. Voico Dobrita, *vornic* in 1458 and clearly senior boyar by 1461; and Iova, at first *comis* (Master of the Horse) and later *vistier* (Treasurer) survived. The others have gone and it is reasonable to suppose that most of them perished in the Easter coup.

Treptow believes that the removal of the boyars was not as vicious nor sudden as the folktales tell. Individuals are listed again in the Council under Ţepeş' brother Radu after 1462, implying that they were either out of favour or out of the country during the Impaler's reign, not rotting at the top of a stake.

There was one boyar, however, whom Ţepeş singled out for punishment: Albu cel Mare. His death, and that of his family, appears in Number Seven of the 'Saxon' stories: 'He had a big family uprooted, from the smallest to the largest, children, friends, brothers, sisters and he had them all impaled.' The fact that Albu called himself cel Mare, the Great, may be indicative. He saw himself as a king-maker, an over-mighty subject, and a document dated 1 April 1551 in the reign of Prince Mircea Ciobanul puts his end in context:

> In the time of Vlad *Voivod* Ţepeş, there was a boyar called Albu cel Mare, who took the . . . villages [Glodul and Hintea] by force and devastated the holy monastery [of Govora] . . . In the days of Vlad *Voivod* Ţepeş, this boyar . . . tried to take the throne from him . . .

Whether Albu's attempt was an act of organized boyar resistance against the Impaler's centralist policy and his emasculation of the class or whether he was simply another Dăneşti rival, the result was the same. Albu himself, his relatives, his friends, all died in the same vengeful 'wipe-out'. His children would have grown to be adult rivals; his sisters would have bred those children. Everybody had to die.

There are conflicting theories as to Ţepeş' treatment of the boyars as a group. He clearly did not eliminate them all, either by impalement or castle-building. Neither is the situation of replacement clear-cut. One view is that, having removed the boyars, Ţepeş brought in his own relatively humble men whom he could trust, rather as the Tudors were to do in England thirty years later. There was inevitably an element of this, the usual nepotism and cronyism, the hallmark of many governmental structures, past and present. Whereas Ţepeş might not have wished to reduce the feudal powers of the boyars (powers which were in fact relatively new since feudalism was only now establishing itself in Wallachia), he certainly introduced new men, some of them from the ranks of the *moşneni*, the smallholding peasantry. The debate focuses on the speed and scale with which this was done.

Particularly sinister in the light of the *voivod*'s reputation was his creation of new hirelings. The *vitesji*, in effect an officer corps for his army, was recruited not from the boyars, who had their own agendas, but from the *mosneni*. Such men could be used either to hold a border castle against the Turks or crush an internal revolt. The new promotions also gave rise to the notion that the Wallachian army was a peasant body, which, while not altogether accurate, has a certain basis in fact. The *armas* were the rough equivalent of a secret police today – Ceauşescu's Securitate of the 1980s would have recognized their role. Many of them, like the men given the grisly task of disposing of the Russian royal family in 1918,[12] were foreigners, (gypsies, Hungarians, Tartars, Serbs) and thus would be more likely to carry out atrocities on Wallachians, if ordered to do so, with fewer qualms than native troops. In a letter written to Braşov, probably in 1458, Ţepeş refers to his former wine-supplier Stoica as *Armasul*, but the Stake-Master was not included in the Council until 1478, by which time the Impaler was dead.

Much has been made of Ţepeş' relationship with the Church. His own personal faith is a closed book. His father, as a member of the Dragon fraternity, was a Catholic. The Impaler may have taken up the Islamic religion during his time in Edirne, which could explain his position as an officer in the Turkish army (we know after all that George Kastrioti, Skanderbeg, did the same). The Serbs, however, were regarded as an almost pagan society within the Balkans; the Wallachians were more firmly rooted in the Orthodox Church.

Like most medieval rulers, Ţepeş was a staunch patron of the Church. At Tîrgsor, in the church of St Nicholas, stands the inscription 'By the Grace of God, I, *voivod*, ruler of Ungro-Wallachia, the son of the great Prince Vlad, have built and completed this church on 24 June 1461.' This may have been in atonement for the killing of Vladislav II, which legend says happened nearby, or in celebration of the event. If so, that too was standard medieval practice. In England, Edward IV went to great trouble and expense to move the body of his rival, Edward, Prince of Wales, killed at Tewkesbury in 1473, to a better mausoleum. William of Normandy, four centuries earlier, had built Battle Abbey on the crest of the hill at Senlac where his enemy, Harold Godwinson, had been cut down. Ţepeş founded a monastery at Comana, gave grants of land and tax exemptions to others at Tismana, Cozia and Govora, and greatly extended the island monastery at Snagov. He also gave large donations to Mount Athos in Greece, the spiritual centre of the Eastern Orthodox Church outside Russia.

Foreign policy had a significant influence on the Wallachian Church. The Metropolitan was appointed before 1453 by the Patriarch of Constantinople, but the fall of the Byzantine capital in that year brought about a change. To the west, the creeping encroachment of Hungary, under the charge first of János Hunyadi, then of his son Matthias Corvinus, meant that Catholicism was seeping into the Impaler's principality. Many of the horror stories found in 'Saxon', Russian and Romanian versions deal with Ţepeş' clashes with Catholic monks – Brother Jacob from Melk may well have been a survivor – and they speak volumes for the anti-Catholic and therefore anti-Hungarian stance that the *voivod* adopted. It was under Vlad Ţepeş that the first Wallachian, Abbot Iosif, was made Metropolitan in April 1457. Previous incumbents, appointed by Constantinople, had been outsiders. All this is very much in keeping with the Impaler's centralizing policy. Church and state went hand in glove in Wallachia, as in the rest of Europe. As he appointed his own boyars and officials, so he began to appoint his own church hierarchy, especially in the spiritual wilderness in which the collapse of Constantinople had left him.

The other element in Ţepeş' reign is the substance of the 'Saxon' horror stories relating to Transylvania: 'In the year of our Lord 1456 Dracula did many dreadful and curious things.' The documents tell us that the *voivod*'s targets here were particularly Braşov (referred to by the German name of Kronstadt or Burzenland) and Sibiu (Siebenburgen, the seven cities). Both these towns were in the Amlaş and Fagaras duchies which Hunyadi and Vladislav II had taken from Vlad Dracul. By the 1450s Transylvania was wholly dominated by the 'alien' German or Hungarian merchants and landowners; the Romanians themselves were barely subsistent and had no legal rights. Early in his reign, Țepeş was at pains to continue the cordial relationship with the 'Saxon' towns that he had briefly enjoyed in 1448. On 10 September 1456, styling himself, 'Vlad, Prince of Wallachia and ruler of Fagaras, your brother and friend in all', he wrote to the elders of Braşov, 'You brethren, friends and neighbours who are truly l oved . . .'. Certainly, Țepeş was asking for help, but he was also trying to unite the Transylvanians with his own people in a great cause. What he wanted was a show of strength to give the Turks pause in what appeared to be a renewal of hostilities against both Wallachia and Transylvania.

In the previous month, Sultan Mehmed advanced along the Danube to take Dar-ne-jihad, the battlefield of Holy War, George Branković's city of Belgrade, the white city. Built on high ground where the Danube and the Sava meet, it was a strategic point south of the Hungarian plain, leading north via undulating valleys where a large, predatory army could never be stopped. Made aware of Mehmed's advance by scouts and spies, János Hunyadi hurried to defend the five-gated walls of its island fortress. Either by accident or design, the janissaries were allowed to break through the breaches their cannon had made and began to ransack and loot the town with its ramshackle houses and twisting lanes. They were suddenly attacked by an organized band of citizens led by Hunyadi, using muskets against the Turks who by this stage expected civilian submission.

The janissaries broke up in panic, the braying of their regimental bands and the screaming of their generals failing to hold them. Mehmed, never the gentleman his father was, hacked with his scimitar at his flying troops.

Twenty days later and a bare fortnight before Țepeş was writing to Braşov, János Hunyadi died. Whether from plague or dysentery, the 'white knight' had gone. And the Balkans had need of new warlords.

Țepeş asked Braşov for 200 men, fifty if that was all they could manage. There was nothing odd about this request. Constantinople unsuccessfully, Belgrade successfully, had seen its citizens man the walls. Medieval towns had walls built for that purpose. In England, in time of need, kings made similar requests; it was only the outbreak of plague in the city that prevented the citizens of York from marching to the aid of Richard III at Bosworth in 1485. Ţepeş wanted the Braşovians to move fast. His letter was dated 'the Friday after St Mary's Day', and he wanted the troops by the following Sunday, nine days away. There is no record of whether this contingent was sent, but presumably it was, because soon the Impaler signed an agreement with the city promising aid against the Turks and giving their merchants rights to trade freely in his Wallachian cities of Tîrgoviste, Tîrgsor and Rucar. He was to be given asylum in Braşov should the need arise. It is likely that similar arrangements were made with other cities, such as Sibiu.

So what went awry? How did this ostensibly friendly relationship end? Romanians believe, in keeping with their view of Vlad Ţepeş as a national hero, that he was protecting Wallachian interests against the avariciousness of the foreigners. In that the foreigners were members of the wealthy merchant class, there is even an element of class warfare here, 500 years before Nicolae Ceauşescu tried to muscle in on the act with commemorative postage stamps of the Impaler,[13] portraying Ţepeş, in communist literature, as a class warrior. It is true that the first punitive measures against the 'Saxons' were economic, but that was merely because Ţepeş wanted to hit them where he knew it would hurt most: in their purses. The impalements would come later. The real reason for the *voivod*'s actions against the 'Saxon' cities, which earned him the reputation 'berserker' and 'bloodthirsty madman', is that he suspected those areas, quite rightly, of plotting with his rival, the future prince Basarab Laiota.

The position was complicated by affairs in Hungary, which had suffered for years an ongoing feud similar to that of the rival Draculeşti and Dăneşti families in Wallachia. On the one hand were the Hunyadis, László and Matthias, the sons of János, the elder boy carrying on his late father's role as commander of the Hungarian armies. On the other was the Habsburg King, Ladislas Posthumous, and the Cilli family to whom he was related. The murder of Count Ulrich Cilli in László's city of Belgrade had led to the execution of László and the imprisonment of Matthias in March 1457. Their torch had been taken up by the in-laws of János Hunyadi, his widow Erzsebet and her brother Mihail Szilágy.

Vlad Țepeș was in the dilemma found so commonly in the Balkans, and in feudal Europe generally, of having sworn fealty to one side – in this case the Habsburgs – and owing allegiance to the other – here the Hunyadis – for help in gaining the throne. This link with the Hunyadis is rather difficult to grasp. After all, János was in the background at least over the deaths of Vlad Dracul and Mircea, but the new *voivod* seems either to have been unaware of this or happy enough to forgive and forget. Whatever the truth, the lines were drawn up. The Holy Roman Emperor, Frederick III, supported Ladislas and, by definition, so did the 'Saxon' towns in Transylvania.

The first spark of open trouble came in the summer of 1457 when the citizens of Bistrița revolted against Szilágy over alleged misappropriation of funds. This has a very modern ring to it and it may be that the townspeople had simply had enough of the warlord's high-handed rule. Backed by Țepeș, Szilágy sacked the town and burned the houses of the ringleaders. The other 'Saxon' cities rallied together after Bistrița and received support from the Szekler leader Count Oswald of Rozgony, anxious to prove his worth as Ladislas Posthumous's new commander in the Carpathians.

Brașov backed Țepeș' Dănești rival Dan III, whose brother the Impaler had killed at Tîrgsor. He was even crowned in the Orthodox cathedral outside Brașov with all the panoply of state and using Țepeș' own title. Dan's temporary capital was outside the city walls on a hill that would become notorious in the Impaler legend – Timpa.

Sibiu, for reasons that are unclear, did not join Brașov in supporting Dan, but backed another claimant, 'a priest of the Romanians who calls himself a prince's son'. This was almost certainly Vlad Calugarul, the monk, Țepeș' half-brother by the Wallachian peasant woman Caltuna. Calugarul set himself up at Amlaș and gained support from disaffected boyars and 'Saxon' merchants, furious that Ţepeş had dropped the trading concessions he had given them the previous year.

So by 1457 the Impaler was faced with no fewer than three rivals, Dan III, Vlad the monk and Basarab Laiota. At first, he tried diplomacy, sending boyars from the Council to both Sibiu and Braşov. Rather like the British ultimata to Germany which preceded both world wars in the twentieth century, there was no reply. The result was Ţepeş' first devastating raid on the 'Saxons' in the spring of 1458. The villages of Satul Nou, Hosman and Casolts were burned to the ground by his cavalry, and the supporters of Vlad the monk were butchered. Bod was totally destroyed, Talmes left blazing and its people hacked 'like cabbage' in the town square. Merchants who were now expected to sell their wares at the specified towns of Tîrgoviste, Tîrgsor and Cîmpulung at below the market value were rounded up for non-compliance and, according to the 'Saxon' accounts, impaled by the roadside or boiled in cauldrons. The young men whom it was claimed had been sent to Wallachia to learn the language were likewise executed, quite simply because they were clearly spies.

The international chess game of politics moved on. On 9 December 1457 Ladislas Posthumous, shown in contemporary portraits as a rather effeminate young man with flowing blond curls, was suddenly taken ill and died the same day, probably poisoned. His place was taken by the election of Matthias Hunyadi, the remaining son of the 'white knight' who now took the surname Corvinus, 'the crow', the great black bird that bedecked his shield and banners. Mihail Szilágy, the new king's uncle, now brokered peace between Ţepeş and the 'Saxon' towns; and an uneasy peace ensued. Matthias Corvinus sent his ambassador Benedict de Boithar to open negotiations with the Impaler, while Szilágy signed a treaty with Braşov. The deal was that Ţepeş should restore the town's trading rights in exchange for the surrender of the pretender Dan III and his boyar followers. 'Know that I shall keep the word ordered by my brother and lord Mihail Szilágy', Ţepeş wrote on 1 December 1458.[14]

By the winter of 1459, this promising new start had collapsed. Dan and his boyars were not forthcoming and Corvinus, keen to stamp his own imprint on his kingdom, dismissed Szilágy as commander in Transylvania. As well as threatening to skewer de Boithar on the highest stake he had, Ţepeş hit the Braşov suburbs like a whirlwind. Attacking at night, his cavalry clattered across the wooden bridge and burned the stockade that gave flimsy protection to Dan III's enclave on Timpa Hill. It was here that the inhabitants were impaled in large numbers as the chapel of St Jacob burned to the ground. According to the poet Michel Beheim, the Impaler sat at a table in the open air and mopped up from his plate the blood of his writhing victims. The boyar who complained of the foul stench was impaled higher than the rest.

Vlad followed up his attack with another on Braşov itself, looting and burning the church of St Bartholomew and carrying away its holy relics. But Dan and his supporters were long gone, armed with plenty of propaganda against his rival. On 2 March 1460, Dan wrote to the burghers of the damaged city, sympathizing with the fact that they had been victims of:

> untold abuses, damage hardly reparable, sad murders, mutilations, sorrows, being grieved, mercilessly killed, destroyed, maimed and tortured . . . by the unfaithful cruel tyrant Dracula, who calls himself Vlad, prince of that country . . . He did this following the teaching of the Devil . . .[15]

Probably hoping to emulate Hunyadi's success in 1448, Dan launched a counter-offensive against Ţepeş later that month, taking the often fought-over Amlaş and Fagaras on the way. The clash with the Impaler, probably near Rucar, was a failure, however; only seven of Dan's boyars scrabbled to safety. Dan himself was forced to dig his own grave and a mass for the dead was said while he was still alive. According to Beheim at least, Ţepeş hacked off his rival's head himself.

With their claimant dead, Braşov now sent a fifty-five-man embassy to the Impaler, led by Johann Gereb of Vingard.

Ţepeş held them at Tîrgoviste and set out to eliminate his second rival, his own half-brother, Vlad Calugarul. On 24 August 1460, St Bartholomew's Day, the Impaler burned the corn standing in the fields beyond the walls of Amlaş and, again according to the 'Saxon' tradition, slaughtered 30,000 inhabitants. Şercaia, the territory of the rebellious boyar Bogdan Doboca, was devastated, the villagers being hanged on hooks and pitchforks. Beaten down by the Impaler's overkill, Braşov took the hint and concluded a treaty with Ţepeş on 1 October. The terms of the treaty provided that there was to be an exchange of prisoners; that the *voivod* would release Gereb's embassy; that Braşov would hand over rebel boyars and merchants; and that full trading rights were to be restored. Ţepeş would be paid for the cost of a standing army of 4,000 men to 'guard' the Seven Fortresses. And he would pay the town for war damage.

Curbing the power of the boyars and bringing the German merchant class to heel as he did has led many Romanians to see Vlad Ţepeş as a Robin Hood, a man of the people. This is to misread medieval history. The peasantry in Wallachia may have constituted nearly 90 per cent of the population, and there were times, as in the Bogomil disturbances of the 1430s, when they could be troublesome. They also constituted, as in all other medieval states, the numerical bulk of the *voivod*'s army. But they were also cannon fodder. They died on the ramparts of castles that they themselves had built. They grew the grain that was the food supply of the state. They cleared forests for the *voivod* and built the monasteries he endowed. To a prince the peasantry were an accepted fact of everyday life. Deferential by nature, they pulled off their caps and knelt in his presence, overawed by the God-given role that he played. He was their lord in every sense. He could read and write. He could buy any one of them a thousand times over. He could outride and outfight any of them. And he had the power of life and death over them all.

Ţepeş had no need to curry favour with these people any more than any ruler did. Murad II may have regarded his slaves as his brothers, but they were still technically slaves and he showed no inclination to set them free. If Ţepeş elevated such men to positions of authority it was for his own purposes, to outmanoeuvre recalcitrant or rebellious boyars. If he refused, as he did, to send the boy tribute to the Turks, the reason was not because he cared for the boys and their families; it was because he wanted to offend the Turks. If he meted out punishment for wrongdoing equally to boyar and peasant alike, it was because he expected absolute obedience to his will from everyone.

One story, found in the 'Saxon', Romanian and Russian chronicles that relates specifically to the peasants, is the tale of the old, the lame and the sick who were invited to dine in a great hall at Ţepeş' capital of Tîrgoviste. Having fed them and got them drunk, the Impaler's attendants locked the doors and set the house alight. In the folktales, Ţepeş justified his actions: 'These men live off the sweat of others, so they are useless to humanity. It is a form of thievery . . . They are worse than robbers. May such men be eliminated from my land.'[16] Romanian historians from the Ceauşescu era, anxious to find in the Impaler a hero on a white horse, have posited that his intention here was to wipe out bubonic plague, the ever-prevalent Black Death which had probably claimed Hunyadi and was a constant source of fear. We know that victims of *pestilencia* throughout Europe were treated with appalling cruelty, whipped out of settlements, stoned, walled up alive. We know, too, that burning the clothes and bodies of the infected was tried, as one of many desperate remedies, at various places where the disease raged. Even so, the theory seems a little far-fetched. No one would have allowed plague victims to enter a major town, especially the *voivod*'s capital, because the belief – and the reality, depending on the strain of the disease – was that the plague is highly infectious.

Another theory suggests that Ţepeş committed the crime to eradicate poverty in Wallachia. If so, this seems draconian[17] in the extreme. All medieval (and many modern) states were faced with poverty on a massive scale. In England, the solution to the wandering bands of 'sturdy beggars' was the Elizabethan Poor Law of 1601. In Wallachia, according to this theory, it was mass murder.

Ţepeş' foreign policy had to focus on the Ottoman Turks. He had spent years with them, his family had fought them. And for the time being he needed to keep them at arm's length. Accordingly, between 1456 and 1459 he sent his emissaries to Mehmed's court, now at Constantinople, and probably sent his *Comis* personally to pay the tribute. In 1460 it suited both men to conclude a treaty. Nine articles covered the essentials of their relationship.

In the first, the Turks were not allowed to enter Wallachia, except for diplomatic missions specifically allowed by Ţepeş. The payment of the tribute – 'totalling 10,000 *galbens* from our treasury' – was to be paid at Tîrgoviste from now on, and the Turkish ambassador responsible for its collection was to be escorted from Giurgiu to the capital and back again, a receipt being issued for the money as it left the country. The second article gave the *voivod* total independence, allowing him to make war with his neighbours and giving him 'the power of life and death over his subjects'. Article Three insisted that any Wallachians adopting Islam when south of the Danube should revert to Christianity on their return to avoid friction – a provision that may tell us a lot about Ţepeş' personal views on religion. The Fourth Article allowed Wallachian travellers in the Ottoman Empire to be exempt from Turkish taxation and to be allowed to wear their own dress. The 'horror' stories of the Impaler, of course, record that the *voivod* himself was a stickler for protocol of this type, nailing heads and torturing people who were improperly attired. 'The prince', said Article Five, 'shall be chosen by the Metropolitan, the bishops and the boyars.'[18] This was in marked contrast to what would follow two years later when, effectively, Ţepeş' younger brother Radu was placed on the Wallachian throne by Mehmed. Should there be a dispute between a Turk and a Wallachian, Article Six contended, the case should be tried by the prince himself. Turkish merchants' rights were carefully controlled by Article Seven. They could cross the Danube and sell only in specific places and leave again quickly. There was to be no 'sight-seeing'. Article Eight added that those merchants could not take Wallachians with them when they left, nor would they be given a special place for prayer. Lastly, the sultan's government did not have the right to act against any of the Impaler's people or take anyone out of Wallachia.

The agreement seems heavily weighted in Ţepeş' favour, but it was assumed that the cash tribute and boy levy would go on as before, and Mehmed needed a quiescent European frontier because he was about to make war in Asia. He concluded a similar treaty with Skanderbeg in Albania.

We know almost nothing of Vlad Ţepeş' private life, but we can assume that by the time of the Turkish treaty he was married to his first wife, whose name is unknown. She was probably Wallachian or Transylvanian and may have been the noblewoman who committed suicide in 1462. Fedor Kuritsyn, who met members of the Impaler's family at Matthias Corvinus's court at Buda in 1480, is probably right when he says the pair were not married. Under Wallachian law, as we have seen, a son of a liaison had equal inheritance rights with a legitimate child. Mihail was the son born of this relationship and would follow his father in almost every particular. Raising rebellious boyar armies against Dracula's successors, he took the Wallachian throne in 1508 and held it for less than two years. He received almost as bad a press as the Impaler. Known as 'the evil one' he:

> took all the boyars captive, worked them hard, cruelly confiscated their property and even slept with their wives in their presence. He cut off the noses and lips of some, others he hanged and still others drowned.[19]

By this time of course, the horror stories of his father were already international best-sellers and it is likely that Mihail was happy to bask in the notoriety, in that it usually got results. He was stabbed to death by an assassin in 1510. The direct descendants of this branch of the family died out in 1632.

The story of Dracula's second marriage to Matthias Corvinus's cousin Ilona Szilágy will be dealt with in the next chapter, but Kuritsyn wrote of the family:

the king [Corvinus] took his sister [Dracula's widow] with her two sons to Buda in Hungary. One of these sons is still in the retinue of the king, the other, who was residing with the Bishop of Oradea [in Transylvania] died in our presence. I saw a third son, named Micahel [Mihail] here in Buda. He had fled from the Sultan to the Hungarian king. Dracula begot him on a young lady when he was not married.[20]

We cannot know how many mistresses the Impaler took to his bed. One hopes that they were not all as unlucky as the one whose body he ripped open to disprove her pregnancy.

By 1462, Vlad Ţepeş had centralized power in his own hands at Tîrgoviste, although increasingly he began to favour the more southerly town of Bucharest. He had controlled his boyars and regulated trade with the 'Saxons' in Transylvania, bringing them to heel. He had executed one rival to his throne and terrified the others. Allying with Mihail Szilágy, and through him King Matthias Corvinus of Hungary, he had protected his western frontiers. But to the south, despite the treaty of 1460 which both signatories knew was no more than a temporary truce, the situation was unresolved. There, poised on the Danube, waited Mehmed the Conqueror.

# 10

# ENEMIES OF THE
# CROSS OF CHRIST

In the early hours of Thursday 29 May 1453, the feast day of Saint Theodosia, Byzantium and its way of life came to an end. The shock waves reverberated throughout the civilized world: the empire that had lasted almost exactly eleven hundred years was no more. Since 2 April, a vast Ottoman army, perhaps as many as 100,000 if one includes camp followers, led by Sultan Mehmed II, had been camped on the landward side of the great city of Constantinople. Prowling the Sea of Marmara and the Golden Horn were the war galleys of the admiral Hamsa Bey, blocking escape routes by sea and ready to tangle with the Venetian warships which formed part of the city's defences.

Those defences were still impressive. There was an inner and outer wall built to facilitate artillery fire, with a deep moat between the two. The inner wall had ninety-six towers, each of which could be held independently of the wall below it. There were eight major gates and a number of posterns which could be used as sally ports from which the defenders could reach out and strike the attackers. The perimeter of the city's walls was twenty-eight miles long, and the wall itself was enormously thick at the most likely attack points.

Constantinople had been besieged before, usually unsuccessfully. It had held out in 626 against the Avars and Slavs and twice against the Arabs, in 669 to 677 and 717–18. Although it was taken by the 'Latin' crusaders in 1204, it was won back by the Byzantine Emperor Michael Palaeologus on 25 July 1261. Bayezid the Thunderbolt's siege had lasted for eight years, but his defeat by Timur-i-Leng in 1402 had forced him to abandon it.

There were to be no more reprieves for Byzantium; in many senses, the fall in 1453 was inevitable. The split with Rome in the eleventh century had led to an irretrievable isolation for the city which no badly attended and half-hearted councils of reconciliation could repair. Almost the only western nation to defend Constantinople was Venice – but even its war galleys were penned in by the May of '53 by the brilliant transportations of Turkish vessels overland on rollers to the Golden Horn. One of the reasons for Turkish military superiority in this period was their capacity to adapt. Already a formidable land force, they copied the style of Venetian warships and created an equally formidable navy that would not be checked until Lepanto in 1571.

Attacks on 12 and 17 May had been beaten back, but the defenders of the city, under the Emperor Constantine Palaeologus and the Genoese *condottiere* Giovanni Giustiniani could not have numbered more than 7,000. When the attack began about half past one in the morning of 29 May, the churches of the city rang their bells, both as a siren to the inhabitants and as a cry to God for salvation. Old men, women and children hurried to the walls, to plug holes with timber and stones, anything to keep the invaders out. On the ramparts, their menfolk waited in silence as the deafening roar of the Ottoman attack echoed and re-echoed around the moonlit walls. They saw the waves of *bashi-bazouks*, the ragtail mercenaries, Germans, Hungarians, Slavs, Italians, anxious to earn the sultan's promise of a great prize to be the first into the central stockade. Beyond them, a solid line of military police whipped the first wave on with thongs and maces.

For nearly two hours the attack went on, scaling ladders clattering against masonry, culverins and matchlocks roaring in the darkness, guttering torches sailing through the air to ignite thatched roofs and dry timbers. Mehmed pulled his first wave back and sent in his steady Anatolian troops to hit the

Gate of Saint Romanus. Drums and trumpets bellowed and screamed as this disciplined, instinctive force lodged its ladders on Constantinople's walls. By now the Ottoman artillery was having its effects on the inner as well as the outer wall. A giant cannon rocked back on its huge carriage on the ridge of Rumeli Hisar, the Fortress of Europe. It had been dragged there by sixty oxen and fired cannon balls weighing twelve hundredweight for a range of over a mile; ironically, the cannon had been built by Urban, a Hungarian gunsmith who had first offered his services to the emperor: Constantine, strapped for cash, had turned him down.

Still, the walls held. The emperor himself led a determined counter-attack that drove the Anatolians back from a breach the guns had made. Now Mehmed sent in his janissaries, the elite backbone of his army, fresh troops who would crash through the gaps in the stonework against an exhausted force who had been fighting now for four hours. The *condottiere* Giustiniani, of whom Mehmed had muttered, 'What would I not give to have that man in my service?'[1] fell back, his breastplate and ribs shattered by a musket ball. Even the emperor's urging could not make him stay and he let his Genoese mercenaries carry him down to a waiting ship, deserting the city as the sheer weight and determination of the janissaries, anxious to find Paradise, forced the defenders to waver.

Like Horatius over the Tiber 'in the brave days of old', Constantine, his cousin Theophilus and comrades Francisco of Toledo and John Dalmata stood in the path of the oncoming hordes. The emperor tore off his eagle insignia and the mob engulfed them all.

Crescents and horsetails now fluttered over the city in the red-gold of a May dawn, and Mehmed unleashed his troops for the customary three days of looting. The soldiers killed anyone on the ramparts or in the streets, hacking down men, women and children indiscriminately. The blood ran down the steep cobbled streets that led from Petra to the Golden Horn. No one made an accurate count of the dead. Women and children were cut down where they huddled, praying to St Theodosia even at this late hour to save them. Some were literally torn apart by *bashi-bazouks* and Anatolians fighting over them like the spoils of war they were. Antony Beevor's recent book on the fall of Berlin in 1945 has caused something of a stir, with its graphic account of mass rape by the Red Army. The same happened in Constantinople, but too long ago for us to have the same outrage of memory and the same sense of shock.

Countless icons and relics were smashed and burned – to us the priceless artefacts of history, to the victorious Turks alien trinkets without worth. The holiest of all were said to be hidden in the warren-riddled walls of the cathedral of the Holy Wisdom (Hagia Sofia in Greek) against the day when Christian Constantinople comes again to Muslim Istanbul. In that church, with the sunlight streaming in through its astonishing glass dome, Mehmed, soon to be styled the Conqueror, walked to the high altar. He threw a handful of dust over his turban in humility before Allah for giving him this victory. He quietly pondered the few cowering priests hiding behind pillars and faced Mecca while an *ulema*, a Muslim scholar, intoned that there was no God but Allah and that Mohammed was his prophet.

The head of Constantine Palaeologus was brought to the sultan's tent. Washed and embalmed, it was placed first on a pole in the Forum of Augustus in the city, then taken as a prize around the courts of Islam. The head of Vlad Ţepeş would be sent to Mehmed's palace twenty-four years later.

The portrait of Mehmed II by Gentile Bellini shows a sophisticated man with a sharp, aquiline nose, soft brown eyes and a receding chin disguised by a full, pointed beard. As a child he had been wayward and idle, his lessons driven home with the whip. At the age of twelve, he was made regent in Rumelia while Murad, his father, was fighting enemies in Karamania. The janissaries despised the child, perhaps because they saw in him a streak of viciousness wholly missing in his father. As a teenager, he appears to have developed homosexual leanings, and one of his targets was Radu Dracula, the hostage brother of the future Impaler. Five days after the fall of Constantinople, he demanded that Constantine's chief minister or megadux Lucas Notarus surrender his pretty fourteen-year-old son to the sultan, along with the equally attractive child of Andronicus Cantacuzenius, the emperor's chief steward. When Notarus refused, Mehmed had both boys decapitated in front of Notarus and then executed him too. Likewise, the son of the chronicler George Phrantzes died because he refused to bend to the sultan's will.

Mehmed had become sultan in the winter of 1451, when Murad died. Spurred on by a God-given belief in his superiority and realizing that Constantinople was actually more bluff than substance, he launched his attack on the city with much preparation; and its capture turned him into the most popular of the Ottoman rulers. There is no doubt that Mehmed was the real founder of the Ottoman Empire. He called himself the 'Sovereign of Two Lands' – Rumelia and Anatolia – 'and of the Two Seas' – the Mediterranean and the Black. As Jason Goodwin says in *Lords of the Horizons*:

> Turnstile of the continents, seal of empires, geomantic paradise, Constantinople was a place of absolutes. It was either very hot or very cold. Here Europe and Asia met.[2]

After May 1453 the city did not become Istanbul but Konstantiniyye, and by 1455 Mehmed had completed his astonishing new palace in the old Tauri forum within its walls on the site of an abandoned monastery. But he did not like it, and four years later began on a new one overlooking the Sea of Marmara that would become the legendary Topkapi on a hill of olive groves, the Palace of Felicity, a paradise on earth.

Vlad Țepeș was in Sibiu when he heard of Constantinople's fall. The news probably reached him – from Venetian sailors struggling home via the mountain pass at Turnu Roșu – how Hamsa Bey, the Turkish admiral, had sunk their galleys, how Mehmed had ordered the impaling of their captain, Antonio Rizzo, and had his body displayed on a stake in full view of the city walls.

Mehmed *el fatih*, the Conqueror, would fail to take either Belgrade or Rhodes in the years ahead before Vlad Țepeș, *voivod* of Wallachia and lord of Amlaş and Fagaras, decided to attack him along the Danube. In 1459, the humanist Pope Pius II, who as Eneo de Piccolomini already had a reputation as a traveller, scholar, writer and man-about-many-towns, launched a new crusade. It was a singularly bad omen that on 1 June, when his congress opened at Mantua, not a single delegate turned up. The fresco in the Siena Cathedral, showing a less-than-rapt papal audience, is based on events four months later, by which time some of Europe's leaders had sent their emissaries. Clearly, crusading as an ideal of chivalry on a par with the quest for the grail was dead. There was no Peter the Hermit now to lead the dewy-eyed Christians across lands longing to be freed and to be part of the kingdom of Christ. Everyone now knew that the Red Sea would not part for them. In most states of Europe, nationalism was fast becoming reality; Christendom was as vague and obsolete a term as the Flood.

What many Western European rulers chose to ignore, however, was that ultimately the Ottoman threat was a threat to them all. There are echoes of this in the appeasement policy followed by Britain and France in the 1930s, reflected in the frequently asked question in the Commons at that time, 'What have we got to do with Poland?' Was it only Pius who had noticed that Mehmed the Conqueror was now calling himself the Eastern Roman Emperor because he worshipped in the mosque of Hagia Sofia? His war fleet of nearly eighty galleys commanded the Black Sea, forcing tribute from the Genoese colonies on its shores and from the kingdom of Trebizond and the Romanian principality of Moldavia. His white-helmeted janissaries had smashed their way into Smeredevo, the last Christian Serbian stronghold, and all the lands south of the Danube were in Ottoman hands, like a great stain spreading west. Pius warned:

> Every victory for [Mehmed] will be a stepping-stone to another, until after subjecting all the Christians of the west, he will have destroyed the Gospel of Christ and imposed that of his false prophet over the entire world.[3]

# Enemies of the Cross of Christ

The delegates who heard him, from Hungary, Burgundy and Milan, shuffled in embarrassment – their 'elsewhere' faces apparent in the Siena fresco. The Holy Roman Emperor, Frederick III, promised 32,000 footsoldiers and 10,000 horses. But they were not forthcoming. Gregor von Heimburg from 'the Germanies' muttered about internal unrest. Alfonso the Magnanimous of Spain, who might have been earnest in support, had died the previous June while planning an attack on Genoa. His illegitimate son, Ferrante, was embroiled in a succession squabble over Naples with Charles VII of France, who in turn was pinned down keeping his obnoxious son Louis from the throne of France. The English, torn by the Wars of the Roses that would decimate their nobility, sent no one at all. Sigismundo Malatesta, the *condottiere* from Rimini, summed up the feeling of most Italian states when he said, 'I serve him who pays me more.'[4] In the following year he was paid to fight the pope himself and Pius excommunicated him. Of the Western powers, only Venice, already threatened and damaged by the Turks, offered a genuine force – 8,000 sailors for their galleys, 50,000 horse and 20,000 foot. The catch was that they demanded money from the papal coffers to meet the costs. And Pius's coffers were empty. George Poděbradý, the Hussite King of Bohemia, had his own internal troubles to sort out and in view of his faith, his relations with Rome were strained; Pius's successor, Paul II, would excommunicate him in 1464. Nearer Wallachia, Casimir the Great, King of Poland, was involved in war with the Teutonic Order, driving its knights west across Prussia in the previous year. Ivan III, the Grand Duke of Muscovy, had his hands full with religious dissent and the Tartar tribes still raiding his eastern frontier. Stefan of Moldavia, the cousin whom Țepeș had helped to the throne two years earlier, was going head to head with Matthias Corvinus over the Hungarian king's support of those who had murdered his father.

It must have struck Pius as ironic that eastern Muslims, as appalled by the warlike Ottomans as he was, should have been the most enthusiastic to join his crusade. Mehmed's brother-in-law, Uzun Hazan, of the White Sheep Uzbeks of

Iran, promised Pius 5,000 battle-hardened troops. Dadian Liprait, King of Mingrelia on the Black Sea, offered men. The lord of Karaman in Trebizond spoke of 40,000. It is curious to think that had all three offers materialized, Mehmed would have faced a force three times the size of his own, and, as with Bayezid the Thunderbolt and Timur-i-Leng, the Ottoman subjugation of the Balkans would have come to a crushing halt.

At Mantua, in January 1460, Pius declared a three-year crusade. Anyone who took the cross would be a warrior for Christ and have his sins pardoned. To finance the crusade 100,000 gold ducats would have to be raised; and the Order of St Mary of Bethlehem was inaugurated to give the venture holy substance.

The Morea, the last Byzantine stronghold outside Constantinople, fell to the Turks in March 1461. By that time, not a single gun had been limbered, not a single sword sharpened. A number of potential crusaders, including Matthias Corvinus, had accepted Pius's gold, but they were doing precisely nothing. Alone of the Christian leaders, Vlad Ţepeş went to war.

Romanian historians have explained the Impaler's motives in 1462 as a genuine crusading urge, a wish to uphold the oath he inherited through his father from the statutes of the Dragon Order to defeat the 'enemies of the cross of Christ'. The truth is that Ţepeş was a realist. Despite the treaty with the Turks two years earlier, geography and history combined to tell the *voivod* that Mehmed was a megalomaniac who would never be content to have his horizons limited by the Danube. Beyond the Danube lay Wallachia. And Ţepeş knew that his army was a fraction of the size of the Conqueror's. Unsure of Hungarian help from Matthias Corvinus, his only hope was to strike first and strike hard.

Several historians have assumed that Mehmed's aim was to make Wallachia a Pashalik or province of his empire. But this does not seem to have been the case. Technically Ţepeş was a vassal of the Conqueror, and should have continued to pay him an annual tribute of 10,000 *galben* and five hundred *boys* under the *devsirme* system. The *voivod*, perhaps genuinely busy with subjugation of the boyars and the 'Saxon' cities, had paid nothing since 1459, and flatly refused to send any Wallachian children. Significantly, alone of the Christian rulers, Ţepeş knew Mehmed personally: he knew his vanity, his ambition and how to provoke him to a fight. In November 1461, he sent a letter to the Conqueror explaining that he could not pay the tribute, neither could he pay it in person at Constantinople as had been the custom. The dust was still settling over his Transylvanian dispute; the time was not right, 'for if I should leave my country my political opponents would invite the Hungarian king to rule over my domains'.⁵

Tursun Bey, secretary to the sultan's council and subsequently historian to Mehmed's successor, Bayezid II, explained:

> He [Ţepeş] said he had no more resources to pay the tribute, for the Hungarian army was strong and represented an obstacle in his way. He also said the Sublime Porte [Constantinople] was too far for him to come and that he had spent everything he had in battles that year . . . He neither came nor paid the tribute. Then he had to be punished and destroyed.⁶

Ţepeş had visited the Turks on a diplomatic mission before, in Varna, with his father when he was eleven years old. Those years may well have warped his life and he was not going back. Mehmed was at Constantinople; and so too was Radu cel Frumos, Ţepeş' younger brother, now twenty-six and probably as ambitious and proud as the Impaler he had not seen for twelve years. 'We marched forward', wrote Konstantin Mihailović, a janissary who had entered the sultan's service under the boy-levy, 'to the Wallachian land after Dracula; and his brother ahead of us.'⁷

In an extraordinary duel of wits that would grace any Cold War spy story, Ţepeş allowed himself to be lured to the fortress of Giurgiu on the Danube, which his grandfather had built and the Turks had captured, in order to show his good faith to Mehmed, to whom he had promised, in the fullness of time, 'many children and horses . . . and I will also . . . add gifts of my own'.[8] This was in accord with Article One of the treaty of 1460 but in fact he was well aware that the sultan's emissaries, the admiral at the Siege of Constantinople and now his chief falconer, Hamsa Bey, and Thomas Catavolinos, a Byzantine renegade, were planning to take him prisoner. He explained what happened in a letter to Matthias Corvinus, whose aid he still desperately wanted, on 11 February 1462:

> . . . the Turks, the most cruel enemies of the Cross of Christ, have sent their highest ranking messengers to convince us not to keep the peace and the agreements that we made with your Majesty . . . By the grace of God, while we were going to that border [the Danube] we found out about their deceit and trickery and it was us who captured Hamza-Bey . . . near the fortress that is called Giurgiu. . . .[9]

With him, the *voivod* had brought a cavalry force, evidently in Turkish armour because they were able to intermingle with the crowd in the fortress and take it: 'The Turks opened the gates of the fortress at the shouts of our men . . .'. Ţepeş burned Giurgiu, one of the most important of the Ottoman strongholds on the river, as it had once been his grandfather's.

> And we killed the men and women, old and young, who lived from Oblucita and Novoselo, where the Danube flows into the sea, to Rahova, which is near Chilia, down to the villages of Samovit and Ghighen, 23,884 Turks and Bulgarians in all, not including those who were burned in their houses and whose heads were not presented to our officials.[10]

The Impaler's attack along the Danube took place in a bitterly cold winter. The sluggish river was frozen for much of the 800 miles his cavalry covered in two weeks, which enabled the horsemen to strike at bridgeheads, crossing places and ports such as Turnu, and cross into the forests of the Wallachian plain before the Turks could organize their defence. Mehmed himself, with the bulk of his army, was tied up against the revolt by the White Sheep Uzbeks in the East; so Ţepeş for now had time on his side. His letter to Corvinus continued:

> First, in the places called Oblucita and Novoselo there were killed 1,350; and 6,840 at Darstor, Cartal and Dridopotrom; likewise 343 at Orsova and 840 were killed at Vectrem; 630 were killed at Turtucaia; likewise 210 were killed at Marotin; 6,414 were killed at Giurgui on both sides of the river and the fortress on the Danube was conquered and taken. The commander of the fortress was killed . . . and the commander of Nicopolis, the son of Firuz-Beg was also captured and beheaded; and of the Turks stationed at Nicopolis, all the most important were killed with him. Likewise 384 were killed at Turnu, Batin and Novigrad; at Sistov and in two other villages near it, 410 were killed; likewise, the crossing point at Nicopolis was burned and completely destroyed; the same at Samovit; and at Ghighen 1,138 were killed; at Rahova 1,460 . . . and the crossing point was completely burned . . .[11]

With what may be an example of Dracula's black humour and the greatest example of understatement in medieval history, he concluded: 'Therefore, your Majesty should know that we have broken our peace with [the Turks].'[12]

Hamsa Bey and Thomas Catavolinos were marched in shackles back to Tîrgoviste and impaled on high stakes.

Ţepeş knew that his action would whip Mehmed into a fury and that full-scale retaliation would only be a matter of time. His letter to Corvinus made the position clear: 'When the weather permits, that is to say in the spring, they will come with evil intentions and with all their power.'[13]

The *voivod*'s suggestion was that Corvinus should send his army (he was not expecting the king's presence in person) to reach Transylvania by St George's Day (23 April). If that was impossible, then the troops and arsenals from the 'Saxon' cities would be a help: 'And if, God forbid, it ends badly for us, and our little country is lost . . . it will be a loss for all Christianity.'

One of his most trusted lieutenants, Radu Farma, galloped through the snow-drifted passes as best he could to reach Buda.

Europe was ablaze. The half-hearted crusaders could not believe the Impaler's nerve. The man was getting results. Pietro Tommasi, Venetian ambassador to the Hungarian court at Buda, wrote on 4 March, 'The Hungarian king will do all he can to help Dracula.' Travelling home to England from his elongated 'grand tour', the pilgrim William of Wey wrote that in Rhodes:

> the military men . . . upon hearing of Dracula's campaign, had *Te Deums* sung to the praise and honour of God who had granted such victories . . .[14]

But Ţepeş needed halberdiers, pikemen, arquebusiers and light cavalry, not *Te Deums*. He sent emissaries to the Tartars of the Crimea, to Armenia and Georgia, all of whom lay in the potential path of Ottoman expansion.

But it was Corvinus he really wanted. Sadly, the son of the 'white knight' was no crusader. Cautious and clever, Corvinus turned procrastination into an art. He had been elected king four years earlier, but, without the famous crown of St Stephen, his role was neither fully legal nor sanctioned by God. The crown was in the hands of Emperor Frederick III. Much of the cash that the hopeful Pius had sent to Buda for crusading purposes would be spent on buying it – and the emperor did not come cheap. For the time being, the only Hungarians at Ţepeş' disposal were the garrison at Chilia on the Danube delta; and their presence there would cost the *voivod* a valuable ally.

The size of the army that Mehmed the Conqueror led against the Impaler can never be accurately gauged. The Greek Laonic Chalkondyles, commenting on the invasion of Wallachia in the early Mohamedan spring, wrote:

> People say that this army was very large, second only to the one the Emperor took against Byzantium. This camp is said

to have been more beautiful than other camps and to have been well supplied with weapons and equipment, the army being as large as two hundred and fifty thousand men.[15]

Tursun Bey, better informed, perhaps, and closer to the action, wrote years later:

> When the spring of the year 866 [1462] came, the colours of triumph waved on their way to Wallachia. An army of almost thirty tümen (300,000) crossed the Danube; the land of Wallachia shone in the presence of the Sultan . . . The whole sky seemed to move. The army looked like powerful waves on the sea.[16]

Unfortunately for us, of course, Tursun Bey was in the propaganda, not to say the poetry, business and the educated guess of Tomassi, the Venetian ambassador at Buda, of 90,000 is probably more realistic. Even this conservative estimate, however, gave the Turks three times the Impaler's strength.

One who knew this army well shortly before Vlad Ţepeş became its hostage as a child was Georgius de Hungaria:

> When recruiting for the army is begun, they gather with such readiness and speed you might think they are invited to a wedding and not to war. They gather within a month in the order they are summoned [Matthias Corvinus's crusaders took nearly a year], the infantrymen separately from the cavalrymen, all of them with their appointed chiefs, in the same order which they use at encampments and when preparing for battle . . . with such enthusiasm that men put themselves forward in place of their neighbours and those left at home feel that an injustice has been done to them. They claim they will be happier if they die on the battlefield among the spears and arrows of the enemy than at home among the tears and slavering of the old women. Those who die like this are not mourned, but are hailed as saints and victors . . .[17]

A detailed estimate of the size and structure of Mehmed's army comes from 1475, the year in which Vlad Ţepeş was unleashed against them for a second time. Then there were 6,000 janissaries, 3,000 *kapikulu* cavalry, 22,000 European *sipahi* cavalry and 17,000 Anatolian *sipahi*. By the time of Suleiman the Magnificent and his defeat of Hungary at Mohácz in 1526, the size of the Ottoman army had doubled.

At the heart of Mehmed's army were the janissaries, a highly trained and efficient body of infantry whose origins may lie in the reign of Orhan, the son of Osman who founded the Ottoman state. These men were co-opted by means of the *devsirme*, the boy levy, and their rigid education, which would be criticized as brainwashing today, made them eager to accept the Koran and the sultan's orders. Tolerant and sympathetic to other faiths in the areas they conquered, the Turks welcomed 'Christian' renegades into their service – Bogomil heretics from Serbia; refugees from Constantinople; even Jews, who had a greater acceptance from Allah than ever they did from the God of the Christians. Boys selected for the *acemi oglan* or military service were chosen for their bearing and strength. Honesty, loyalty and good manners were their watchwords, and they learned riding, wrestling, archery and sword-play exactly as the Dracula brothers had experienced at Edirne under Murad II. The most promising were groomed for the sultan's personal cavalry, the *kapikuli*, which had parallels in various households of the kings of Western Europe.[18] Those who had not qualified were given specialist training as armourers, gunners and drivers. Even the 'ordinary' janissaries completed a six-year training that included mathematics.

The ritual of joining the janissary corps was deeply symbolic. Graduates, every bit as proud and trained as those at Sandhurst or West Point today, lined up in front of their company officer and were given the tall, distinctive white cap of their corps. Each man would kiss the officer's hand, saluting him as 'travelling companion'.

The janissaries were organized into companies known as *artas*, each consisting of about fifty men, and bearing in mind Napoleon's famous (if probably apocryphal) comment about an army marching on its stomach, its officers had curious culinary ranks! The sultan was 'the father who feeds us', the colonel was 'the soup maker', the major 'the master cook', the junior officers 'head scullions'; then there were 'barrack-room chiefs', 'heads of water distribution', and the imams were 'the prayer leaders'.[19]

The janissaries on the march as they arrived to find their Danubian fording places burned by Ţepeş must have been an incredible sight. At their head was the Imam Azam, the white silk banner of the faith. Inscribed in gilt curls was the legend, 'We give you victory and a sparkling victory. It is God who helps us and His help is effective. Oh, Mohammed, you have brought joyful news to the Believers.' Other banners were stars, crescents, moons, hands, boots, spearheads and animals. Traditionally, a day ahead of the army marched the carriers of the *tug*, the horsetail banner. One wonders if the Impaler cut them down in the Danube's reeds.

Bertrandon de la Brocquière saw these men in action. They wore:

> . . . two or three thin, ankle-length cotton robes one over the other, for a coat they wear a felt robe called a capinat. It is light and very water-proof . . . They wear knee high boots and wide breeches . . . into which they stuff all their robes so that they will not get in the way when they are fighting or travelling . . .[20]

The *capinat* was woven in wool by Jews from Thessalonika; the *bork* or white cap was fronted by a spoon, another culinary symbol. Officers' jackets were trimmed with fur of fox, sable, lynx or squirrel. Boots were always of red leather, except for the senior officers who wore yellow.

The weaponry of the janissaries varied enormously and reflects their ability to learn fast from their enemies. For long-distance killing the curved short bow was carried by infantry and cavalry alike. The superb drawing of a seated officer by the Italian artist Gentile Bellini, who also painted Mehmed, shows just such a weapon, with quiver and arrows slung from a waist belt. At close quarters, the curved sabre, with a sharp point and single-edged blade, was the favourite, but daggers, either straight or curved, were also carried. Ram's-head maces and heavy battle-axes could crunch through sallet and skull of a Wallachian, and any one of a variety of pole-axes like the glaive or halberd could wrench a fully armoured boyar out of the saddle and disembowel him in seconds. Mail-shirts were worn when pitched battle was likely, with reinforcing plates of iron on the chest, back and arms. Most impressive of all was the janissaries' rapid assimilation of firearms. They probably first saw them in use by Hunyadi at Varna in 1444, and called them blowpipes. These were the clumsy forerunners of the matchlock, the first recorded use of which is in 1475. But Europeans marvelled at the janissaries' aim with these 'inventions of the devil'.

The other units of Mehmed's army, his cavalry and the outriders of Anatolia, were less disciplined but reliable nonetheless, and good soldiers. They had the advantage over European armies of the best horses in the world, the small, fast and patient Arabs. The cavalry were skilled archers, firing from the saddle at the gallop, wearing mail-shirts and conical copper helmets with adjustable nasals. Known as *sipahi*, they wore animal skins over their armour, probably as much to reduce the heat on the metal as to appear fierce in sight of the enemy. Most of them hoped to be timar-holders, owners of plots of land similar to the feudum or fief of western feudalism. 'Take a Turk from the saddle', ran an old saying, 'and he becomes a bureaucrat.' De la Brocquière wrote of the soldiers:

> They are diligent and get up early in the morning. They are frugal when on the road and live on only a little food, a little badly baked bread and some raw meat, dried a little in the sun, or some curdled or otherwise prepared milk, some cheese or honey or grapes or fruit or grass, or a handful of flour, from which they make porridge for six or eight men a day.[21]

At a respectful distance from the soldiers came the camp followers that dogged any medieval army; in fact, these were the essential 'support services' of the army – the sword-cutlers, bowyers, blacksmiths, silk merchants, pharmacists, bakers and tailors without whom the military effort would soon grind to a halt.

A vital service was provided by the Ottoman equivalent of regimental bands, the *mehterhane*. Using drums, cymbals, trumpets and clarinets, they stood on the field of battle in a semicircle around the seated kettledrummer. Cavalry units had mounted bands, some of these with the drums slung across the humps of Mehmed's dromedaries. Most of the instrumentalists were Greek, but the volume had an important psychological role. 'Five hundred trumpeters,' wrote Evliya Celebi two centuries after Ţepeş, 'raised such a sound that the planet Venus began to dance and the skies reverberated . . .'[22]

We know the names of Mehmed's troop commanders who crossed the Danube in late September 1462. There was the Grand Vizier Mahmud and with him Evrenos Ali, Turahanoglu Omer, Nesuh of Albania, Delioglu Umur of Janina and, most chillingly of all, perhaps, in his borrowed eastern armour, Radu cel Frumos, Dracula the Handsome. Their target was not the subjugation of Wallachia, but the removal of its *voivod*, 'the wicked horseman', as Tursun Bey called him, 'that bloody tyrant and merciless Infidel', Vlad Ţepeş.

The Impaler's army is far more obscure than that of the Conqueror. Many foreign visitors had had the opportunity to observe the Ottomans first hand, and were fascinated by them. Wallachia, on the other hand, was a small frontier state lost in its own mountains. It did not possess the grandeur of the Hungarian or Polish armies and warranted little comment from contemporaries. Of those who wrote about Ţepeş' 1462 campaign along the Danube, William of Wey heard about it second-hand on the island of Rhodes; Chalkondyles, Dukas, Kritoboulos of Imbros and George Phrantzes were Byzantine bystanders; the others were Turks or Turkish supporters who were either there with their own agenda (Tursun Bey and Konstantin Mihailović) or later court historians who simply copied the earlier accounts. All of them concentrated, with reason, on the Impaler's incredible tactics, saying almost nothing about the composition of his army.

Ṭepeş commanded his troops himself from the front and there is no doubt about either his extraordinary courage or his skill as a soldier. We have no depictions of the Impaler on the march, but it is likely that he wore, in battle at least, the expensive fluted plate armour of 'Gothic' type. Such suits cost a king's ransom, and the finest examples come from Augsburg, Nuremberg (where his father had been invested with the Dragon insignia), Landshut and the Austrian city of Innsbruck. These 'Gothic' suits were the best examples of the armourer's craft, lighter than the weight carried by an infantryman in the First World War or the Falklands, and hinged to allow total freedom of movement. The Impaler would have used a lance for initial contact with enemy cavalry, a wooden, iron-tipped pole fifteen feet long, and, for closer work, a battle-axe, mace or sword. This last was the knightly weapon *par excellence*, like that of Sigismund, founder of the Dragon Order, and now the civic sword of the City of York, is the simple 'cruciform' type, with a wide, tapering, double-edged blade, a hilt made for use with one or both hands and a slim quillon (cross-piece). There was already the tendency by the 1460s to curve these quillons to form better protection for the hand. On the march, it is likely that Ṭepeş wore only part of this armour, perhaps with a leather jerkin or jack. We know that he dressed as a Turk from time to time, both as a subterfuge (as at Giurgiu) and also as a result of living among them in his teenage years.

His personal bodyguard, smaller certainly than Mehmed's *kapikuli*, were mercenaries, some of whom were Wallachian. Certainly by 1475, a hardcore of these were lent to him by his cousin Stefan of Moldavia, although, as we shall see, this is not true of the earlier campaign. Some boyars rode with Ṭepeş – the messenger Radu Farma was one – and brought with them their retinues, much after the fashion of the feudal levies of the West, the armed retainers, say, of Warwick the Kingmaker in England or Gilles de Rais in France. The retinues' loyalty was questionable because they were taught to follow their lord and to watch for his banner in battle. In an age before nationalism, patriotism was very narrow, and few Christians could match the religious zeal of the sultan's janissaries. The boyars may well have worn 'German' armour, but over it they dressed in their long Byzantine robes.

The nature of the terrain in which he was fighting and of the campaign in which he fought meant that Țepeș relied far more than the Turks on his cavalry. We cannot be sure about his horsemen. A century after the Impaler, it was impossible to distinguish Wallachian horsemen from the Hungarians to their west and the Russians to the east. After the Wallachian victory over the Turks at Calugareni in 1595, virtually the entire army was mounted. They had learned their skills from the Turks, training their horses to walk like camels, moving both legs on one side at the same time. Three years after Țepeș' death, Matthias Corvinus wrote to King Frederick of Naples who had been patronizing enough to send him a Spanish riding master:

> With the horses which we trained ourselves we defeated the Turks, subjected Siberia and vanquished all before us, honourably by means of our own horses. We have no desire for horses that hop about with bent hocks in the Spanish fashion; we do not want them even as a pastime, still less for serious business.[23]

Like Corvinus' own armoured hussars (light cavalry), Țepeș' horsemen probably rode the tough little sturdy ponies of the tarpan breed, now largely localized to Poland, of thirteen or fourteen hands high, normally dun in colour with a pronounced dorsal stripe. In today's Romania, such horses are called Hușuls, ideal for mountain work, sure-footed and needing very little water. They are related to the wild Przewalski breed with its two extra chromosomes.

The rest of the army comprised fighting men raised under a sort of levy *en masse* not known in the West. There, 'liveried retainers' of a lord, or more rarely from a town, took the field under the bastard feudalism that had developed in the late Middle Ages from a purely land-based custom. Țepeș' army, like any medieval army, was backed with its camp followers.

The numbers are difficult to ascertain. Fedor Kuritsyn talks of 30,900; Domenico Balbi, the former Venetian ambassador to Constantinople, put the number at 30,000; the ever-conservative Pietro Tomassi at 24,000. A certain proportion of the Impaler's army was made up of men from the towns, from Sibiu and Braşov, from Tîrgsor and Tîrgoviste, from the newly burgeoning Bucharest which lay on the Danubian plain, right in the path of Mehmed's invasion force. It is possible that the richer 'Saxon' towns had the money to pay foreign mercenaries – few armies were without them – like the French and Burgundian *jacquerie*, the Italian *condottieri* and, a new force emerging to strike terror into cavalryman and footsoldier alike, the brightly coloured, pike-carrying Swiss *Landsknechte*.[24]

Ţepeş had two advantages over the Turks. First was the element of surprise which had made the Danube raids so successful. Now, of course, that was gone and his was essentially a defender's role against the Ottoman invasion. Second, he knew better than Mehmed the territory over which battles and skirmishes would be fought. True, the Turks had Radu with them, but we have no evidence that he was a soldier, and he had not seen his homeland for nearly twenty years and never as a man, with an adult's perception. Ţepeş used scouts, local men who knew every ravine and precipice, the water sources and the fertile villages, to go ahead of his army and especially along the river bank. Throughout the September of 1462, the Danube was scanned day and night.

The drill used by the bulk of the *voivod*'s army, which would have been composed of footsoldiers, was probably little different from the Ordinances of Charles the Bold of Burgundy, themselves written, usually late at night by the insomniac duke, during the 1460s:

> In order that the troops may be better trained and exercised
> . . . the captains of the squadrons are to . . . practise
> charging with the lance, keeping in close formation . . . to
> withdraw on command, to rally . . . and to withstand a
> charge . . . The pikemen must be made to advance in close

formation . . . [and] kneel so that the archers can shoot over the said pikemen as if over a wall. The archers must also learn to place themselves back to back in double defence or in a square or a circle, always with the pikemen outside them to withstand the charge of the enemy horse.[25]

We have no record of the books that Ţepeş owned, but perhaps one was the popular *Regulae Bellorum Generales* of the Roman writer Vegetius, who had said, 'Only a few men are brave by nature – good training increases their numbers.'[26]

The Wallachian footsoldiers wore long white tunics tied at the waist with belts and thick animal hides to protect them from Turkish lançe thrusts or sword cuts. This was a variant of the jack or brigandine worn throughout Europe, a sleeved garment made of up to thirty layers of wool and buckled under the armpits or down the front. A sensible footsoldier would have worn some kind of sallet or kettle-hat, an iron headpiece with sloping sides to deflect blows.

A curious reference to Ţepeş' army can be found in the 'Saxon' stories which began to circulate shortly after the 1462 campaign, according to which he forced a contingent of gypsies into his fighting units (although this was probably the normal enlistment process of the levy *en masse* of the time) and:

> clothed them all in cowhide and similarly their horses as well. And as they came upon one another, the Turkish horses shied away and fled because of the cowhide clothing which their horses did not like.[27]

The story goes on to recount the deaths of both retreating Turks and attacking gypsies by drowning in the nearest water supply, so this incident *may* refer to the parched summer of 1462. It is, however, a classic of the anomalies and *non sequiturs* of the 'horror' stories. It is highly unlikely that a gang of pressed men, which the tale says the gypsies were, would have been given expensive horses; and the strange reference to cow-hide frightening the *sipahis'* horses makes no sense at all.

As in the Ottoman army, the weapons carried by the Impaler's troops would have varied enormously. It is possible that some of the archers used crossbows, highly favoured by the Germans, the Italians and the Swiss. Cumbersome and slow to fire, these weapons fired quarrels or bolts, short, wooden-flighted arrows that could punch a hole in the most expensive plate armour. Modern experiments with reconstructed bows have produced an average firing rate of four bolts a minute. Other archers would have carried the longbow, made famous by the English, traditionally made of supple yew and six feet long. The arrows, a 'cloth-yard' in length, with shafts of ash or witch-hazel and goose-feather flights, could reach a target 350 yards away. An experienced bowman could fire fifteen arrows a minute. Ţepeş' pikemen carried the same halberds, glaives and bills as their Turkish opponents, and daggers or short swords for in-fighting. Handling a pole-axe was difficult and took precision timing, especially being able to hook the twelve-foot weapons into the neck or armpit of a well-armoured opponent.

We do not know what artillery the Impaler had with him. The towns of Braşov and Sibiu made guns, and it is conceivable that their guildsmen brought with them one or two bombards, or cannon. But these guns were usually used for sieges, their stone or iron shot smashing through masonry as the huge guns of the Turks had done at Constantinople. One such monster, called Griete, was fired in 1411 at Bourges, the Duke of Berry's capital. An eyewitness wrote, 'when it was fired the thunderous noise could be heard four miles away and terrorised local inhabitants as if it were some reverberation from Hell.'[28] The only recorded uses of handguns by the Wallachians refer to their use as the Turks crossed the Danube and it may be that Ţepeş dispensed with them later. His was a hit-and-run campaign, a masterly piece of guerrilla warfare; and unreliable firearms, whatever their weight, would merely slow him up.

The rations for Ţepeş' men would probably have been less frugal than those of Mehmed's. Unlike the Muslim Turks, the Orthodox Wallachians drank alcohol, carried in barrels or goat-skin sacks. Bread, biscuits, pork, beans and cheese would have been their staple diet, but raids on villages in Turkish-held Bulgaria produced chickens, eggs and beef. Hunger was a weapon in itself, and Ṭepeş used it very effectively against an army whose very rank titles were linked with food. And throughout the long, hot summer, his men lay in the Danube's reeds and watched. And waited.

# 11

# IMPALER PRINCE

In the first week of June 1462, Mehmed's horse-tail advance guard reached Vidin, one of the few Danubian crossing points the Impaler had failed to destroy. The Grand Vizier Mahmoud had sent these scouts ahead to reconnoitre, and they had come back with the depressing news of the extent of Ţepeş' raids along the river. There is some confusion in the accounts as to how the Turks got there. Laonic Chalkondyles refers to their ships, as though they sailed or rowed up the Danube, which is entirely feasible given their command of the Black Sea and its being turned, as the cliché has it, into an 'Ottoman lake'; but the Turkish chronicles themselves make no mention of a seaborne attack. Konstantin Mihailović of Ostrovitza, however, makes the point clear:

> When night began to fall, we climbed into our boats and floated down the Danube and crossed over to the other side several miles below the place where Dracula's army was stationed. There we dug ourselves trenches so that cavalry could not harm us. After that we crossed back over to the other side and transported the janissaries over the Danube and when the entire infantry had crossed, then we prepared and set out gradually against Dracula's army, together with the artillery and other equipment that we had brought with us.

This crossing was possibly a second attempt, the Wallachians having driven the Turks back in an earlier clash, with volleys

of arrows. But this seems unlikely. Ţepeş knew the Turks'
propensity for night attacks (he was soon to use the same
tactic himself) and surely would not have let the enemy get
such a foothold on the Wallachian bank. 'Having halted,' the
Serbian janissary went on, 'we set up the cannon but not in
time to stop three hundred janissaries from being killed.'

At some point, Ţepeş' scouts down river must have spotted
the amphibious landing; and the Impaler struck. The honesty
of Konstantin's account is refreshing, in contrast to the clear
propaganda of the Turkish sources:

The Sultan was very upset by this . . . as he witnessed the
great battle from the other side of the Danube and was
unable to come over himself. He was afraid that all the
janissaries might be killed.

Ţepeş' best bet was to hit the Turks while most of their
army was still across the river. Amphibious operations and
river crossings were notoriously difficult, and the army on
water, however temporarily, had the disadvantage. So, Harold
Godwinson should have stopped William of Normandy on
the Pevensey sands in the early autumn of 1066; Rommel and
von Runstedt should have halted 'D Day' on 6 June 1944 on
the Normandy beaches. Unlike the earlier and later defenders,
Ţepeş had not been caught napping; he was simply
outgunned. Mihailović continued:

Seeing our side was greatly weakening, we defended
ourselves with the hundred and twenty guns which we had
brought and fired so often that we repelled the prince's
army and greatly strengthened our position. And Dracula,
seeing that he could not prevent the crossing, withdrew.

It is this that makes it unlikely that the Impaler had much
artillery with him. Mihailović does not mention it at all, but
perhaps against Mehmed's impressive cannonade of a
probable 120 pieces the Wallachian guns were too puny to
commit to paper. The sultan crossed the Danube and
distributed 30,000 coins to his troops, a bonus over and

above the *ulufe* or thrice-yearly salary paid to the janissaries.

Now, the die was cast. Ţepeş was facing an army, organized and equipped far better than his own and probably three times its size. He had received no reply to his letter asking help from Matthias Corvinus in February, and trouble was breaking out to his north-east, and from an unexpected source, from his cousin Stefan of Moldavia. Chalkondyles takes up the story:

> [Dracula] divided his army in two, keeping one part with him and sending the other against the prince of Black Bogdania [Moldavia] to keep him back if he tried to invade the country. Because this prince [Stefan] had had a misunderstanding with Vlad he was at war with him and, sending messages to Sultan Mehmed, he said that he was also ready to join him in his war against Vlad.[1]

Because Chalkondyles is the only source contending that Stefan offered his services to Mehmed, most Romanian historians have doubted its validity. Kurt Treptow, however, is quite prepared to believe it, less in the spirit that Stefan joined forces with the Infidel against his own cousin, but that he put Moldavia and his own interests first. In no sense were the two principalities one – the fact that each had its own ruler is proof of that. This was not yet an age of nationalism, although some Romanian historians would turn Ţepeş into a nationalist, nor, as we have seen, was the unifying concept of Christendom particularly strong. Essentially, fifteenth-century politics was a melting pot in which every ruler was for himself. Even so, Chalkondyles' assertion casts doubt on most historians' assertions that Stefan was truly a 'great' ruler in the accepted sense of the term. It also makes nonsense of the title *Athleta Christi* (Christ's Champion) given to him by the Pope.

Stefan's bone of contention with Ţepeş was the fortress of Chilia on the Danube delta. It was vitally important to the Moldavians that they, rather than the Impaler's people, control it. On 2 April 1462, the governor of Caffa wrote to Casimir of Poland, highly concerned that these Christian princes were at loggerheads:

I understand that Stefan, Prince of Moldavia . . . is fighting with Vlad *voivod* who makes happy war with the Turks. This quarrel not only helps the Sultan but, what is more dangerous, if the Turks enter in these two Wallachias, it will be a great danger for us and for other neighbouring countries.[2]

But the quarrel went beyond the acquisition of Chilia. On the broader canvas, Ţepeş and Stefan had drifted apart since their time at Suceava, when the Impaler had been on the run. The latter had now thrown in his lot squarely with Matthias Corvinus and Hungary; Stefan sided with Casimir of Poland and paid a yearly tribute to the sultan. 'In the month of June on the 22nd day,' reads the Moldavian-German Chronicle, '*voivod* Stefan came in front of Chilia, but he could not take it and was shot in the left ankle . . .'[3]

Domenico Balbi confirmed the military pincer movement: 'the naval fleet of the sultan, together with the prince of Moldavia, went to attack the fortress of Chilia, they stayed there for eight days, but they were unable to do anything'.[4]

In January 1465, Stefan finally took the fortress at the second attempt, but by that time, the harm had been done. Ţepeş had been obliged, back in the summer of 1462, to detach 7,000 men to his eastern frontier to defend it against possible attack; this was 7,000 he did not have against Mehmed's janissaries.

Ţepeş' war of attrition now began. Outnumbered, abandoned by one ally, Corvinus, and fighting another, Stefan, he was forced to adopt desperate tactics. As his army withdrew northward, skirmishing with Mehmed's cavalry on the flanks and his janissaries in the centre, he carried out a scorched earth campaign, burning villages and crops in their pre-harvest glory. Boyar and peasant alike grabbed what belongings they could and went with him, leaving nothing but destruction for the Turks to find, burned out villages and demolished walls. Animal corpses were thrust into wells and used to dam rivers. Artificial marshes were created on the Danube's flood plain to slow the Ottoman advance, and pits were dug with sharpened stakes in their bases to catch the unwary horseman who rode too fast and too far. Michael Ducas wrote:

> Thus, having crossed the Danube and advanced for seven days, Mehmet II found no man, nor any significant animal and nothing to eat or drink.[5]

Just as the previous winter had been particularly cold, so the summer of 1462 was particularly hot. It is thought that the humid continental climate of Wallachia in the Impaler's time is much the same as it is now, the intervening centuries having been particularly cold. Because of this, the West's usual four seasons are today often seen in Wallachia merely as two – summer and winter. The highest ever recorded temperature, at Ruse on the Danube, in July was 42°C (108°F). In the mountains, the air was cooler and the rainfall heavier, but after the cold winter of 1461–2, there could still have been snow in the ravines and gulleys until July. Tursun Bey wrote:

> When they got closer to the established place [i.e. a head-on confrontation with Ţepeş], the front line of the army announced that there was not a drop of water to quench their thirst. All the carts and animals stopped there. The heat of the sun was so great that one could cook kebabs on the mail shirts of the *gazi*s [warriors]. This is why the Sultan accused the commanders of carelessness. At the same time the scouts were scolded and punished.[6]

This was an army that prided itself on its commissariat, where food and water for men and horses was an essential requirement. 'In this parched plain,' wrote the chronicler Hodja Hussein, 'the lips of the fighters for Islam dried up. Even the Africans and Asians, used to desert conditions, used their shields to roast meat.'[7]

Relatively safe in the cool of the oaks in the Vlasia forest and with plenty of water and food, Ţepeş' cavalry harassed the struggling Ottomans, galloping out from thickets, loosing arrows, cutting down stragglers, a hit-and-run tactic that the Turks had rarely faced. There is a theory that Ţepeş in effect used germ warfare against the Turks by paying infected Wallachians, disguised as Ottomans, to mingle with the invaders and spread disease among them; suitably high wages were paid to these men. Such tactics sound rather unlikely. Lepers were visibly ill and everyone, Turks and Christians alike, shunned them, stoning them in their bleeding rags and kicking them out of civilized society. If, as some contend, the victims had tuberculosis or syphilis, these diseases are not highly contagious, unless we accept the western mythology about the sexual preferences of Mehmed's janissaries. In any case, for syphilis to have a debilitating effect can take twenty years. Mehmed's campaign was over by August!

According to Tursun Bey, Mehmed detached part of his force to tackle the 7,000 waiting near the Moldavian border in the east. Waiting silently and hidden by reeds on the edge of a forest, the Ottomans, under the leadership of Mehmed-Pasha, ambushed the little command. The troop commanders named are listed by Tursun, leading the left and right wings. Caught utterly by surprise, the Wallachians tried to fight their way out, but they were clearly heavily outnumbered and 'the victorious *gazis* slaughtered the Infidels with their bloody swords as if they had cut cucumbers'. Tursun Bey estimated that only 700 of the 7,000 escaped and that the Turks 'loaded the heads of the Infidels on their camels and mules. Besides this each soldier put on top of his sword [presumably the blade tip] the head of an Infidel; their swords looked like snakes with the heads of men. The sky was an amazing sight.' So far, so dramatic, but Tursun Bey gets carried away with his narrative:

> hundreds and thousands of Infidels were brought in chains to the victorious Court. After the evening service, torches were lighted and the triumphant Sultan sat on his chair. Then the Infidels, resembling dragons and as evil as Ahriman [a Persian god of evil] were brought to him.[8]

Laying aside the Turk's obvious exaggeration in numbers, the defeat of Țepeș' 'second army' probably did take place. It was as well for the Impaler that Stefan of Moldavia had no plans to invade the neighbouring principality. The survivors of the battle were executed 'with [the janissaries'] bloodthirsty swords'.

Perhaps in retaliation for this defeat, perhaps because Mehmed was marching on Tîrgoviste, Ţepeş decided on the famous night attack of 17 June. According to the papal legate Niccolò Modrussa, who interviewed the Impaler at the Hungarian Court at Buda years later, the Wallachian force, numbering by this time about 24,000, found themselves in rough country with the Carpathians at their back. The Turks had looted towns already and carried off Wallachian children as tribute. Using Turkish arrows torn from the bodies of the dead, Ţepeş unleashed a cavalry force, perhaps 7–8,000 strong, and rode hell for leather through the Ottoman camp.

Mehmed's camp was far more than a mere huddle of tents; it was a symbol and microcosm of Ottoman society. 'I think there is no prince', wrote Chalkondyles, 'who has his armies and camps in better order, both in abundance of victuals and in the beautiful order they use in encamping without any confusion . . .'9 The camp was built at noon, the professional handlers of canvas, skins, banners and guy ropes breaking their backs in the midday sun. The Grand Vizier's tent was purple, those of the beys yellow or red. Pietro della Valle saw an Ottoman camp in the seventeenth century, when the crescent was about to wane, but Mehmed's must have been similar. The vizier's tent was half a mile in circumference, entered by a series of rotundas and screened by smaller green tents, perhaps for camouflage. Columns supported the high, vaulted roof and carpets were strewn everywhere. The sultan's tent was larger than the rest, with its distinctive six horse-tail banners flapping overhead. Around it, in three circles, stood a series of war-wagons with guns mounted, a tactical trick the Turks had borrowed from Jan Žižka and the Hussites. A solid rearguard of janissary tents lay beyond that, but the strength of the camp was at the front, covering the ground from which an attack was most likely. Wings of *kapikuli* and provincial cavalry had their multi-coloured canvases on each side of the great circle, ringed as it was with the commissariat and Mehmed's personal bodyguard in two concentric circles. In the centre, guarding the main approach to the sultan, were alternating rows of artillery, infantry and janissary tents. A screen of advance guard tents faced the potential enemy and two huge rotating circles of cavalrymen, walking their horses slowly, kept watch.

Țepeș' veterans heard the whole camp at prayer an hour before sunset, the imams intoning towards Mecca. A cannon was fired, as was the custom, and the troop commanders called good fortune and long life to the sultan. With no alcohol and a disciplined regime, the Ottoman camp was utterly unlike the Christians' army.

The story of the night attack is a classic example of propaganda and historical skulduggery. The Wallachian version, as related by Modrussa, ran:

Dracula carried out an incredible massacre without losing many men in such a major encounter, though many were wounded. He abandoned the enemy camp before daybreak and returned to the same mountain from which he had caused such terror and turmoil. I learned by questioning those who had participated in this battle that the sultan lost all confidence in the situation. During the night, the sultan abandoned the camp and fled in a shameful manner. And he would have continued this way, had he not been reprimanded by his friends and brought back, almost against his will.

Țepeș had planned a two-pronged attack, his boyar Gales hitting the camp from the rear. The boyar seems not to have done this, however, perhaps panicking at the last moment, leaving the *voivod* outnumbered. Modrussa's bias is evident. Mehmed II may have had his faults, but losing his nerve was not one of them.

Tursun Bey has such a different account that we must wonder if he was talking about the same battle:

[The Wallachians] first encountered the army from Anatolia and they read verses of welcome and death to them, as they deserved . . . They were adequately welcomed; their mouths were filled with spears . . . Most of them were wounded or killed while they were trying to run away. In the confusion of the darkness they advanced towards the centre of the [camp] thinking that it was the way out . . . When numerous candles and torches were lit in each tent . . . the mean Infidels lost their heads and scattered, having lost all presence of mind . . . Most of them, leaving their horses and trying to escape, entered the Turkish tents . . . Their defeat was so great that even ten-year-old children who were apprentices and servants in the army [the *devsirme*] killed many Infidels twice as powerful as themselves.[10]

Tursun Bey's account is clearly fictitious. Ţepeş was brought up amongst the Turks, and he would have briefed his cavalry accordingly. There are even suggestions that he personally wandered the lines himself, in typical Turkish disguise, reconnoitring before the attack took place. The Wallachians made for the centre of the camp, because that was where the sultan's tent was pitched and he was their target. A cavalryman would not *abandon* his horse to escape, but use it for a fast getaway. And the comment on the prowess of ten-year-olds against the Impaler's hard riders is simply laughable.

Luckily, we have the honest and straightforward Mihailović, who was sleeping in his janissary's tent that night, to strike a likely balance:

Although the Romanian prince had a small army, we always advanced with great caution and fear and spent nights sleeping in ditches. But even in this manner we were not safe, for during one night, the Romanians struck at us. They massacred horses, camels and several thousand Turks. When the Turks had retreated in the face of the enemy, we [janissaries] repelled the enemy and killed them. But the Sultan had incurred great losses.[11]

There is no doubt that the night attack came dangerously close to succeeding. Had Ţepeş, thundering through the camp, hacking right and left to the Turks' terrified cries of 'Kaziklu-

Bey! Impaler Prince!', managed to reach Mehmed, the result may have been a foregone conclusion. As it was, the gamble failed and the Impaler may have been wounded as his cavalry fought their way out against enormous odds. 'It was all the fault', ranted Tursun Bey, 'of that wicked man with broken wings [a reference to his dragon standard?] and a heart pierced by the spears and swords of brave soldiers.'[12]

What a gift for the vampirologists – Dracula's heart pierced!

Whether Ţepeş was pursued into the Carpathians immediately by Mihail-oglu Ali-Bey as the Ottoman sources insist, or whether the Turks licked their wounds and were too terrified to follow, as Modrussa's version contends, the fact was that Mehmed's advance continued. Some sixty miles from the *voivod*'s capital of Tîrgoviste, the advance guard came upon a sight possibly unique in the annals of warfare. It is not found recorded in any Ottoman chronicle, but Chalkondyles recounts how:

> the [sultan's] army came across a field with stakes, about three miles long and one mile wide. And there were large stakes on which they could see the impaled bodies of men, women and children, about twenty thousand of them . . . The [sultan] himself in wonder, kept saying that he could not conquer the country of a man who could do such terrible and unnatural things and put his power and his subjects to such use . . . And the other Turks, seeing so many people impaled, were scared out of their wits. There were babies clinging to their mothers on the stakes and birds had made nests in their breasts.[13]

The forest of the impaled is one of the lasting, ghastly images of Vlad Ţepeş. He was not going quietly into that good night. Tursun Bey knew exactly where he was going:

> Trying to escape from the lion's claws, he had chosen the claws of a bird of prey. The Hungarian king [Matthias Corvinus] took him prisoner. And there he sent his soul to Hell.[14]

The end of the campaign of 1462 is seriously disputed among Romanian historians. The chronology of Constantin Rezachevici, for instance,[15] leads us to believe that the sickening sight of the field of the impaled was the last straw in a psychological battle Țepeș had been waging since the previous year. Not only were Hamsa Bey and Catavolinos rotting there, but Țepeș' own people, his women and children, their flesh hanging in tatters as ongoing meals for the crows and Carpathian vultures. There is every likelihood that Mehmed's army was ill with any one of a dozen infectious diseases that followed medieval armies – the plague, dysentery, malaria – and this is why he did not sack Tîrgoviste but turned south to Braila, which he destroyed, and then back across the Danube, leaving Radu the Handsome to take the Wallachian throne. The sultan was back in his old palace at Edirne by 11 July. Florescu and McNally have taken up this suggestive narrative wholesale; and other western historians, for example the military expert Tim Newark, have also accepted this version of events.

Rezachevici's narrative continues that Țepeș won victories over his brother's Turkish-backed force in August and on 8 September, the monks on the island of Rhodes 'tolled the bells and have sung *Te Deum* to worship the glory of the Romanian prince'.[16] Both Barbu T. Campina and Nicolae Stoicescu have elaborated on this theme, contending that what led to Țepeș' downfall was the defection of the boyars to the more reasonable and infinitely less terrifying Radu.

Kurt Treptow, however, argues more convincingly that this defection would not have happened had the Impaler genuinely been victorious. The night attack was a gamble, and failed. And having failed, Țepeș knew all too well that his small and increasingly exhausted force had nothing left to throw at the Turks. Endless guerrilla raids in an interminable partisan war was the best he could do. Given this situation, the boyars lost heart. The bulk of the Turkish army had gone home, Radu (after all the son of the great Dracul too) was at Tîrgoviste and his known friendly relations with the Turks would mean, perhaps, stability and a few years of peace, even if that peace came with the inevitable strings of the yearly tribute and the *devsirme*.

There was also a feeling, perhaps less well defined and certainly not quantifiable today, that Ţepeş was betraying his Wallachian and Orthodox trust by allying himself with Corvinus.

The facts bear Treptow out. By the end of August, Radu ruled Wallachia and his brother had retreated north to his mountain stronghold on the Argeş. According to the folktales – there are no Turkish accounts of these 'mopping-up' operations – Radu followed him and positioned his guns on the spot at Poenari still called 'the field of the cannon'. The Romanian stories tell that a spy in Radu's camp got a message to the castle by means of an arrow through a window of an imminent attack the following day, and Ţepeş and his followers escaped, reversing the shoes of their horses to confuse the trackers they knew would come after them. Such a ruse is almost certainly mythical. If Ţepeş' men rode Arabs, it would be feasible because Arab horses' hoofs are surprisingly circular. If they were Tarpans, the shoes would not fit. The other curious folktale refers to the Impaler's wife or mistress (it is unclear which), who told him on the night before the attack that she would rather be food for the fishes of the Arges River than be taken as a slave by the Turks. Accordingly, she threw herself from the battlements into what is still known locally as Rîul Doamnei, the princess' river.

All we can be sure of is that Ţepeş escaped, clambered down the precipitous gorges and raviñes to reach Königstein, one of János Hunyadi's old fortresses in Fagaras. He waited here for news of the king of Hungary, who was due to meet him at Braşov, to the north.

Matthias Corvinus had probably never intended to clash directly with the Turks. As Machiavellian as any Renaissance prince, he watched and waited to see which way the wind blew. His kingdom would have cause to regret this in the next generation, when an estimated 90 per cent of the Hungarian army, including its King Louis II, were cut down by the troops of Suleiman the Magnificent at Mohácz in 1526. On 15 July Corvinus left Buda with a large army and all the panoply of war. He had only reached Szeged, still on his own soil, by 10 August. He crossed into Transylvania by mid-September and waited throughout the whole of October at Sibiu, deliberating his next move. Mehmed, of course, had gone home before Corvinus had even set out.

Finally, at Braşov in November, Corvinus met Ţepeş, who had recently moved into Prince Dan's old Wallachian suburb of Scheii, outside the walls. Negotiations between them dragged on for five weeks before Corvinus sent the fierce old Hussite warrior, Jan Jiškra, to arrest him. Exactly where and how this happened is unknown, and the ostensible reason for it completely out of keeping with what we know of Vlad Ţepeş. This theory is based on a series of three documents, dated 7 November 1462, that had come into Corvinus's possession. One was addressed to the sultan, another to his Grand Vizier Mahmoud and the third to Stefan of Moldavia. All three purported to have been written by Ţepeş, using such crawling and unlikely terms as 'emperor of emperors' and 'lord and master' in connection with Mehmed. The letters offered the Impaler's military service on the sultan's behalf against the Hungarians and even offered to kidnap Corvinus in person. The consensus today is that these letters were forgeries. Only copies survive, but the Latin is bad, the style clumsy and the idea hardly consonant with a man who had made it his life's work to cement a principality and take on an enemy (the Turks) whom he clearly detested.

Florescu and McNally believe that the author was probably Johann Reudell from the Black Church in Braşov, using a corruption of his own surname – 'Rothel' – as the place from which the supposed Ţepeş letters were sent. The burned and the impaled of Braşov were having their revenge at last.

The real reason (leading to the possibility that Corvinus dictated the letters himself) is that the Impaler was now an embarrassment to the Hungarian king. He was a political refugee, still no doubt intending to force Corvinus to commit himself to Pius II's crusade against the Turks. Corvinus needed hard evidence to explain to Pius – and anyone else who raised eyebrows at his lacklustre performance – that he had been threatened by treachery and forced to act against the prince of Wallachia, and in so doing, spend a great deal of the money he had dedicated to crusade. In fact, of course, Corvinus had spent this money on buying the crown of St Stephen, which gave him full validity as king.

The Impaler had risen twice as Wallachia's prince: now he was a prisoner once more.

The years that followed are a closed book in the life of Vlad Ţepeş. We are not even sure how long he remained a prisoner of Matthias Corvinus, but the best guess is that he was released, on certain conditions, in 1475. It seems likely that his confinement was one of comfortable 'house arrest' rather than a musty prison cell, first at Alba Iulia, then at the fortress of Vac before being taken to the summer palace at Visegrád on the Danube. This was the 'paradise on earth' referred to by Castelli, the envoy of Pope Sixtus IV, the thirteenth-century castle undergoing Italian landscaping during Corvinus's reign. Much of the palace that Vlad Ţepeş would have known was later destroyed by a century and a half of Turkish occupation, but recent restoration gives us a clear picture of Corvinus' eye for architecture.

We know that Ţepeş was not kept with other prisoners in the rather forbidding King Solomon's Tower on the crest of the hill, and that he had his own apartments and, within reason, the freedom of the place. Corvinus may well have amused himself – and Ţepeş – by wheeling him out occasionally to overawe guests. Everyone had heard of the Impaler prince. Niccolò Modrussa spent hours talking to him about the Turkish campaign; at least one anonymous artist painted him. At some point, perhaps in 1474, Ţepeş was given his own house in Pest, across the river from Corvinus' capital at Buda. It was here that the folktales tell of the bizarre incident in which a thief was chased by constables through Ţepeş' courtyard. Ţepeş killed the leading constable with his sword. When challenged by Corvinus' magistrates to explain himself, he alleged that the man had clearly committed suicide by daring to invade the territory of a prince. Corvinus is said to have laughed this off.

While Ţepeş may have accepted this gentle incarceration with whatever patience he could muster, the world moved on around him. In June 1463, Matthias Corvinus paid 80,000 gold coins, much of it papal crusading money, to buy the glittering crown of St Stephen from the Holy Roman Emperor. Reports tell that 3,000 knights carried it back to Buda, where Corvinus was crowned the following year in the cathedral of Esztergon.

The fall of Chilia to Stefan of Moldavia in the winter of 1465 saw the emergence of conflict between the 'Black Bogdan' (Stefan) and Corvinus. The war that erupted was brief enough, with Stefan's forces victorious at Baia-Mare towards Christmas 1467. Three years later, the usual entanglements among the Romanians led to open warfare again as Stefan took on Radu Dracula with the intention of replacing him with his own puppet, Basarab Laiota, one of Vlad Ţepeş' rivals ten years earlier. By the end of 1473, Tîrgoviste and Bucharest had fallen to Stefan and even Radu's wife, Maria Despina, and his daughter Maria Voichita were in Stefan's hands. By January 1475, all that Radu held of Wallachian soil was the fortress his grandfather had built at Giurgiu on the Danube; and it was there that he died, unloved and unmourned, allegedly of syphilis, in that month. His faithful monks, no doubt used to burying Draculeşti, laid his body to rest in the monastery of Tînganu.

The problem that arose now for Corvinus was that Basarab Laiota had thrown in his lot with the Turks. It was probably at last dawning on the Hungarian king that the former buffer state of Wallachia was buffer no more. The Moldavians held Chilia, guarding the entrance to the Danube, but the prince of Wallachia was once again paying the annual tribute and the *devsirme* to Mehmed. Corvinus's back door was ominously open: the man to close it was Vlad Ţepeş (he had nearly done so in the night attack on the Ottoman camp in June 1462). But Ţepeş was a maverick, and Corvinus knew how the man could turn on his former captors. Accordingly, he renewed a proposition that had been floating around for some time, that Ţepeş marry Corvinus's cousin, Ilona Szilágy, the daughter of the Impaler's old comrade from the Transylvanian days. This meant the conversion of the former *voivod* to Catholicism.

Corvinus had already tolerated the 'horror' stories about

the Impaler in his own demesnes, stories propagated through the German presses of Augsburg, Nuremberg and Landshut. That was at a time when he wanted the world to think the worst of his prisoner. Now, he was quite prepared to let the Orthodox Church hang Țepeș' soul out to dry over the heresy of his conversion. In 1462 he needed the man under relative lock and key; now he needed him out and unleashed. We need not see Țepeș as a gullible dupe in all this. It is likely that personal faith was not a major issue for him; he certainly knew the consequences of heresy from his churchmen in Wallachia. Furthermore, he was a member of the Dragon Order and had already made Catholic vows there. Perhaps the most important consideration of all was that marriage to Ilona Szilágy would give him his freedom: two sons were born to the couple in the imposing house in Pest where they lived, sons who would carry on the Dragon code and the blood of Dracula for a thousand years.[17]

The Impaler's last campaign began on 18 July 1475. In that year the Ottomans took the Crimea, bringing them ever nearer to a confrontation with Russia that would last four centuries. In the West, the papacy was on the march again. Although Francesco della Rovere, now Pope as Sixtus IV, was not the crusader that Pius had been and was more interested in the papal indulgence of nepotism and patronizing the arts by building the Sistine Chapel, he nevertheless 'called the kings of Christendom for swords about the cross'. Venice, already under renewed threat from Mehmed, was waiting. So was Stefan of Moldavia. 'We are ready', wrote Stefan, 'to resume the struggle for the defence of Christendom with all the power and heart which Almighty God had chosen to invest in us.'[18]

Now that Basarab Laiota had effectively joined the Turks, Stefan could afford, in fact needed, a rapprochement with Țepeș. He sent Ion Țamblac, a trusted aide, to Corvinus early in June and the Hungarian king began the usual crusade-launching process. The 'Saxon' towns were once again asked for money and equipment, the Hungarian Diet was summoned to pledge its support and Corvinus raised a tax of a gold florin per household throughout his kingdom. Țepeș was given command of the army that Corvinus sent to Turkish-held Bosnia. Striking out from his headquarters at Arghis, he had marched to Merghindel by October and joined forces with Corvinus to inflict a defeat on the Turks in the town of Sabac on 8 February the following year. Corvinus then went home, which seems rather precipitate bearing in mind that the rest of Bosnia was still in Ottoman hands; and he left command of the army to Țepeș.

Using a ruse that had worked before, the Impaler sent a body of Hungarian troops wearing Turkish turbans and tunics to mingle in the streets and squares of the silver-mining town of Srebreniča. This 'Trojan horse' caused mayhem inside the town walls while Țepeș' cannon blasted the masonry from outside. As always, the Impaler's vengeance was terrible. At Srebreniča, at Zwornik and at Kuslat, the grim picture was the same. As the papal legate, Gabriele Rangoni, wrote to Rome:

He tore the limbs off Turkish prisoners and placed their parts on stakes . . . and displayed the private parts of his victims so that when the Turks see these, they will run away in fear.[19]

The spring of 1476 saw Țepeș back in Transylvania. The tide of war and politics had turned again in his favour. At Turda he received not only the good wishes of Stefan of Moldavia in his forthcoming struggle with Basarab Laiota, but, more practically, an army of over 20,000 men under the command of Stephen Báthory. In the Magyar town, ringed with gorges and honeycombed with deep and gloomy caves, Țepeș weighed his options. The real commanders, in terms of experience and knowledge of the country, were the Impaler himself and Vuk Branković, the son of George, who had long held Belgrade. Their plan, to join forces with Stefan of Moldavia before advancing against Mehmed, was blocked by Turkish initiative: the Turks struck first, defeating the Moldavians at Valea Alba in July. But Țepeș' arrival reversed the fortunes here and the Turks were driven back out of Moldavian territory to the Siret River – the second time that the Impaler had come to the aid of his sometimes less than grateful cousin.

The campaign now switched to a sustained attack on Laiota. Ţepeş and Báthory marched from Transylvania with about 35,000 troops; Stefan brought 15,000 from the east. It was a classic pincer movement. On 7 October, Ţepeş wrote to Braşov, whose houses he had once burned, whose people he had once impaled:

> With faith in the Lord Jesus Christ, I, Vlad *voivod*, by the grace of God, Prince of all Wallachia, My Majesty [had he learned this phrase at Buda?] gives this order to the honest, faithful and good friends . . . to the country, to the twelve councillors and to all [in the] great fortress of Braşov . . .

Ţepeş proposed a deal in return for their support against Laiota. All previous customs duties on goods and all taxes were to be wiped out so that Braşovian merchants could trade freely throughout Wallachia. In return he expected their full support in not sheltering his enemies, as they had done in the past, warning that 'If anyone should not respect [this arrangement] they will receive the wrath of My Majesty. It cannot be different . . .'[20]

A month later, Ţepeş had caught up with Basarab Laiota. Reports to Matthias Corvinus at Buda confirmed that the pretender's army, 18,000 strong and reinforced with Turks, had been decisively beaten at Rucăr. Casualties were heavy on both sides, but by 8 November, Ţepeş was again writing to Braşov, this time from his old capital of Tîrgoviste. He had not seen it since July 1462:

> Herewith I give you news that I have overthrown our foe Laiota who fled with the Turks. Thus God has given you a free path. Come with bread and goods and you will eat now that God has given us a single country.[21]

Nine days later, Carstian, the governor of Tîrgoviste, wrote to Braşov with news of the Impaler's capture of Bucharest:

Therefore I ask you to give praise to the almighty God with organs, songs and bells, as we have done in our country which is also yours. And you must know that the boyars of all the country have sworn allegiance to Vlad voda . . .[22]

The last weeks of Țepeș' life are shrouded in mystery. With Stephen Báthory's army now back in Hungary and Stefan of Moldavia's marching home to the east, the man who was now prince and *voivod* for a third time was exposed to the dangers he had always faced. There is a kind of monotony in Balkan politics, a ghastly sense of *déjà-vu*. The boyars who had opposed him in the early part of his second reign had largely been disposed of and replaced. Yet it is clear that even those replacements, presumably trusted men, hand-picked by Țepeș, had gone over first to Radu and some to Laiota in the years since Corvinus took the Impaler prisoner. A bodyguard of 200 Moldavians was left behind by Stefan to defend the *voivod*; whether Țepeș had asked for these or Stefan had offered them with a vague sense of unease, we do not know.

At the end of December 1476, Basarab Laiota launched a counter-attack against the Impaler, now based in Bucharest, dangerously near to the Danube. Previous rivals had been killed – Dan and Vladislav – but Laiota had slipped through the net. The clash itself was no more than a skirmish. This was not a great and desperate gamble like the night attack on Mehmed's camp. Even so, Țepeș would go out in a blaze of glory. According to the Russian Kuritsyn – who had met the Impaler's widow and children at Buda, as well as the remnants of his Moldavian bodyguard – the *voivod* had gone to the top of a hill, alone, to watch the fighting below. One of his own men, confusing him for a Turk, hit him with a lance. Under sudden attack from all sides, Țepeș defended himself with his sword, cutting down five assailants before he died.

This account makes little sense. The only reason Țepeș would have moved to higher ground is to reconnoitre, and he would not have done that alone. True, he often wore Turkish armour as a ruse, but that would have been pointless in a skirmish with Laiota in open country. It is likely that his attacker was an assassin and that the man saw his chance in the clash of arms, almost certainly killing Țepeș from behind. According to one legend, his head was hacked off and taken back to Mehmed, who had it displayed at Constantinople, appropriately, on a tall stake visible in the heart of the city.

Vlad Dracula was dead. The world would spend the next five centuries resurrecting him.

# 12

# IN THE COMPANY OF CAIN

After my death, whoever the Lord God grants the throne of Wallachia, whether it be one of my sons or relatives or, for our sins, one of another family, if he will strengthen, protect and renew this deed of mine, may God grant him His support; but if he will not renew and strengthen it and ruins and destroys it, let God destroy and kill him in the body in this world and in spirit in the hereafter he will be in the company of Judas and Cain and of all others to whom it was said: his blood be on them and on their children, as it is and will be, forever . . .

This extract, written during Vlad Ţepeş' second reign in Wallachia and now housed in the archive at Bucharest, is a *hrisov*, a grant of lands to a boyar family. In that sense, it is typical of earlier documents issued by his predecessors, but the case of Ţepeş, it takes on a special meaning: is the phrase 'for our sins' merely the empty phrase it has become today, or did the Impaler expect little mercy from his God because of the bloody actions of his life?

In February 2002, in the early stages of writing this book, Slobodan Milosević went to trial in The Hague in Holland. He faced sixty-six charges covering three countries across which Ţepeş once rode. In Bosnia, he conspired, said the prosecution, to wipe out Moslems and Croats over a three-year period in the 1990s. In this case there were two charges of genocide, ten of crimes against humanity, eight grave breaches of the Geneva Convention and nine violations of the laws and customs of war. In Croatia, where non-Serbs were 'ethnically cleansed' between August 1991 and June 1992, there were two counts of crimes against humanity, thirteen violations of the laws and customs of war and nine grave breaches of the Geneva Convention. In Kosovo, with its twice-fought-over field of blackbirds, 800,000 Albanians were expelled in six months of 1999. In this instance there were four counts of crimes against humanity and one violation of the laws and customs of war.

Geoffrey Nice QC, outlining sample crimes for the benefit of the Court, chose, apparently at random, that committed on 20 November 1991, when 255 non-Serbs from the general hospital of Vukovar in Croatia were transported to a farm some three miles away. Here, beaten and tortured for hours, the hapless group were divided into huddles of ten or twenty and shot. Their bodies were dumped, Nazi-style, into a mass grave. In Bosnia on the same day, said Nice, a heavily pregnant woman was forced out of her village home by Serb troops and had to give birth to her baby in the woods nearby, without help, without medical facilities, without a roof over her head. She was one of forty-five local people promised Red Cross help by Serb paramilitaries. Instead, they were taken to a house with a strange smell. The smell came from the floor and its carpets, which had been soaked in petrol. The doors were locked and someone threw in a match. 'They were all burned alive,' Nice told the court. 'The baby's screams were heard for some two hours before it, too, succumbed.'[1] And on that same day in Kosovo, to the background whine and thump of artillery shells, Serb forces roamed the villages, shooting men and raping women. One woman, separated from her twenty-year-old daughter in the panic, eventually found her body along with seven others she recognized at the bottom of a well, probably thrown in alive to die of thirst and starvation. The *Daily Mail*'s banner headline screamed, with deep relevance to this book, 'Calculated cruelty, medieval savagery'.

In the same issue, criminologist Brian Masters wrote an

analysis of Slobodan Milosević, the 'butcher of Belgrade', that beautiful city once owned by another tyrant, George Branković, and saved from Turkish destruction by János Hunyadi, the 'white knight'. Masters told us that the names of hundreds of Milosević's victims are listed by the prosecution and their ages written alongside. There are many young children among them, randomly slaughtered by a megalomaniac. Masters was clearly horrified by sitting in the same room as Milosević. He is:

> not a monster who can be readily labelled as such. He shows no signs of psychopathic disorder. Nor does he appear to be a Jekyll and Hyde, or one of Dostoevsky's characters in the grip of a compulsion; he is not a bloody maniac by night and harmless statesman by day. He does not show the signs of the necrophiliac character who cherishes death and loves the proximity of corpses. There is no evidence that he is a sadist, bent upon causing pain and watching its effects in order to find peace within himself. He is not a serial killer or mass murderer . . . It is not suggested that he personally strangled, shot or torched his victims . . .[2]

The final chapter attempts to put Vlad Ţepeş in the context of his crimes, to decide whether he was a 'prince more sinned against than sinning'. But first we have to plumb the depths.

Benjamin Disraeli once said that there are 'three kinds of lies: lies, damned lies and statistics'. And nothing is more difficult to deal with than crime statistics, especially if we take into account the vagueness of medieval arithmetic. At the end of any medieval battle the clerks and heralds of the winning side would comb the field looking for corpses. They recognized the nobility by their coats of arms, embroidered on jupons or tabards or painted on the shields still strapped to their bodies. The common soldiery, even those who wore the livery or crest of the house they served, were rarely counted. Writing of a battle fought sixteen years before Ţepeş' birth, Shakespeare's famous Agincourt roll call from *Henry V* reads, on the French side:

This note doth tell me of ten thousand French
That in the field lie slain; of princes, in this number,
And nobles bearing banners, there lie dead
One hundred twenty six; added to these,
Of knights, esquires and gallant gentlemen,
Eight thousand and four hundred . . .

Various famous French names are listed as Henry says 'Here was a royal fellowship of death.' The English list is unbelievable by comparison:

Edmund the Duke of York, the Earl of Suffolk,
Sir Richard Ketly, Davy Gam, esquire:
None else of name; and of all other men
But five and twenty. O God, thy arm was here . . .[3]

And so was the English propagandist's! Shakespeare's 'none else of name' says it all; the brutal and licentious soldiery were expendable.

If we examine English battles contemporary with the Impaler's reign of terror we find the chroniclers' figures are fairly consistent. There were an estimated 2,300 dead after the second Battle of St Albans on 17 February 1461. By this time, the practice was developing of butchering prisoners after a battle because they were a nuisance and expensive to feed. The figures are much heavier for Towton in the following month (in fact, this is the bloodiest battle on English soil), partly because of the topography of the field – Bloody Meadow was a murderous cul-de-sac created by a loop of the River Cock and by high ground, into which the losing Lancastrians were driven – and partly because it was fought in a snowstorm, making visibility and escape difficult. But Towton illustrates the statistics problem very well. The Tudor historian Polydore Vergil estimates 20,000 dead and wounded on both sides, Yorkist and Lancastrian. The contemporary Croyland Continuator claims 38,000; Edward Hall an oddly precise 36,776; and the contemporary letters of Margaret Paston 28,000. Interestingly, none of the above was present at Towton: the Continuator was probably a politician away from the action; Polydore Vergil was writing fifty years after the event, as was Hall, and for the next generation.[4]

Medieval chroniclers, who were hardly ever eyewitnesses to events, embellished numbers for effect. In their accounts, a particular hero could kill a thousand men in the course of a battle – physically impossible given the weapons of the time – and perform astonishing feats. In England, the fictional Guy of Warwick killed the enormous, and equally fictional Dun Cow (the Lambton worm), that ravaged the neighbourhood of the town. John Lambton slew a dragon which was causing equal havoc in his neck of the woods. And all this was recorded as hard fact, without any shred of doubt or qualification.[5]

What, then, are we to make of Vlad Țepeș' own statistics, written in his letter to Matthias Corvinus in February 1462? At Oblucitza and Novoselo, 1,350; at Dirstor, Cirtal and Dridopotrom, 6,840 and so on. The tally cited by the Impaler, over a two-week killing spree and involving eighteen specified villages and towns, is an astonishing 20,019. This, however, is a rough estimate: Țepeș' grand total is '23,884 Turks and Bulgars'. We cannot dismiss these figures as lightly as we can those of the Croyland Continuator or Polydore Vergil. Țepeș was present at the action. Radu Farma, the boyar who took the letter to Corvinus, had carried with him two bags of heads, noses and ears. What was the point of this? Was Țepeș trying to impress the uncrowned king of Hungary? He needed his support in what would be a desperate war against the Turks. It is difficult to see how these grisly statistics and the even more grisly bag-contents would help. Presumably, it showed Corvinus that the war had really started and that the Impaler meant business; but it could equally have convinced the wary procrastinator that the *voivod* did not need his help after all. The account of Antonio Bonfini at Corvinus's court suggests that it was Țepeș' excessive cruelty that led the king to imprison him for so long. Certainly, these seemingly exact figures are unusual, perhaps even unique in medieval history. We have no way, of course, of verifying them.

If we turn to what could be termed Țepeș' 'peacetime' slaughter and look at the 'Saxon' stories which were already circulating by the time of his imprisonment by Corvinus, a different pattern emerges. Where numbers of sufferers are mentioned, rather than the ubiquitous 'all' or 'many', we are given the following statistics: two pretenders (Vladislav II and Dan II), a gypsy; two priests (one with his donkey); the putatively pregnant mistress; the boyar who complained of the stench of decaying corpses; the wife of the man with the overly short shirt; 200 poor people burned in a Tîrgoviste hall; 600 merchants from the Thunow and Pregel districts in Wuetzerland; 400 young men who had come to Wallachia to learn the language; 500 boyars who could not tell him how many princes had ruled Wallachia in their lifetime; and 30,000 killed at Amlaş on St Bartholomew's Day 1460. Even without the indiscriminate slaughter of Christians, pagans and Jews at Nicopolis (which could be said to be an act of war because this was 1462 and part of Ţepeş' raid along the Danube), the figures total 31,707.

If we scale up the 'alls' and 'manys' that are listed in the 'Saxon' tales, we have an estimate of around 100,000 victims of Ţepeş' 'calculated cruelty; medieval barbarism'. And many people have casually accepted this figure as the truth. Miranda Twiss,[6] for instance, accepts the 500 boyar impalements at Tîrgoviste (this figure does not include their families), and the knifing of Ţepeş' mistress who claimed to be pregnant. The interjection by Miss Twiss of words like 'perhaps' 20,000 forming the forest of the impaled and 'it is rumoured that' over 30,000 died on St Bartholomew's Day gets a little lost when we are faced with the enormity of these figures in print.

Two examples of analysis cast doubt on the sheer scale of Ţepeş' depravity. The first is the practical consideration of the prince's palace at Tîrgoviste, the ruins of which still remain. It is most unlikely that 500 boyars, as well as their wives and families (and no doubt retainers), could have fitted inside the Great Hall: it had room for 200 people at most. The courtyard outside, which is the scene of the impaling of the 500, could probably hold thirty or forty upright stakes. The 'Saxon' stories (and the Russian versions agree) say that this impalement was instant, rather than carried out in batches over a period of time. Such slaughter is simply not possible.

The second factor is the likely population of Wallachia in Vlad Țepeș' time. A reasonable estimate is that the Impaler's principality was about 48,000 square miles of territory with approximately 3,220 towns and villages; but it may have been smaller still, around 29,560 square miles. The towns were tiny by modern standards, and the villages often merely clusters of huts near a water source. Various historians estimate, but do not give their sources, that the total population of medieval Wallachia was about half a million. If this is correct, then Țepeș' death rate becomes ludicrous. We are asked to believe by the 'Saxon' chroniclers that in the St Bartholomew's Day attack at Amlaș alone, where 30,000 perished, the Impaler was wiping out 6 per cent of the country's entire population. If we extrapolate further, that Țepeș' total body count is over 100,000, then we are talking about 20 per cent, the equivalent in Britain today of 12 million people! *Today*, of course, it could be done, using modern killing methods, even those as relatively unrefined as the bullets of the Nazi *Einzatsgruppen* or the Zyklon B pellets of the death camps in the 1940s. The sheer *mechanics* of impalement, however, tell a different story.

If we analyse the 'Saxon' stories – echoed of course in the Russian and Romanian versions – we can build up a body of evidence which helps us outline Țepeș' psyche. Of the thirty-two tales, eleven have a proven basis in fact, whereas thirteen can be regarded as examples of gratuitous viciousness. The innocuous young people, it was said up to 400 men, who had come to learn the language and customs of Wallachia were almost certainly spies; that is certainly how Țepeș saw them. The method of execution – they were locked in a room and burned alive – was not new, and was used also by Slobodan Milosević more recently; but Țepeș' execution methods were far more ingenious than that.

> . . . he had a big copper cauldron built [one of the 'Saxon' stories tells us], and put a lid made of wood with holes in it on top. He put the people in the cauldron and put their heads in the holes and fastened them there; then he filled it with water and set fire under it and let the people cry their eyes out until they were burned to death.[7]

And then he invented frightening, terrible, unheard of tortures. He ordered that women be impaled together with their suckling babies on the same stake. The babies fought for their lives at their mothers' breasts until they died. Then he had the women's breasts cut off and put the babies inside head first; thus he had them impaled together.
And then he put many people on spinning wheels and killed them.

And then this Dracula would roast little children and force their own mothers to eat them. And he ordered that the breasts of many women be cut off and he forced their men to eat them . . .

Antonio Bonfini, the Hungarian court chronicler, adds in relation to Ţepeş' behaviour:

And then he often peeled the skin off the feet of Turkish prisoners and covered their wounds with salt, then brought goats to lick their salted soles.

Torture, 'even unto death', was widespread in the Europe of Vlad Ţepeş: it was not formally abolished in 'Germany' until 1831, in Russia until 1847. In fact the earliest known official abolition in Western Europe was in Scotland in 1708. Various statesmen lied about this, for example, Sir Thomas Smith, Secretary of State to Elizabeth I of England:

Torment or question, which is used by the order of the civil law and custom of other countries, to put a malefactor to excessive pain . . . is not used in England . . . beatings, servitude and servile torment and punishment [the state] will not abide.[8]

Lopping off ears and noses was standard practice for minor infringements the world over. In England nearly half a century after Ţepeş' death a Dr Leighton had both ears cut off and both nostrils slit open. He was also branded on both cheeks for writing seditious materials during the brief 'reign' of Lady

Jane Grey. In another English case in 1552, a fraudster had his ears nailed to a post in Cheapside. The only way to cut him loose again was by slicing off his ears.[9] In France, twenty years after Țepeș' death, the 'spider king' Louis XII passed laws known as *essorillement* in which servants lost ears for dishonesty; a third offence meant execution. Such mutilations were also commonplace in the East. In Egypt, adulterous women had their noses cut off[10] and as late as 1779 a horrified visiting Englishman wrote, 'He who commits a rape on a free woman has his privities cut off, that it might be out of his power ever to perpetrate the like crime . . .'[11] The Turks themselves hacked off hands and feet. According to Grafton's Chronicle, when they invaded Austria in the early seventeenth century they:

> comitted such cruelties and tyranny as never hath bene heard nor written, for of some they put out the eyes, of others they cut off the noses and eares, of others they cut off the pappes and ravished virgins and of women great with child, they cut their bellies and burnt the children.

Did they learn all this from Vlad Țepeș?[12]

A common punishment in the Turkish army was to whip the soles of a soldier's feet so that marching was excruciating. The 'goat-licking routine' described by Bonfini was used extensively in France. French victims were tied to a bench and had their feet soaked in salt water before the rasping tongue of the goat caused acute agony.

Flaying, which features in the canon of Țepeș' crimes, was also popular in France, the skin being removed from the top of the head first, and so on down. Few survived beyond the flaying of the chest. In 1366 the Count of Rouci died this way, for treason during the Hundred Years War. Similarly, burial alive, such as was inflicted on the Impaler's brother, Mircea, was a standard method of dispatch by the Inquisition in Western Europe. The last known instance of it featured Anne van de Hoor, from Malines in the Netherlands, who was buried up to her chin. Refusing to recant, her torturers/executioners merely shovelled on the soil until she died of suffocation. Death by burning was of course a punishment usually reserved for heretics, to prepare them in what remained of this life for the flames of Hell to come in the next and as purification of their sins. In the appalling *auto da fe* of sixteenth-century Spain, thousands came to their deaths, with dozens being burned together as public entertainment. An estimated 13,000 heretics died this way between 1481 and 1517.

Țepeș' fiendish cauldron had its echoes too. For sixteen years in the reign of Henry VIII of England murder by poisoning was punished in this way. Because the targets of Richard Roose were the family of the Bishop of Rochester, the king took exception and had the crime made one of high treason by Act of Parliament in 1513. Various methods were used, including immersion in boiling water, the rather grimmer method of heating cold water or the use of boiling oil or tallow (candle-wax) instead. Similar systems were in use in France until its final abolition by law in 1791. Eleven years after Vlad Țepeș' death, such an execution went horribly wrong in Tours, when Loys Secretan, a coiner, was immersed in this way by the local executioner, Denys. Secretan's ropes worked loose in the bubbling water and he kept bobbing to the surface, screaming for help. The crowd took pity on him, hauled him out and kicked the executioner to death.

The 'spinning wheels' of which the 'Saxon' stories speak was widely used in Western Europe, but not England. The victim was spread-eagled, usually naked, onto an iron-flanged cartwheel and the limbs repeatedly struck with hammers or iron bars until the bones broke. A skilful practitioner could achieve this without breaking the skin. In France, the wheel was mounted horizontally on a post while the executioners went to work on arms and legs with an iron bar three feet long and two inches square. By the late eighteenth century this was a more common method of execution than the more conventional hanging used elsewhere. In Germany, the wheel was fixed to a tripod so that a good view could be had by the spectators on every side. Regulations here specified that forty blows were to be given, only the last one aimed at the nape of the neck to snap the spine and deliver the *coup de grâce*.

The Holy Inquisition, already active in Țepeș' time against heretics like the Hussites in Bohemia, the Bogomils in Serbia and Wallachia and the Lollards in England, was developing such torture and execution methods to a fine art. Because for the Church it served a purpose – to root out heresy which subverted God's laws – an intellectual justification for it was promoted, to which Vlad Țepeș may have subscribed. Woodcuts of the torture implements used at Bamberg in Germany in 1508 include all those employed by Țepeș, except one – the stake for impalement.

It is this means of execution that marks Vlad Țepeș out from all the other ghastly array of pain that haunts the late Middle Ages. We have established already that life was cheap, and that in Wallachia, as in most European states, the word of the ruler was law. These were the necessary ingredients, the background against which impaling could take place. *The Devil's Dictionary*, originally written in 1911 but not published until 1993 has this definition:

> Impale, v.t. In popular usage to pierce with any weapon which remains fixed in the wound. This however is inaccurate; to impale is, properly, to put to death by thrusting an upright sharp stake into the body, the victim being left in a sitting position. This was a common mode of punishment among the nations of antiquity . . .

But was it? The dictionary goes on to quote China and other parts of Asia, where it 'is still in high favour' and claims that until the beginning of the fifteenth century it was 'widely employed in "churching" heretics and schismatics'. An authority called Wolecraft refers to impalement as 'the stoole of repentynge' and that, rather as the gallows was 'the drop' and being broken on the rack was 'marrying the Duke of Exeter's daughter' (in England), impalement was known as 'riding the one-legged horse'.

In 1995 the world's first Dracula conference was held in Romania, at which experts lectured on a number of related themes.[13] One speaker, Professor Lloyd Worley of the University of Northern Colorado, as well as investigating the 'prenatal and natal foundations of the vampire myth' through literature, pathology and psychology, also looked at the act of impalement in some detail. Worley's description of the act is markedly different from the woodcuts produced to accompany the 'German' horror stories of Ţepeş at the turn of the fifteenth/sixteenth centuries. Impaling, says Worley, was:

> the thrusting of a long stake or shaft through the anus [in the case of women sometimes through the vagina], through the intestines to the diaphragm muscle. The naked victim was then hoisted upward and the pole fixed in the ground. Subsequent writhing eventually forced the stake upward to pierce the heart, causing death (if the victim had not already died of shock or blood loss). Even after death, the impaling process continued, with gravity often causing the stake to exit through the mouth.[14]

The 'Saxon' stories imply that Ţepeş invented those 'terrible, unheard of' tortures. But this is simply not true. Assyrian bas-reliefs as early as 700 BC show Israelites impaled by King Sennacherib after he had taken their town of Lachish. The term for this is *al ha-es*, meaning 'hanging on a pole', and the phrase is vague enough to mean hanging by the neck by conventional methods. Worley quotes the authority of the Dead Sea Scrolls found at Qumran, probably dating to the second century before Christ. The Bible itself makes a number of references to impalement, with examples in Deuteronomy, Joshua, Esther and Ezekiel. It is clear from these examples – 'And if a man have committed a sin worthy of death and he be put to death and thou hang him on a tree' – that the punishment was known before Sennacherib, but this verse from Deuteronomy sounds suspiciously like hanging a body from a gibbet, a punishment widespread throughout Europe until the eighteenth century. Worley makes it clear, however, that in the original Hebrew the word loosely translated as 'tree' is in fact 'staff' or 'timber', and the term 'to hang' actually means to 'fix' or 'make firm'. It is possible that the Egyptians used impalement as a form of punishment for a crime, but likely that Sennacherib was the first to use it as

Ţepeş did, as a means of instilling psychological terror into his enemies, be they Ottoman Turks, shifty merchants from Braşov or treacherous boyars. As a warlord and conqueror, the Assyrian king faced many of the same problems as Ţepeş, eventually being murdered by one of his sons, in 681 BC.

The horror of impaling was carried over into the New Testament, at least as a folk-memory, and the victim was deemed to be 'accursed of God'. The Romans of course used crucifixion as an alternative method, and vague references to Celtic practices by both Julius Caesar and by Strabo, the Greek geographer, if they were talking about impalement, were regarded by the Romans as horrific. There are no known references to impalement throughout the 'Dark Ages', despite appalling atrocities by various nomadic bands of warriors, including the Dacians, in what would become Wallachia. Steven Runciman in his monumental history of the crusades refers to a band of Franks on their way to Jerusalem, marching through Hungary and impaling a boy whose village they were looting. Worley conjectures that this was possibly learned from the Turks, although he concedes that there is no hard evidence for this. The fact that Venetian sailors running from captured Constantinople in 1453 made a great deal of the impalement of their captain, Rizzo, suggests that such was a rare and perhaps even unique spectacle. The very fact that Mehmed II's invading army in 1462 does not seem to have used the technique surely speaks volumes for the fact that it was not a Turkish custom, even in a war of attrition. When Vlad Ţepeş was finally killed, allegedly by a Turkish assassin, it was his head that was taken back to the sultan's court, not his entire impaled body.

The mechanics of impalement are problematic and make it doubly difficult to accept the ludicrous body count of the 'Saxon' stories. When they and others calmly say 'Dracula impaled them', the reality of course is that several men and probably horses would be needed for each impalement. This was presumably the role of the *armas*, a sort of execution squad cum private army 500 years before the Tottenkopf SS. The most probable method was to pin the victim, already naked, to the ground by sheer weight of numbers and hold the legs apart by means of ropes attached to the horses. The stake, presumably a reasonably stout, straight but not too large tree-trunk, was oiled and inserted through either the anus or vagina. The problem with this method is resistance. The tip of the stake would probably meet bone at some stage and, even if not, it would take considerable force to insert the wood through the tough sphincter muscle, yards of twisted gut and the even more formidable diaphragm. Even the grain of the timber would be a problem here, because wood is by no means as penetrative as metal (hence the need for iron-tipped arrows and spears). If the impalement was carried out with the victim lying horizontally on the ground, four men would have been needed to hold the victim down and a fifth to insert the stake. The woodcuts show an altogether easier and more likely process (which would also explain how babies could be impaled with their mothers) of driving a stake through the body either from the chest or back, like insects on a display board.

I put the impalement problem to physicist Brian Bond, who, after deliberation, suggested a 'nutcracker' force theory. He hypothesized that three growing trees, forming a rough 'L' shape, could be used and a long tree-trunk cut down and laid between two of them. Experienced men – the *armas* – would exert leverage on the free end of the trunk and this would have the effect of driving the impalement stake as though with a mallet into the orifice of the victim, who would previously have been tied on the ground by the ankles to two other trees. Experts, Bond believes, could carry out this operation in about five minutes, although, of course, large numbers would be needed and, at least in 1462, time was of the essence. The method recorded by Dr Meryon in Syria in 1813 of draping a victim over a saddle on the ground, slitting the anus and using a wooden mallet, would not seem to be very efficacious given the numbers involved.

According to some theorists, victims could linger for days like this, although there are all kinds of question marks over how the stake, with the weight of their victims, could be anchored firmly in the ground. We know that crosses for crucifixion were hauled upright by means of ropes and pulleys, with the victim in place, but the horizontal beam of the cross made this relatively easy. If we take 'the forest' of the impaled literally, then perhaps living trees were used with the branches cut off. Again, we have the impossibility of being able to hoist the victim onto the top of such a tree. No contemporary records give us any indication of the *height* of the stake, but even a six-foot trunk would cause enormous problems. And it is worth remembering that this 'forest' was created by an army retreating in front of an oncoming and much larger Turkish force. Tursun Bey, who was with Mehmed's army, specifically refers to a 'field' of the impaled, implying that the stakes were not growing, but driven into the ground.

Such preparation, cutting down trees, lopping off branches, stripping victims, holding or tying them down, inserting the stakes and somehow hoisting them into position would be at best a lengthy and extremely difficult process.

In one sense, then, the tortures and executions ordered by the Impaler were probably carried out by other people; he himself was physically removed from the crime. Even so, at only a few yards or feet remove rather than miles, he was a different kind of mass-murderer from, say, Adolf Hitler, Josef Stalin or Slobodan Milosević. There is little doubt that Hitler condoned wholeheartedly the 'final solution' that exterminated over six million Jews, but there is no evidence that he ever entered the gates of a death camp. There is a world of difference, in terms of psyche, between a Hitler and a Ţepeş. The law and social morality might brand them equally guilty, but the Impaler was a hands-on murderer. There are a handful of telling clues that help us to understand him.

His black humour, referred to in the various stories, just *may* have a basis in fact; similar characteristics are found in several murderers. 'What a nuisance they are!' he is supposed to have complained to a boyar as they walked below the twitching bodies dying on their stakes and, with an even more sinister connotation, 'How beautiful they look.' This is the stuff of twentieth-century serial killers like Ed Gein, who wrapped himself in his victims' skins, and Jeffrey Dahmer, who kept severed heads in his fridge. Ţepeş seems to have had a strangely puritanical streak at odds with his depravity, and this too is a not uncommon trait of sex killers. According to the tales adulterous women in particular were singled out. Their breasts were sliced off, and their vaginas cut out. One faithless wife was impaled in a square in Tîrgoviste with her skin lying on a table nearby. The mistress who lied to the *voivod* by telling him she was pregnant suffered disembowelling at the Impaler's own hand. Because we know almost nothing about his sex life, not even the name of his first wife, this line of enquiry leads to a dead end.

Another tale about Țepeș may hold a clue to what sort of man he was. This time, the source is not the obvious paranoia of the German merchants but Fedor Kuritsyn, who almost certainly interviewed people who had spent a great deal of time with the Impaler at Buda. The Russian envoy wrote:

It is said of him, that he could not cure himself of the evil habit of catching mice and having birds bought at the market place so that he could punish them by impalement. He cut off the heads of some of the birds; others he had stripped of their feathers and then let loose.

Another version of this, and one unlikely to have come from Kuritsyn, occurs in a letter from Gabriele Rangoni, the Bishop of Erlau and papal legate, to Pope Sixtus IV in the year of Țepeș' death:

Unable to forget his wickedness, he caught mice and, cutting them up into pieces, stuck them on small pieces of wood, just as he had stuck men on stakes.[15]

The problem with psychoanalysis is that it is all things to all men. Even experts cannot agree among themselves (a loophole that lawyers in criminal cases use today): the expert witness for the prosecution is countered by the expert witness for the defence. And that is before we get into the realms of Freud and Jung! The historian, however, has to try. We cannot make sense of Vlad Țepeș unless we try to see beyond the monster of legend and the dark, saucer eyes of the Ambras portrait.

Animal torture, especially in young people, is one of the three warning signs of the potential serial killer known by American psychiatrists as the 'triad'. We know so little of Ţepeş' childhood that we cannot apply the other two signs – bed-wetting and obsession with fire; and of course the animal mutilations at Buda, if they really happened, took place when he was in his thirties and early forties. American psychotics like Henry Lee Lucas and Jeffrey Dahmer both tortured animals to death. Edmund Kemper was fascinated by cats, burying one alive before digging it up and decapitating it. Peter Kurten, the 'monster of Dusseldorf' in Weimar Germany, slaughtered sheep while having sex with them and once decapitated a swan, drinking the blood from its severed neck. If the tale of Ţepeş eating al fresco among the corpses of his staked victims and mopping up their blood with his bread is true, then we have another obsession, what criminologists call 'haematomania', an extremely rare obsession with blood.

Many of the 'Saxon' and other stories deal with enforced cannibalism, the Impaler presiding over one set of victims obliged to eat others. Recent studies on this bizarre form of behaviour have established that it was probably common in primitive cultures at the mercy of the weather and bad harvests. Classic tales of survival, from the Donner wagon train marooned in the Rocky Mountains in the 1840s to the Andes plane crash in 1972, bear witness to the fact that even this last of all taboos can be broken in moments of necessity. Psychopaths like Fritz Haarmann, who sold human flesh on the black market in interwar Hanover, and Albert Fish, who stewed twelve-year-old Grace Budd in his life-long search for sexual kicks, are the reality on which Thomas Harris's appalling Hannibal Lecter is based. Even so, we only have the lurid 'horror' tales of the Impaler as evidence of this particular perversion.

Criminologist Colin Wilson rates Timur-i-Leng as 'the most spectacular sadist in world history', with Vlad Ţepeş a close second. Like many modern authorities, Wilson is perfectly happy to accept the exaggerated statistics of slaughter. So Timur, according to legend, bricked up 2,000 prisoners at Sabwazar in 1383 and made a pyramid of 5,000 decapitated heads at Zirih. He slaughtered 100,000 prisoners at Delhi, and at Sivas in Anatolia 4,000 Christians were buried alive. So Țepeș' 'estimated' 100,000 victims are included by Wilson, who assumes that the Impaler received harsh treatment at the hands of the Turks during his teenaged captivity which left him warped – which may indeed be the case. If Radu was the victim of Mehmed II's homosexual urges, was Vlad a similar target? True, the Wallachian was a year older than the sultan's son, but we cannot know what pressures he was under during his years as a prisoner at Egrigoz and Edirne.

Did Țepeș' obsession with impalement and blood have a sexual element? In their book *The Dracula Syndrome*, writers Richard Monaco and William Burt examine seventeen twentieth-century cases of murder with 'vampiric' associations, dividing them up into psychopathic, perverse and cult causation. We need to establish at this stage something that will be analysed in more detail in the final chapter. There is only one reference to Vlad Țepeș in the Monaco/Burt book; there is no mention of him at all in the hundreds of Internet interviews which Tony Thorne carried out with the 'generation dead', mostly West Coast vampire-obsessed teenagers today. Modern historians, especially Romanian historians, of the Ceaușescu era and since the collapse of Communism have been at pains to separate the *voivod* of Wallachia from Bram Stoker's creation. But Bram Stoker did not 'create' Dracula; he stole him from the folklore tales of Arminius Vambery and merely transposed ideas, merging the *varcolac* and *strigoi*, creatures of the Romanian night, with a real historical character. The obsession with blood – the haematomania of which Wilson writes – is common to the *voivod* and the Count. The means of execution of the vampire – the stake through the heart – is clearly a variant of impalement. The decapitation of vampires as the final means of destruction was the fate of both Vlad Țepeș and his father. During the day, the vampire traditionally sleeps in a mouldering coffin – he is buried alive, as Vlad's brother Mircea was. His 'return from the dead' to rule Wallachia, not once, but three times; his attacks *by night* on the Turks; his ownership of not one 'Castle Dracula' but several; all this has an obvious correlation with

Stoker's fiction. Pretending that the novelist merely took the name and nothing else is preposterous. That said, we can attempt to explore Ţepeş' psyche as far as we can.

An analysis of two other historical multiple murderers may help us understand the Impaler. In the cases of Gilles de Rais and Elizabeth Báthory, we immediately run into the same problem we have with Vlad Ţepeş – the unreliability of contemporary evidence. De Rais was Gilles de Laval, Baron de Rais, who was executed in France when Vlad Ţepeş was nine. Accused by the Catholic Church of being a:

heretic, apostate, conjuror of demons . . . accused of the crime and vices against nature, sodomy, sacrilege and violation of the immunities of Holy Church,[16] during his trial in September 1439, de Rais was charged with 'having taken innocent boys and girls and inhumanly butchered, killed, dismembered, burned and otherwise tortured them . . . and has foully committed the sin of sodomy with young boys and in other ways lusted against nature after young girls, spurning the natural way of copulation . . .'

In echoes of later child killers like Peter Kurten and Albert Fish, de Rais is said to have confessed to his servant Henriet:

that he took more pleasure in the murder of the said children and in seeing their heads and limbs separated from their body, in seeing them die and their blood flow, than in having carnal knowledge of them.

Incredibly, there are echoes of Ţepeş' method of impalement – the stake thrust through the anus which has vague links with the supposed sodomy of Gilles de Rais. It is interesting, however, that whereas de Rais' crimes were overtly sexual in nature, those of Ţepeş were not. What is even more interesting is that the very Church that condemned de Rais recently overturned all charges against him, pouring huge doubt not only on the charges, the evidence of the 110 prosecution witnesses at his trial, but the alleged confession of de Rais himself.

No such pardon has been given to Elizabeth Báthory. Many books refer to her as 'Countess Dracula' because of her obsession with blood, and some claim that she was a descendant of Ţepeş. She *was* a descendant of Stephen Báthory, who had fought alongside the Impaler in his last campaign and she *did* rule in Transylvania, which probably explains the confusion. It was probably Elizabeth Báthory whom Sheridan Le Fanu had in mind when he wrote his best-selling *Carmilla* in the 1870s. Colin Wilson paints a cheerful picture of the dysfunctional family from which she came – 'her brother was sexually insatiable, one uncle was a devil worshipper and an aunt was a witch and a lesbian'.[17] Báthory stood trial – or rather, not, as she refused to attend in person or offer a plea – in the winter of 1611, accused of the murder of over fifty young girls. Her motive was not directly sexual (despite her obvious lesbian relationships with various maids) but she believed that she could remain ever-youthful by drinking the victims' blood and bathing in it. Her accomplices were either beheaded or had their fingers torn off. Báthory was walled up alive with only a small hole for the delivery of food until her death in August 1614.

What is common to all three 'monsters' – Ţepeş, de Rais and Báthory – is that because of their status and the physical enormity of their crimes, they had to have accomplices. Someone had to carry out the impaling, the procurement of children and the draining of blood; all three, according to contemporary evidence, had any number of servants willing to do that.

Modern 'vampire killers' normally have no such aid. And it is ironic that, for the purposes of this book, although we know a great deal about what motivates such people, the structure of today's society means that it is impossible to reproduce a Ţepeş unless they can be found in the 'banality of evil' in instances like Milosević. Such killers are by their nature loners – they do not have feudal minions to do their bidding. As Benjamin Disraeli observed as early as 1831,[18] 'The Age of Chivalry is past. Bores have succeeded to dragons.' Many of the killers cited by Monaco and Burt are not truly vampiric – their blood-fetish is only a by-product of the greater elements of sadism involving degradation and power.

Tony Thorne cites nine authenticated cases of vampire murders in Britain and America over the last ten years, all of them involving disturbed teenagers and all of them motivated by gang culture and the need for acceptance. He cites the 1920s cases in Weimar Germany of Karl Denke, Georg Grossmann, Fritz Haarmann and Peter Kurten as probably genuine examples of 'haematomania', while admitting that the term itself is at best pseudo-scientific. The case of John George Haigh would seem to be marginal. His motive, in the Britain of 1949, for killing Olive Durand-Deacon and the McSwanns was purely financial. His confession – 'I shot her in the back of the head. Then I fetched a drinking glass and made an incision in the side of her throat and collected a glass of blood, which I drank' – was probably an attempt to prove insanity and avoid the rope. It failed.

So where can psychoanalysis of a man dead for five and a half centuries take us? If we follow the precepts of the now outdated and frequently attacked Sigmund Freud, we make little headway because we know almost nothing about Vlad Țepeș' childhood, and it is from childhood that Freud says all our troubles arise. Other than what may be the puritanical streak we have observed in his punishments for immorality among women, we know little about Țepeș' sexuality. It may even be that the murder of his mistress was committed, if at all, in the heat of the moment, because she had ridiculed him by lying. We cannot get far because we have no idea of the content of the Impaler's dreams. In Freudian terms, a simplistic answer to Țepeș' 'problem' is that he lacked a super-ego which in most people controls their external actions and takes them along conventional paths of what is acceptable – clearly, even by fifteenth-century standards, mass impalement was not. If we accept Freud's version, Țepeș was driven by the Thanatos instinct, essentially an aggressive death-wish aimed at others. Intriguingly, Freud used the mass trauma of the First World War to analyse the effects of slaughter on human beings. Individuals, he observed, and indeed whole states, discarded morals at the drop of a hat and used war as an excuse for aggressive, brutal behaviour. When he looked more broadly at society's role in controlling human beings, he decided that one major task was to control the baser instincts, which include what he called *lustmord*, the enjoyment of killing. Clearly in Ţepeş' time, when the leader of the Catholic Church called for a crusade to kill the Infidel and the followers of Mohammed were offered paradise by way of jihad, there was little chance of peace in the world of Vlad Ţepeş.

We are even more at sea with Freud's one-time friend and protégé Carl Jung, because even though the man's intellectual interests were more wide-ranging than Freud's, embracing archaeology, astrology, alchemy and world religions, he again relied heavily on the portents of dreams, his own driving him in a certain direction. He did, however, specifically address the problem of evil – 'where love stops,' he wrote, 'power begins and violence and terror'. But, once again, as we know little about Ţepeş' loves, to put the man on the psychiatrist's couch is self-defeating. He may have been schizophrenic; he may have been self-delusional; he may have been a raving lunatic – we simply do not have the evidence to be sure.

Of two things we can, however, be sure: Vlad Ţepeş was a mass-murderer and a psychopath. Opportunities for mass murder were rare in the past. Today, because of the technology of mass destruction, they are far easier. A terrorist bomb, for instance, with the simplest trigger mechanism, is capable of killing dozens in a single blast. The spectacular attacks on the World Trade Center in New York on 11 September 2001 killed over 3,000 people. To men like Vlad Ţepeş, with unrestrained power on the one hand and opportunities to wage war on the other, there were outlets for sadistic impulses, and they could act accordingly. Today, as psychologist Professor Adrian Furnham of University College, London, explains, 'A psychopath doesn't have to be violent or dangerous,'[19] although of course many of them are. American psychologists use a sixteen-point scale of criteria identified by the American Psychiatric Association. These concern the subject's sex life, consistency in work behaviour and other points that sound banal when applied to a fifteenth-century warlord. Other criteria, however, make good sense from what we know of the Impaler's actions. Clearly, he was 'impulsive' and 'reckless'. His ripping open of his mistress, his nailing the Turkish emissaries' turbans to their heads, his attack in 1462 along the Danube – all this and more betokens a man who does not always weigh things rationally. Lying is another characteristic trait of the psychopath – Ţepeş' evasiveness in failing to pay direct homage to Mehmed at Constantinople, in which he basically pleaded an unstable principality, could well be an example. 'Illegal behaviour' must be viewed by different standards from our own. In Wallachia, he *was* the law, but he certainly broke the basic structure-bonds of Christianity with his wholesale slaughter, especially in respect of women and children. He clearly 'took risks', another psychopathic trait – but then, what medieval ruler did not? Even the cautious time-server Matthias Corvinus was eventually forced into action against the Turks. Ţepeş' attack on Mehmed was foolhardy in the extreme; he was gambling on Corvinus and Stefan of Moldavia's support and got neither. He evinced an obvious 'lack of shame and remorse' throughout his career. He saw impalement and similar methods of execution as a fact of life as well as of death and rather seemed to relish the notoriety the killings gave him. Those who see in Ţepeş' endowments of monasteries some attempt to atone for his actions and to throw himself on the mercy of God in abject fits of remorse have misread the signs; all medieval rulers gave freely to the Church – it was expected. A 'failure to learn from experience' and 'poor judgement' can also be laid at the Impaler's door. Many writers on him say that his Turkish prison experiences as a boy taught him to trust no one. But the facts of his life prove that he did. He trusted János Hunyadi, he trusted Matthias Corvinus; he trusted Stefan of Moldavia; and presumably, many of the boyars he had elevated in the 1450s. He was to be betrayed by them all. Oddly, something that sounds very modern – a 'failure to honour financial obligations' – fits Ţepeş perfectly. He refused to pay Mehmed his yearly tribute and consistently reneged on various trade deals with the merchants of Transylvania. He did exhibit acute 'pathological egocentricity'. Who else but

Țepeș could kill the constable rather than the thief as a hue and cry took place through his garden at Pest? The Impaler himself would never have called his 'anti-social behaviour' 'unmotivated'. He killed the poor because they were a blot on the Wallachian landscape. He killed 'Saxon' merchants because they were bleeding his country dry. He killed Catholic monks because at that time in his life, his alleged Orthodox upbringing made this acceptable. He killed Turks because they were the enemy. We may put a different gloss on all these actions today.

Finally, the hypothesis that Țepeș' impaling may have been the twisted result of impotence, that in Freudian terms, the stake represented the phallic imagery of the maypole, a kind of sex substitute, cannot be proven.

> But his fiercest fury was directed against women. He seems to have been darkly jealous of the perpetuation of the human race. Wives and concubines were strangled, sawn asunder and buried alive if they showed signs of pregnancy . . . Contemporary Arab chroniclers, pondering upon the fierce and gloomy passions of this man, arrived at the conclusion that he was the subject of a strange disease, a portentous secretion of black bile producing the melancholy which impelled him to atrocious crimes.[20]

This passage is not about the fifteenth-century Wallachian *voivod* but about the Arab Ibrahim ibn Ahmed, who lived 600 years earlier. It would be of little comfort to the victims of either of them to know that, historically, in the annals of murder, Vlad Țepeș was not alone.

# 13

# RESURRECTING DRACULA

Draculaland was under way. Sighişoara, the birthplace of Vlad Ţepeş and one of the most beautiful surviving medieval towns in Europe, was until recently to be home to a theme park, Hollywood style. It was to bring much-needed cash to the ailing Romanian economy.

In November 2001 *The Hollywood Reporter* covered an unseemly row between movie moguls Universal Studios and the Romanian tourist board. Draculaland was estimated to cost $40 million, and Universal claimed that Dracula was theirs. The classic elements in the film *Dracula* – the cape, the widow's peak, the blood-filled eyes, the fangs – are, said Universal, their copyright and that Romania would have to pay for their use. Veronica Miclea, head of the Romanian Tourist Office in Prague, The Czech Republic, countered with:

> Dracula is our trademark because Dracula belongs to Romania. [Universal] borrowed from us our Dracula and did these films, but forgot he is our character. When you say Dracula, you think of Transylvania; it is Romania.

Nobody in all this squabbling seems to have remembered the intervention of Bram Stoker. How long will it be before the Dublin government wants a slice of the action? And bearing in mind where the Count's ship washed ashore in the novel, what will be the claims of Whitby Borough Council?

Romania hoped to make a killing. A million extra tourists were expected to visit the park scheduled for opening in

2003: two new airports and a road and rail link were under way. As *The Hollywood Reporter* says an estimated additional $20 million in tourism revenue would be an important kick-start to further investment. The take-home pay of the average Romanian is $125 a month.

In January 2002 *The Spectator* painted a more gloomy economic picture. Agathon Dan, the Romanian tourist minister, found it difficult to interest foreign investors.[1] The investors seemed unimpressed with the theme park's attempt to recreate a 'Horror Castle', in which electronic effects would terrify visitors, and an 'Institute of Vampirology', complete with Vlad's torture chamber, where the Impaler 'skinned, boiled, burned, fried, buried alive, blinded, impaled, strangled and cut off the noses, ears and genitalia' of his victims.[2] Dan returned to Bucharest claiming victory, how-ever, and batted aside opposition from feeble protest groups. His determination was summed up with the phrase 'only God can stop this project now'. Perhaps God did, but He did it in the unlikely combination of Greenpeace, UNESCO and Prince Charles. Greenpeace was particularly concerned that the ancient oak forest, already old when Vlad Ţepeş was born, would be destroyed to create vampire rollercoasters. UNESCO complained about the proximity of such *kitsch* to the superb medieval town. Prince Charles is a patron of a society concerned with the preservation of Romanian heritage, and blasted the ill-advised scheme on a cultural visit last year.

Nothing daunted, Draculaland's organizers say they will simply move it to a site near Bucharest.

What would Vlad Dracula, the *voivod* and prince of Wallachia, have made of all this? And, more importantly, what are we to make of him? First, we must remember that a great deal of the information we have on the man is biased or second-hand. The 'Saxon' stories, circulating from the court of Matthias Corvinus from the late 1460s, emanate from the merchants of Braşov and Sibiu whom Ţepeş had not only controlled commercially with trade treaties, but who had been the target of the *voivod*'s ferocity. The *vornic* (judge) Neagu wrote to the council of Braşov in the late 1470s:

Remember well who started having people impaled . . . You, because you kept Dan [Dracula's rival] among you and this angered Vlad *voivod* . . . [who] . . . came upon you with fire.[3]

The historian cannot dismiss such evidence out of hand. It would be like dismissing the Holocaust because most of the evidence comes from Jewish survivors. We have already established, however, the inaccuracy regarding the *numbers* of Țepeș' victims, and so the 'Saxon' stories become doubly suspect. It was in Corvinus's interests in the 1460s to circulate these distortions with their ludicrous body count, to discredit the man he wanted to keep under lock and key for political reasons. Thanks to the printing press, the Impaler stories took on a life of their own and the presses of Nuremberg and other German cities realized that they were a licence to print money, paving the way for Byron, Polidori, Rymer and Stoker, long before celluloid took over.

The Turkish accounts clearly have a bias of their own. The Impaler was their enemy, and they were only too delighted to blacken his reputation. The earliest of these was written by Tursun Bey, who took part in the 1462 campaign, but the account was not written until well over thirty years later. Asik-Pasha-Zade's account also dates from the very end of the century, but it is clearly a truncated copy of Tursun's. Mehmed Nesri's version is some twenty years later still and yet another variant of the first. The last version, that of Sa'adeddin Mehmed Hodja Efendi, did not appear until 1584. Although we cannot dismiss the Turkish accounts, we have to be aware that distortions accrue in any narrative the further away from the original we get. The Turkish narratives, like Michel Beheim's epic poem, are 'history' only in so far as they were stories for entertainment, and, in the Ottoman examples, recited to glorify Mehmed and Allah. It is interesting to temper the Ottoman accounts with the altogether more honest versions of the Serbian janissary Konstantin Mihailović fighting for the Turks, yet without perhaps their poetry and passion.

The Russian accounts, probably stemming from the work of Fedor Kuritsyn at Buda in the 1480s, are rather more forgiving than either the 'Saxon' or Turkish versions. To the Russians, and to the Dukes of Muscovy in particular, the need for strong autocratic rule was paramount. Statesmen knew that cruelty was sometimes necessary and, had the phrase been current in fifteenth-century Moscow, there would have been much talk of eggs and omelettes.

An interesting parallel with Vlad Ţepeş is his neo-contemporary Richard III of England. Most people's view of Richard, if they have one at all, is that of William Shakespeare – Richard was a malignant murderer, crippled and born prematurely, determined to kill his way to the crown. The body count in the Shakespeare play – eleven – hardly equals the Impaler's grand total; however, even that conservative figure is wildly inaccurate. There is in fact no hard evidence against Richard for any of the murders of which Shakespeare makes him guilty. Shakespeare's Richard is a fascinating character of fiction and melodrama, as is Ţepeş, but this does not make our job of searching the rubble of time for the truth any easier. Shakespeare based his play on the serious historical accounts of Thomas More, Edward Hall and Ralph Holinshed, at least two of whom had access to men who knew the king personally. Such men were John Morton, Bishop of Ely and a notorious enemy of Richard, whose poisonous accusations seem to have been swallowed by the gullible More hook, line and sinker. History, it is said, is written by the victors, and that is certainly so with Richard III and Vlad Ţepeş. Shakespeare, as well as gleefully regurgitating the 'histories' whose biased narratives he ransacked for a gripping drama, was working indirectly for the family who had overthrown the last of the Plantagenets. Had Richard defeated Henry Richmond at Bosworth, or had Vlad Ţepeş killed Mehmed II in the night attack on his camp, our versions of both men would have been radically different.

'Nobody troubles about daily deaths . . . in the middle of a daily massacre' wrote Graham Greene in *Ministry of Fear* in 1943. He was talking about murder in war-time Britain, but the words apply equally to late medieval Europe. Ask any member of the public today whether our society is more violent and anarchic than any in the past and the answer will be, 'Yes, it is.' Historians take a longer view. We are crushed by the sheer scale of atrocities today; 3,000 dead after two aircraft crashed into the World Trade Center in New York in September 2001; 80,000 died in minutes in the heat of Hiroshima on 9 August 1945; 130,000 in Dresden on St Valentine's Day 1945. The estimated casualty roll for the six years of the Second World War is fifty-five million. We have become numbed by all this. Casualty rates, lists of bombings, executions by paramilitaries, deaths through rioting – they filter through our television sets or our newspapers with only slightly more concern than the latest Dow Jones figures on the stock market.

Despite the scale of modern atrocities, we *are* still shocked by these things. Generations have passed since the Second World War, yet there is still today a sense of unease in Britain about the Germans. We still stand in horror when we see, even for the umpteenth time, those 747s plough like arrows into the rippling skyscrapers of the 'Big Apple', the nickname, ironically, so similar to that given by the Ottomans to their capital – the Red Apple. We shake our heads at the pictures of shattered Omagh and any of us older than ten at the time remember exactly where we were when, in six seconds in Dallas, someone blew the back out of John Kennedy's head and a dream died.

Medieval men had no time for such maudlin sentiment. And if we are to understand Ţepeş the man we have to acknowledge and accept this. Medievalists like M.M. Postan and Johan Huizinger are quick to point out that the Middle Ages was rich in culture, with a dynamic economy and laudable aims – there was, after all, a twelfth-century renaissance before the more famous rebirth of the sixteenth eclipsed it. The point at issue, however, is that life to the Impaler's contemporaries all over Europe, whatever their social status, was nasty, brutish and short. In England, in the year that Ţepeş first became *voivod*, Margaret Paston wrote to her husband:

I recommend me to you and pray you get some crossbows and windses [firing mechanisms] to bed with them and quarrels [bolts] . . . And also I would ye could get 2 or 3 short pole-axes to keep doors with, and also many jackets (padded) if ye may.[4]

This letter was written seven years before the Wars of the Roses erupted, and yet a knight's constant care was to defend his home against the threat of attack from any quarter. The same Margaret Paston spoke of her son's education, urging the boy's tutor to 'truly belash him till he will amend'. Elizabeth Paston, at twenty, was getting much the same treatment; in her case she was being difficult about accepting the much older man her parents had chosen as her bridegroom:

And she hath since Easter the most part been beaten once in the week or twice, and sometimes twice in one day and her head broken in two or three places . . .[5]

War perhaps brought out the worst in people. Of the 1370s, the French chronicler Thomas Basin, Bishop of Lisieux, wrote:

In the opinion of many, the English are not human beings and men, but senseless and ferocious beasts, which go about devouring people.[6]

Basin was no doubt thinking of the sack of Limoges by Edward the Black Prince, that has echoes of Ţepeş' work. According to Jean Froissart:

There was not so hard a heart within the city, an [if] he had any remembrance of God, but that wept piteously for the great mischief that they saw . . . for more than three thousand men, women and children were slain and beheaded that day.[7]

From whatever perspective we view Vlad Ţepeş' age, and whichever European country we choose, the same level of cruelty exists. Historian Jean Benedetti was writing of Gilles de Rais when he said:

He absorbed what his society had to offer, reproduced it and refracted it through his own personality and temperament. When his society finally condemned him, it was not from any genuine sense of moral outrage but . . . for the most hypocritical and cynical reasons. His society never ceased to regard him as one of its own.[8]

Much of the Middle Ages was spent in active warfare. The number of battles and skirmishes in which Ţepeş took part is not recorded, but from 1456 until his capture in 1462 and again from 1475 until his death two years later, the *voivod* was constantly a general, leading troops, sacking towns, orchestrating killing. As Benedetti says, 'War is at worst a kind of organized criminality.'[9] In the decade before the Impaler's birth, the Archbishop of Rheims described the effect of an English attack on the French countryside:

They took women and children, without difference of age or sex, raping the women and girls; they killed the husbands and fathers in the presence of their wives and daughters; they took nurses and left the children behind so that they died for want of food; they took pregnant women and chained them so that they gave birth in their chains; the children were allowed to die without baptism and mother and child were thrown into the river; they took priests and monks . . . ploughmen, chained them up in various ways and in this tortured state beat them so that certain among them, were maimed for life and others driven out of their minds . . . Some were roasted alive, others had their teeth ripped out, others were beaten with huge sticks . . .[10]

This was the norm. Clearly a French army in English territory would behave in the same way.

One of the 'most evil men and women in history', in Miranda Twiss' book of the same name, is Vlad Ţepeş' contemporary, the 'Black Legend', Tomás de Torquemada. Whereas the Paston letters reveal the fifteenth century's readiness for blows and warfare and the various accounts of the Hundred Years War confirm the almost banal routine of violence, Torquemada was a servant of God, in theory the antithesis of evil. As early as 1252 the then pope sanctioned the use of torture in stamping out any kind of heresy. Such hypocrisy is almost unbelievable today. The accused had no defence in ecclesiastical law and was not told the names of his accusers. Torquemada was a 'natural' for the muscular Christianity expected of the Dominican heretic-hunters, the 'Hounds of the Lord'. In the space of two months, between September and November 1481, 298 people had been burned alive in the notorious *auto da fe*, having been charged with worshipping the God of the Jews. Torquemada was in fact an anti-Semite and his targets were the *conversos*, the Jews who had nominally converted to Catholicism. His *Limpreza de Sangre*, far more vicious than any law the Impaler passed and foreshadowing the obsessive racial work of Nazis Himmler and Rosenberg, banned all Jews from office and effectively condemned them to death as heretics. The figures of the early Inquistion, unlike those of Ţepeş' victims, are believable. In Ciudad Rodrigo fifty-two were burned. By the end of 1485 up to 5,000 penitents had to appear each Friday, wearing coarse clothes and whipping themselves. A ghastly list of torture methods was added to the Inquisition's repertoire: water was forced down the throat of a trial victim; the rack pulled joints apart; the *garrucha* lifted the accused slowly by means of pulleys and dropped them quickly, dislocating limbs in the process. Contemporary woodcuts from Spain show these and other methods being carried out by professional Inquisitors, while benign-looking clerics look on. Tomás de Torquemada, unlike Vlad Ţepeş' died peacefully in his sleep; according to Catholic belief, 'in the odour of sanctity'.

There is little doubt that by medieval standards the Impaler was not regarded as out of the ordinary. Clearly the merchants of Braşov, Sibiu and other 'Saxon' towns hated him, and with reason. The Turks were at pains to blacken their enemy. But men who were not the targets of the *voivod*'s wrath could afford to be more dispassionate, and men who fought with him sang his praises. Monasteries blessed him. Anonymous monks carried his body to hallowed ground and buried him. This has led to many Romanian historians not only accepting Țepeș' conduct but finding merit in it. Anton Balota for instance writes:[11]

> the *voivod*'s cruel methods . . . were actually nothing more than the standard practices of their times . . . It is evident that the basis of the conflicts between Dracula and the traders of Brașov were of economic origins and not the policy of a sick *voivod* bent on personal vengeance.

They had, after all, been warned. According to Constantin Guirescu:[12]

> This merit [Țepeș' preservation of Wallachia] overrules the extreme harshness of the punishments which terrified his contemporaries and, in the final instance, causes history to pronounce a positive judgement of Dracula.

Anton Balota goes further than suggesting that the Impaler's means justified his ends:

> It is interesting to note that the contents of the tales about Dracula awakened the interest of authoritarian rulers who considered his personality as an example worthy of being copied.[13]

We have already discussed Tsar Ivan IV of Russia, known as the Terrible, and the similarity of his actions to those of Țepeș. Both men of course faced the same problem – unruly, power-hungry boyars, who played the game of politics for real. In 1538 they poisoned Ivan's mother with mercury and skinned alive her favourite, Fydor Mishurin, leaving his bleeding corpse on display in what would become Red Square in Moscow. Ivan's childhood torture of animals – he would drop cats from the Kremlin's battlements – fits absolutely the obsessions of the sociopath and Țepeș' own alleged behaviour at Buda and Visegrád. At the age of thirteen, so the chroniclers claim, Ivan staged a palace coup with the help of loyal guards and had the boyar leader, Andrew Shuisky, thrown to a pack of starving dogs which tore him apart. Perhaps like Ţepeş, with his puritanical streak and his firm belief in law and order, Ivan came to believe that God was working through him, not only sanctioning his increasing violence, but using the deranged Tsar as his instrument. We cannot be sure how far, if at all, the stories of Vlad the Impaler as collected by Fedor Kuritsyn were known to Ivan, or whether he used them as a blueprint; but if he did not, the metier of his reign followed an extraordinarily coincidental path. The Chosen Council he set up in Moscow was composed of carefully hand-picked men, as was the Impaler's in Tîrgoviste. His *Streltsi* were an elite force of officers, elevated from humble origins, very like Dracula's *vitesji*. As Ţepeş was facing a war on two fronts, against the Turks and the Hungarians (and temporarily three, if we include the brief campaign against Stefan of Moldavia), so Ivan was fighting the Tartars, the Poles and the Swedes.

It was the death of the Tsar's wife Anastasia that tipped him over the edge. There is no exact parallel here, because we know so little about Ţepeş' family life, but in the deaths of his father and brother, we see a personal tragedy that could have had a serious psychological effect on the *voivod*. Ivan's grief turned to paranoia of epic proportions, and among his victims were his subsequent wives. Two died of natural causes. Anna Koltovskaya, however, took a lover who was impaled for alleged adultery with the Tsaritsa, and she too was effectively locked up in a convent. Maria Dolgurukaya was drowned the day after her wedding to Ivan when he discovered she was not a virgin. In February 1565 the Tsar created the *Oprichniki*, secret police who rode black horses and carried brooms and dogs' heads as symbols of their intention to sweep away and destroy any examples of treachery to their master. These hardened criminals were a law unto themselves, and were directly responsible for the deaths of thousands of Russians, boyars and peasants, in orgies of slaughter carried out at Ivan's command; they were the equivalent of Vlad Ţepeş' *armas*.

One of the Tsar's victims was Boris Telupa, a prince who had annoyed him. He was:

drawn upon a long sharp-made stake, which entered the lower part of his body and came out of his neck; upon which he survived for fifteen hours, talking to his mother who had been brought to behold the sight. After her son's death, she was given to one hundred gunners who defiled her to death and the Tsar's hungry hounds then devoured her flesh and bones.[14]

As with Ţepeş, we are quickly into unbelievable figures. Three years after the creation of the *Oprichniki*, Ivan unleashed them onto the city of Novgorod where 60,000 are said to have perished. For five weeks, a daily cohort of citizens was brought before Ivan in the main square, and men, women and children were tortured by flogging, slitting of noses, castration and having their tongues cut out before they were thrown into the River Volkhov to drown. Novgorod was Ivan's Braşov.

Most historians have categorized Ivan IV as insane, partly because he killed his own son in a fit of rage and partly because his rantings were so public. He would bang his head against the stone floor in front of church altars and scream and cry in full view of his astonished and terrified court. There is no record of such behaviour in the accounts of Vlad Ţepeş. Nor do we have any means of measuring his emotions; but perhaps that is the clue to his enduring legacy of evil. No one speaks of his temper, his mood swings, his tears or his laughter. We can only try to measure the man through his actions.

We can also hope to understand the Impaler by comparison with more modern examples of tyranny. The 'Saxon' stories compared him unfavourably with monsters of the past, like Nero and Diocletian; if such comparisons can be made with ancient personifications of evil, why not more recent cases? The comparisons depend on our definition of evil, a very wide concept indeed. At its simplest level, the adjective is defined by the *New Penguin English Dictionary* as 'not good morally; sinful or wicked; arising from bad character or conduct; causing discomfort or repulsion; offensive; disagreeable; pernicious or harmful'. As a noun it is defined as 'wickedness, sin; the fact of suffering misfortune or wrongdoing; something that brings sorrow, distress or calamity'. But these definitions are only of limited use, because concepts of morality differ. Miranda Twiss, for example, includes the schizophrenic Roman Emperor Caligula in the same book as England's King John; one was a certifiable lunatic, the other merely trying to centralize his power, exactly as Vlad Ţepeş was to do, but without impalement. The bloodthirsty Attila the Hun, responsible for the deaths of several thousand, is included in the same pages as Gregori Rasputin, as far as we know guilty of the murder of no one. And this illustrates the point. As Miss Twiss says:

> We do not really understand evil – often taking it as an absolute rather than as a comparative word. Our concept of evil in the twenty-first century is dramatically different from previous centuries.

Thus, any attempt to compare Ţepeş, very much a man of fifteenth-century Europe, with Josef Stalin, Adolf Hitler, Pol Pot and Idi Amin, very much men of the twentieth century, is, in the end, counter-productive; but the question had to be raised. Concepts of morality and *realpolitik* have changed. In regard to war, for example, the Geneva Convention has established a yardstick the Impaler would not have recognized. The revised version of 1929 insists that wounded or sick prisoners of war be respected and protected, not mutilated and killed. Pillage is specifically condemned, while all medieval armies, Christian and Muslim alike, regarded this as a perk. There is some relevance in comparison with all the above dictators, in that they too used terror in their capacity as ruthless heads of state to inspire fear and compel compliance, but there are more differences than similarities. As one of the 'generation dead' interviewed over the Internet by Tony Thorne commented:

> The Marquis de Sade, he was considered a very sick, very evil degenerate at one point; they have *clubs* for that kind of stuff now.[15]

And what sort of yardstick brands Adolf Hitler more of a monster than Josef Stalin? How can we measure the enormity of these crimes against the relatively lesser ones of Vlad Țepeș? People have a habit of forgetting and forgiving in some instances too quickly and in some instances not at all. So Myra Hindley, the Moors' murderess, waited in jail, never to be released. The paramilitary bombers, guilty of many more deaths, walk free: Josef Stalin said, 'A single death is a tragedy; a million deaths is a statistic.'

Or, as Edward Young wrote in the 1740s:

> One to destroy is murder by the law;
> And gibbets keep the lifted hand in awe;
> To murder thousands takes a specious name,
> War's glorious art, and gives immortal fame.[16]

> If any man whomsoever of the house of Israel, and of those come from elsewhere who sojourn among them, eat blood, I shall set my face against his soul and banish him from among his people.[17]

Vlad Dracula has not been banished from his people. The world's first Dracula Congress was held in May 1995, organized by the Transylvanian Society of Dracula, based in Bucharest, together with the Ministry of Tourism and Culture, the Romanian Institute of Military History, the Institute of Folklore and Ethnography and (perhaps inevitably, considering the West Coast obsession with vampires) the Center for Humanistic Studies, Santa Barbara, California. The purpose of the Congress was to evaluate Dracula both as Vlad Țepeș the historical figure who died 500 years ago, and as the literary and celluloid myth of more recent origin. Most of the historical papers were given by Romanian historians, dealing with written and oral sources. Matei Cazacu, for instance, considered Țepeș to have been a pawn in the Machiavellian game played by Matthias Corvinus who, arguably, made the Impaler the first victim of written propaganda. When Corvinus judged the time to be right he unleashed him as a force of terror. Both actions were manipulative, aimed to defend his own kingdom of Hungary. Others stressed Ţepeş' role in the light of incipient Romanian nationalism, as a hero defending his country's cause against bullying aggrandizement on all sides.

The Congress took to the road, moving from Bucharest (only just becoming fashionable in the Impaler's day because of its proximity to the Danube and the likelihood of Turkish attacks) to Braşov, scene of some of the most violent of Ţepeş' outrages, then on to Tîrgu Mureş, Bistriţa and the Borgo Pass.

Romania, with its legacy of Ceauşescu and failed Communism, is anxious in the twenty-first century to make money out of Ţepeş' memory. Ceauşescu propagated the idea of the Impaler as a pseudo-Communist hero fighting the evils of the 'capitalist' foreign merchants of Braşov. On the collapse of the Ceauşescu regime, the *voivod* achieved a new reputation, exemplified by Mihail Ungheanu in his book *The Falsification of Dracula*. The haunted ruins of the palace at Tîrgoviste, the crumbling relics of Poenari over the Argeş, the gaping grave at the island monastery of Snagov – all these are 'open to the public' in a way unthinkable in Ceauşescu's time and certainly in Vlad Ţepeş'. Yet the Romanians persist in divorcing the real flesh-and-blood man from his literary and mythic counterparts. To them he is Ţepeş', the Impaler, not the over-the-top creation of an Irish civil servant, but a prince of his people, a hero on a white horse whose actions, though harsh, are inevitably justifiable against the odds he faced. But, in the end, Vlad Dracula did not preserve Wallachia. His own nature was too unforgiving, his own reputation, whether deserved or not, too terrible. Within less than a generation after his death, his principality formed merely the western edge of the Ottoman Empire, whose conquests continued unabated.

Beyond Romania and the 'land beyond the forests' his legend is different. This was a man who nailed men's hats to their heads, who impaled mothers and their babies, swatting friend and foe alike as if they were flies. Before even more callous mass-murderers came along, he was the bogeyman to frighten us all, and he became over time the dread Count of the undead, the bloodthirsty vampire associated with Bram Stoker, Max Schreck, Bela Lugosi and Christopher Lee. He hovers in the night air of every vampire story written since 1897, and if we cannot see him, it is because he has shifted his shape once again. Gabriel Ronay in *The Shadow of the Vampire* makes some fascinating links between Vlad the Impaler and twentieth-century propaganda. He may be stretching things a little when he equates the Nazi obsession with ritual and purity of blood with the Dracula stories, but is probably quite correct when he refers to the work of the American Army's Psychological Warfare Division which produced posters of 'the Hun' as a monster with fangs and gave their GIs Stoker's novel as reading matter. As he says:

> The rulers who once used Dracula's deeds to justify their absolution have long since gone, together with their once mighty empires. The Russian despots and Nazi Übermenschen who made the myth an important strand in the cultural weave of their societies, have been obliterated. The crusading churches which found the scare engendered by the vampire myth in their dogmatic sparring are now at peace. Only Dracula the Undead lives on . . .

One of the great problems of history is that all too often we can only measure men by their deeds because we cannot know their innermost feelings. We see their faces, painted on canvas or carved into wood and stone, but we cannot see their hearts; and so, in the end, Vlad Ţepeş must remain his country's greatest enigma. Our concept of evil is subjective – each of us has our own interpretation. And the Impaler shows us many facets of his psyche, all of them partially hidden in the mists that curl among the reeds at the Snagov lake where he once lay buried. And hidden, too, by the mists of time. To most of us in the West, brought up on the Stoker and celluloid versions of the Impaler, his name still strikes a chord, still sends a certain shiver down the spine along with the music of the children of the night; the name of Vlad Ţepeş, son of the devil.

# THE DRACULEŞTI OF WALLACHIA

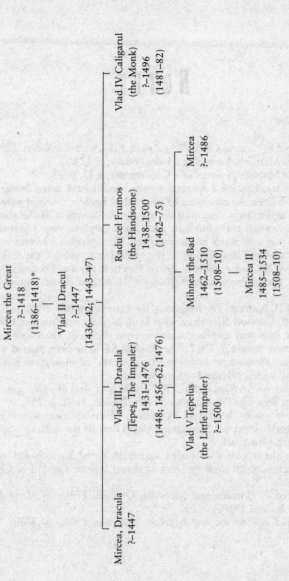

Mircea the Great
?–1418
(1386–1418)*

Mircea, Dracula
?–1447

Vlad II Dracul
?–1447
(1436–42; 1443–47)

Vlad III, Dracula
(Tepeş, The Impaler)
1431–1476
(1448; 1456–62; 1476)

Vlad V Tepelus
(the Little Impaler)
?–1500

Radu cel Frumos
(the Handsome)
1438–1500
(1462–75)

Mihnea the Bad
1462–1510
(1508–10)

Mircea II
1485–1534
(1508–10)

Mircea
?–1486

Vlad IV Caligarul
(the Monk)
?–1496
(1481–82)

*(The direct line of the Dracula family died out in 1659.)*

\* Dates in brackets refer to the years as prince of Wallachia

# NOTES

## Chapter One

1. Quoted in Victoria Clark, *Why Angels Fall*, Picador, 2000, p. 229.
2. Simon Marsden, *Journal of a Ghosthunter*, p. 124/5.
3. Simon Marsden, *Journal of a Ghosthunter*, n.32, p. 23.
4. In theory, Eastern European tombs should have fared better than English ones. An estimated 65 per cent of English medieval sepulchres were deliberately destroyed during the Reformation of the sixteenth century, when grave furniture and Gothic canopies were equated with Popery and the work of the antichrist. They received a second wave of hammer-blow destruction in the rabid Puritanism of the following century. No such systematic destruction took place in Romania.
5. In M. Parker-Pearson, *Archaeology of Death and Burial*, Sutton, 1999, p. 9.
6. D'A.J.D. Boulton, *The Knights of the Crown*, Boydell, 2000, p. 354–5.
7. Charles Dawson discovered what he claimed was the 'missing link', the exact half-way evolutionary creature between man and ape at Piltdown, Sussex in 1912. The cranium has since been proved to be a genuine Pleistocene *homo erectus*, but the all-important jaw-bone 'found' with it belonged to a modern ape.
8. Articles in *Archaeologica* 1934 by Tanner and Wright, quoted in Alison Weir *The Princes in the Tower*, Pimlico, 1992, p. 257.
9. Translation by Raymond McNally of Russian manuscripts in the Kirillov-Belozersky Monastery Collection of the Saltykov-Schedin Library, Leningrad.
10. From the account of Fedor Kuritsyn in the Kirillov-Belozersky Collection. Both these versions of events will be assessed in Chapter Eleven.
11. Quoted in Florescu and McNally, *Dracula: Prince of Many Faces*, Little Brown, 1989, p. 175.
12. Quoted in Florescu and McNally, *Dracula: Prince of Many Faces*, p. 175.

## Chapter Two

1. Tony Thorne, *Children of the Night*, Indigo, 2000, p. 237.
2. Directed by Neil Jordan with screenplay by Anne Rice from her novel, released in 1994.

# Notes

3. Thorne *Children of the Night*, p. 247.
4. Alexander Walker, London *Evening Standard*, 1994.
5. Thorne, *Children of the Night*, p. 248.
6. *Salem's Lot: the Movie* from the novel by Stephen King, Warner/Serendipity Productions, 1979.
7. *The Lost Boys*, directed by Joel Schumacher. Warner, 1987.
8. Quoted in Thorne, *Children of the Night*, p. 249.
9. *Blacula*, written by Joan Torres and Walter Koenig, Movielab, 1972.
10. *The Fearless Vampire Killers* (British title *Dance of the Vampires*), MGM/Cadre Films/Filmways, 1967.
11. *Halliwell's Guide*.
12. Quoted in Nigel Blunden, *Encyclopedia of Serial Killers*, PRC, London, 1996, p. 126.
13. *Dracula: Dead and Loving It*. Polygram/Castlerock/Gaumont/Brookesfilm, 1995.
14. *The Sunday Times*, 1995.
15. *The Vampire Lovers*, MGM–EMI/Hammer, 1970.
16. *Lust for a Vampire*, Hammer, 1970.
17. Thorne, *Children of the Night*, p. 43.
18. Thorne, *Children of the Night*, p. 43.
19. *Dracula*, directed by Terence Fisher, produced by Anthony Hinds. Rank/ Hammer, 1958.
20. David Pirie, *The Vampire Cinema*, p. 124.
21. Quoted in Daniel Farson, *Vampires, Zombies and Monster Men*, Aldus/Jupiter, 1975, p. 40.
22. Christopher Frayling, *Radio Scotland*, Interview, 1997.
23. Basil Copper, *The Vampire in Legend, Fact and Art*, Corgi, 1975, p. 151.
24. *Dracula, Prince of Darkness*, Warner/Hammer/Seven Arts, 1966.
25. Copper, *The Vampire in Legend, Fact and Art*, p. 136.
26. The original quotation from Stoker's novel reads 'I am Dracula. And I bid you welcome, Mr Harker, to my house.' Wordsworth Classic Edition, 1993, p. 15.
27. See Chapter Three.
28. The film was cut by seven minutes before it reached the censors, thereby avoiding further problems. By contrast, James Whale's *Frankenstein*, released in the following year, ran into problems from the National Society for the Prevention of Cruelty to Children because of the now infamous scene with Boris Karloff's monster and the little girl at the lake. In the original screenplay, the mad professor's creation throws her into the water; even Karloff's toning down of this caused uproar.
29. Pirie, *The Vampire Cinema*, p. 54.
30. Sadly, in his *The Vampire*, occultist Montague Summers (1928), referring to the Hungarian's performance in the stage play, calls him Bela Lugoni! Summers, p. 337.
31. Strictly speaking, the very first was George Meliès' *Le Manoir du*

*Diable* of 1886 and the second, the now lost Swedish *Vampyr* of 1912. The first full-length filming of Bram Stoker's novel was done in Berlin in 1920, but was a Hungarian production, *Drakula*.

32. *Nosferatu the Vampyre*, Gaumont/Werner Hertzog, 1979.
33. See Chapter Four.
34. *Shadow of the Vampire*, Saturn/BBC Films, 2001.
35. Farson, *Vampires, Zombies and Monster Men*, p. 42.
36. Letter from Huntley to the author, quoted in Copper, *The Vampire in Legend, Fact and Art*, p. 125.
37. Quoted in Farson, *Vampires, Zombies and Monster Men*, p. 27.
38. For a very detailed breakdown of the various runs see Summers *The Vampire*, p. 335–7. Summers also contends that during the London run, a nurse was on hand for anyone 'overcome owing to the horrors of the drama' (Summers, p. 356) and that later, the whole cast appeared in front of the curtain to reassure the audience that the play was 'comically intended for their entertainment. So gross a lapse of good manners,' Summers goes on, 'not to speak of the artistic indecorum, is hardly credible.'
39. *Bram Stoker's Dracula*, Columbia Tristar, 1992.

*Chapter Three*

1. The vampire as a folkloric myth is discussed in the next chapter, but as I focus largely on Eastern Europe, it is best to discuss this Irish version here. The *Leannan-sidhe* is a faery mistress who lures unsuspecting mortals into an underworld of the ancestral dead. She can change her shape, usually into that of a white fawn or kid, and is particularly drawn to poets or creative people generally. She is invisible to all but her victim. Vampirologist Elizabeth Miller believes that Stoker's *Dracula* has far more in common with Celtic/Gothic traditions than Transylvanian folklore.
2. Christopher Frayling, *Nightmare: The Birth of Horror*, BBC Books, 1996, p. 82.
3. Whitman, son of a New York carpenter, had a number of careers before settling to journalism. His finest collection of poems, *Leaves of Grass*, eventually running to 440 pages, was first published in 1855, although Whitman added to it as his experiences developed. The most telling of these was the four years he spent as a medical orderly with the Union Army in the Civil War, which left him shattered and prematurely aged. He was an invalid and recluse after 1873 and most of his correspondence with Stoker dates from this time.
4. The Pre-Raphaelite Brotherhood dated from mid-century, centring on artists like Burne-Jones, William Holman Hunt, Ford Madox Brown and Dante Gabriel Rossetti. Their themes were usually literary, classical or biblical; romantic medievalism crept into the work of Jones especially.

# NOTES

5. F.K. Robinson, *Glossary of Words Used in the Neighbourhood of Whitby*.
6. Edgar Allen Poe (1809–49), tragically found dead at forty in a Baltimore street, wearing somebody else's clothes, was the acknowledged master of the macabre. 'Weird, wild, fantastic' are the words used to describe him in Chambers *Biographical Dictionary*, 'dwelling by choice on the horrible, Poe's genius was yet great and genuine'.
7. Quoted in Frayling, *Nightmare*, p. 106.
8. All quoted in Frayling, *Nightmare*, p. 106.
9. Summers, *The Vampire*, Dorset Press, 1929, p. 334.
10. Quoted in Daniel Farson, *Vampires, Zombies and Monster Men*, p. 40.
11. James Twitchell, *The Living Dead – a Study of the Vampire in Romantic Literature*, Duke University Press, 1981.
12. Quoted in Frayling, *Nightmare*, p. 107.
13. Frayling, Radio Scotland Interview, *The Usual Suspects*, 23 December 1997.
14. Frayling Radio Scotland Interview, *The Usual Suspects*, 23 December 1997.
15. Bram Stoker, *Dracula*.
16. Frayling, *Nightmare*, p. 74.
17. Quoted in L. Adler and R. Dalby *The Dervish of Windsor Castle*, Bachman & Turner, London, 1979, p. 149.
18. Quoted in Adler and Dalby, *The Dervish of Windsor Castle*, p. 151.
19. Quoted in Frayling, *Nightmare*, p. 82.
20. Summers, *The Vampire*, p. x.
21. From Rymer, *Varney the Vampire*, 1846.
22. Quoted in Clive Leatherdale, *Dracula: The Novel and the Legend*, Desert Island Books, 1993.
23. Review, *Daily Variety*, 1986.
24. Quoted in Radu Florescu, *In Search of Frankenstein*, Robson Books, 1999, p. 98.
25. Florescu, *In Search of Frankenstein*, p. 109.
26. Quoted in Frayling, *Nightmare*, p. 75.
27. *The Diary of John Polidori*, quoted in Florescu, *In Search of Frankenstein*, p. 131.
28. Summers, *The Vampire*, p. 294.
29. Rosemary Herbert (ed.), *The Oxford Companion to Crime and Mystery Writing*, OUP, p. 189.
30. Claire Bloom, *Gothic Horror*, London 1998.
31. Quoted in Leatherdale, *Dracula: the Novel and the Legend*, p. 128.

## Chapter Four

1. Nigel Jackson, *Compleat Vampyre*, Capell Bann, 1997, p. 88.
2. Summers, *The Vampire*, p. 1.

# VLAD THE IMPALER

3. Voltaire (1694–1778) was destined for the bar and a diplomatic career. Instead, however, he became a satirist, and was banished from Paris at the age of twenty for his outspoken criticism. In and out of royal favour, Voltaire spent as much time in exile or the Bastille as he did at court. His tolerance and cynicism in many ways made him the epitome of the Enlightenment.

4. John Locke's expression of classical liberal ideas struck a chord with Voltaire when he was exiled to England in the 1730s. Shaftesbury was the third Earl, a philosopher and politician who had been taught by Locke. John Trenchard wrote at the turn of the eighteenth century, usually as 'Cato', criticizing standing armies and the corruption of government under William III and Anne. He was a keen advocate of freedom of speech. Anthony Collins was a friend and disciple of Locke and a champion of the deistic theory that God's existence could be established by reason, not revelation.

5. Quoted in Jackson, *Compleat Vampyre*, p. 3.

6. Ian Woodward, *The Werewolf Delusion*, Paddington Press, 1979, p. 150.

7. Quoted in Farson, *Vampires, Zombies and Monster Men*, p. 63.

8. As a young historian investigating Victorian death and spiritualism, I visited the cemetery with my wife on a gloriously sunny day in 1975. Special permission had to be sought because of the vandalism of the previous year. Highgate Cemetery was appallingly overgrown, with thick impenetrable foliage blacking out the sun of the June day. Mausolea had been broken into, tombs smashed open and funeral-pall-wrapped cadavers were exposed to the dim light. There were some sepulchres my wife would not let me go near and I was secretly pretty glad of that!

9. Quoted in Farson, *Vampires, Zombies and Monster Men*, p. 15.

10. Gervase of Tilbury (*c.* 1150–1220) was a lecturer on canon law at the university of Bologna. *Otia Imperialia* was a collection of historical and geographical oddities written for the Holy Roman Emperor, Otto IV.

11. Nicholas of Cusa (1401–64) was a contemporary of Vlad Țepeș. Active at the Council of Basle in 1432, he became a diplomat for the pope and was made cardinal in 1448. His best-known work is *De docta ignorantia* (1440) but he also wrote on cosmology and mathematics.

12. Giovanni Cibo (1432–92) was an exact contemporary of the Impaler, but outlived him by sixteen years. A warmonger and crusade-urger, Innocent caused a scandal by rampant nepotism, and his involvement in European politics led to the Vatican being besieged by the Roman nobility.

13. Bill of Innocent VIII, 1484. Quoted in James Sprenger and Heinrich Kramer, *Malleus Maleficarum* with foreword by Montague Summers, Arrow, 1986.

14. Heinrich Kramer was a Dominican from Alsace who became Inquisitor for the Catholic Church in the Tyrol, Salzburg, Bohemia and

Moravia in the 1470s, the decade of Vlad Dracula's death. James Sprenger was born in Basle and became a zealous Master of Theology at Cologne University. An inveterate traveller throughout Germany, he died suddenly in December 1495 and was buried at Strasbourg.

15. Rather alarmingly, the occultist Montague Summers, writing learnedly on vampires in the late 1920s, was impressed by this vicious book, calling it 'supremely authoritative' (Summers, *The Vampire*, p. 165). In terms of the negative influence *Malleus* wielded at the time of the Inquistion, it can fairly be likened to Hitler's *Mein Kampf* as a bible of terror.

16. Quoted in Rossell Robbins, *The Encyclopedia of Witchcraft and Demonology*, Peter Nevill, 1959, p. 254.

17. Guazzo was a Catholic friar operating as assessor in witch trials throughout Germany and Northern Italy in the early seventeenth century. Hopelessly gullible, he was prepared to believe anything: thus, he declared a Belgian had fathered a child by a cow. The offspring grew up instructed as a Christian, but chewing the cud and eating grass! In Guazzo's scheme of things, Martin Luther was the devil's son.

18. Robbins, *The Encyclopedia of Witchcraft and Demonology*, p. 254.

19. Thomas Aquinas (1224–74) was a Benedictine trained at the University of Naples. Canonized in 1323, his writings had huge influence on the Medieval Church, especially the Dominicans, whose order he joined in 1244. He was undoubtedly a first-rate thinker, although his knowledge of Greek and Homer, and indeed of history, was very slight.

20. Robbins, *The Encyclopedia of Witchcraft and Demonology*, p. 256.

21. *The Undead*, London, 1971.

22. Quoted in Jackson, *Compleat Vampyre*, p. 42.

23. Quoted in Jackson, *Compleat Vampyre*, p. 55.

24. Stoker, *Dracula*.

25. Quoted in Jackson, *Compleat Vampyre*, p. 66.

26. The barguest is a black dog found in Yorkshire folklore. Typically, it had huge glowing eyes and presaged death to all who saw it. Shriker is the name given to the creature across the Pennines in Lancashire and Shuck is the East Anglian variant. For a fascinating recital of appearances by mystic hounds, see Janet and Colin Bord, *Alien Animals*, BCA, 1981.

27. Interestingly, Bela Lugosi's eyes were blue. The director of *Dracula* used beams of light shone through a cardboard filter to give them extra reflection.

28. A fascinating and recent example is the 'Foo fighters', unexplained lights that appeared to fighter pilots in the closing stages of the Second World War. For a fuller explanation, see Nick Pope and Mei Trow, *Open Skies, Closed Minds*, Simon and Schuster, 1996.

29. Quoted in Nigel Jackson, *Compleat Vampyre*.

30. Jackson, *Compleat Vampyre*, p. 81–2.

31. Gaius Plinius Secundus (23–79) commanded cavalry on the Danubian

frontier of the Roman Empire and finished his epic *Historica Naturalis* two years before his death. He made no attempt to distinguish between fact and legend, but his work remains a fascinating collection of Roman lore. He died of suffocation in the choking fumes of Vesuvius in the eruption of AD 79.

32. Henricus Agrippa von Nettesheim (1486–1535) was a diplomat, teacher, soldier and an agent of the Emperor Maximilian I. His most famous work was *De Occulta Philosophia*, written in 1510 and enlarged twenty years later. Intriguingly, in connection with the shape-shifting qualities of vampires, Agrippa owned a black dog called Monsieur, which ate from his table and slept in his bed.

33. John Mandeville (probably a pseudonym) wrote *The Voyage and Travels of Sir John Mandeville, Knight* in 1366. The real author was either the French doctor Jehan de Bourgoyne or Jean d'Outrmeuse. The travelogue is mostly a compilation of other works, but involves discussion of Turkey, Persia, North Africa and India.

34. Quoted in Jackson, *Compleat Vampyre*, p. 105.

35. Stoker, *Dracula*.

36. Quoted in Farson, *Vampires, Zombies and Monster Men*, p. 18.

37. Quoted in Thorne, *Children of the Night*, p. 56.

38. Farson, *Vampires, Zombies and Monster Men*, p. 18.

39. Quoted in Thorne, *Children of the Night*, p. 63.

40. Quoted in Thorne, *Children of the Night*, p. 67.

41. Voltaire, *Dictionnaire Philosophique*.

42. Christopher Frayling contends that 'sunlight is Stoker'. In other words, the vampire's inability to cope with daylight is a literary invention for the novel *Dracula*, rather as the *tricoteuses* (knitters) clacking away with their needles as the aristocrats' heads bounced from the guillotine in the Place de la Concorde is almost certainly the invention of Charles Dickens for *A Tale of Two Cities*.

43. Quoted in Farson, *Vampires, Zombies and Monster Men*, p. 31.

44. Jessica Snyder Sachs, *Time of Death*, QPD, 2002.

45. Farson, *Vampires, Zombies and Monster Men*, p. 34.

46. Summers, *The Vampire*, p. 34.

47. Martin Luther launched his attack in 1517 with his famous ninety-five theses nailed to the door of Wittenberg Cathedral. Calvin, Melanchthon, Zwingli and others emerged to become sectarian leaders of the Protestant faith before the papacy launched its counter-attack in the 1540s, exemplified by the burning of heretical books, the creation of the Jesuit Order and the unleashing of the Holy Inquisition.

*Chapter Five*

1. *Herodotus* vol. 2, trans. A.D. Godley, quoted in Kurt W. Treptow, *Vlad III: Dracula*, Center for Romanian Studies, Iaşi, Romania, 2000, p. 21.

# NOTES

2. Aeneas Silvinius Piccolomini, *Cosmographia*, quoted in Treptow, *Vlad III: Dracula*, p. 19.

3. *Slavs and Turks: the Borderlands of Islam in Europe*, the Leisure Hour Office, Paternoster Row, London, 1880.

4. Technically, the legions withdrew on the orders of Lucius Domitus Aurelineaus, the Emperor Aurelian, himself probably a native of Dacia, who abandoned the area to the Goths raiding south. Popular and militarily capable, he was given the title Restituter Orbis (restorer of the world), rather ironic in view of his Dacian policy, and was assassinated by his own officers near Byzantium.

5. Piccolomini, *Cosmographia*, quoted in Treptow, *Vlad III: Dracula*, p. 19.

6. A violent argument seems to be currently raging on the Internet between J.P. Holding and Richard Carrier on the efficacy of this. The links with Ţepeş seem to me far more relevant.

7. Letter from Batu to Bela IV, 1240, quoted in Robert Marshall, *Storm from the East*, BBC Books, 1993, p. 108.

8. Unattributed source quoted in *Storm from the East*, Robert Marshal, BCA, London, p. 117.

9. Victoria Clark, *Why Angels Fall*, Picador 2000, p. 208.

10. *The New Penguin English Dictionary*, London 2000.

11. For instance, the Percy family held the Marcher lordships on the Scots border in return for halting Scots raids. The Earls of Norfolk became Marshals, officiating at royal ceremonies. The Dymoke family eventually became hereditary Royal Champions and so on.

12. Kurt W. Treptow, ed., *Dracula: Essays on the Life and Times of Vlad Ţepeş*, East European Monographs, New York, 1991.

13. Guy Bois, *The Crisis of Feudalism*, Cambridge, 1984.

14. Rodney Hilton, *Class Conflict and the Crisis of Feudalism*, London, 1985.

15. The name comes either from the leather jacks or jerkins worn by the rebels or Jacques Bonhomme, the generic term for a French peasant.

16. Clark, *Why Angels Fall*, p. 208.

17. The town was described by traveller Emily Gerrard in 1883, 'The top-heavy overhanging gables, the deserted watch-towers, the ancient ramparts, the crooked streets . . . all combine to give the impression of a past which has scarcely gone and of a present which has not yet penetrated.' Quoted in Burford, *Hiking Guide to Romania*, p. 277.

18. Letter from Vlad Ţepeş to the Council of Braşov, 1456, quoted from the Latin in Florescu and McNally, *Dracula: Prince of Many Faces*, p. 112.

19. The Cathars (from the Greek meaning puritan) were a late twelfth-century sect later based at Albi in southern France. They were considered heretic by the Catholic Church because they believed in two Gods – the God of the New Testament who created a beautiful, invisible and spiritual world; and the God of the Old Testament, representing all that was earthly and evil. The heresy was crushed by Pope Innocent III in 1245.

20. Matthew Spinks, *A History of Christianity in the Balkans*, Chicago, 1933.

21. From Chedomil Mijatovich, *Constantine, the last Emperor of the Greeks*, London, 1892, quoted in Treptow, *Essays*, p. 72.

22. Flavius Constantinus, *c.* 274–337, was the first Roman Emperor to be baptized, and Christianity became the state religion of the Empire in 324. Having won the throne by intrigue and war – there were for a time five rivals for the purple – he executed his own wife and son for plotting against him.

23. Clark, *Why Angels Fall*, p. 402.

24. From the poem 'Lepanto', by G.K. Chesterton, describing the brilliant naval victory over the Turks by the galleys of Don John of Austria in 1571.

25. In 1943, in removing the Jews of Kraków from their ghetto to the labour camp at Plazsov, the Nazi commandant Amon Goeth told his soldiers that they were ending 600 years of history.

26. The often misquoted line comes from the poem 'To Helen' by Edgar Allan Poe.

## Chapter Six

1. Sheila Bignall, 'Who was Nicolas von Popplau?' *Ricardian Register,* Vol. XXII, No. 3, 1997, quoted in Bertram Fields, *Royal Blood*, Sutton, 2000, p. 280.

2. Quoted in McNally and Florescu, *In Search of Dracula*, p. 79.

3. Not to be confused with the more famous Kronstadt in Russia, the naval base that was the scene of the naval mutiny in 1917.

4. McNally and Florescu, *In Search of Dracula*, p. 87.

5. This translation is by Raymond T. McNally.

6. Quoted in Treptow, *Dracula: Essays*, p. 193–4.

7. The translation is from Peter Panaitescu.

8. Herod the Great, ruler of Palestine in Roman times. He would have been well known to the monks of St Gallen as a tyrant and the evidence against him is quite compelling. Whether or not he sentenced the first-born of every household to death in search of the infant Christ, he certainly slaughtered wholesale on the merest suspicion of opposition to his reign and even ordered the execution of his wife Mariamne and their two sons. Nero, Roman Emperor from AD 54 to 68 AD was certainly, recent research has revealed, more sinned against than sinning. The story of his violin solo while his city burned around him is nonsense, but he was certainly vain, extravagant and sexually debauched. Unlike Herod, who simply issued orders, there is strong evidence that Nero killed his wife Poppaea by kicking her during pregnancy. He executed Antonia, Claudius' daughter, because she rejected his proposal of marriage, and eliminated talented Romans such as Seneca and Lucan probably because they were better writers than he was. Gaius Diocletianus was proclaimed

emperor by the Roman army in 284. An inveterate and successful soldier, he spent much of his time defending his empire and holding it together. The probably reason for his inclusion here is his persecution of the Christians in 303, in which, in four edicts, he attempted to wipe out the sect. The resulting purge created two victims who would become saints by Vlad Dracula's time – the twelve-year-old Agnes, naked and beheaded under the arches of Domitian's stadium, and the soldier Sebastian, riddled with arrows and bludgeoned to death by the emperor's guard.

9. The term berserker is usually associated with the Norse warriors, the bear-shirts whose violence on the battlefield was legendary. Interestingly, Bram Stoker uses the term in Dracula where he wrongly attributes the Count's descent from the Szekelys – 'Here, in the whirlwind of European races, the Ugric tribe [Magyars] bore down from Iceland the fighting spirit which Thor and Wodin gave them, which their Berserkers displayed to such fell intent on the seaboards of Europe . . .'. A better translation for our purposes in relation to the Impaler is 'madman'.

10. Pagans would be those beyond the extent of the Christian Church, the Ottoman Turks to the south-east or the Tartars beyond the Black Sea. Jews, except in Casimir the Great's Poland, were treated with varying degrees of contempt. Heretics, whose definitions would be constantly shifting at the whim of what Orthodox and Catholic doctrine decided *was* heretical, were increasingly the targets of the Holy Inquisition.

11. All translations of the Russian tales are by Raymond T. McNally.

12. Intriguingly, shortly before his hasty and farcical trial in December 1989, Nicolae Ceaușescu offered a bribe to Major Ion Secu, responsible for his captivity, running to one or two million dollars, 'and until I have access to that kind of money, I know a cache here in Voinesti [a village near Tîrgoviste] where I can lay my hands on hundreds of thousands of lei'. Quoted in Behr, *Kiss the Hand You Cannot Bite*, p. 16. Later searches by the new Romanian government revealed nothing.

13. The classic is *Struwwelpeter*, Heinrich Hoffman's tales for children, 1845.

14. There is a similar gulf, for instance, between the Norman and Angevin kings of England, speaking Latin and medieval French as opposed to the Old and Middle English of their subjects.

15. Quoted in Florescu and McNally, *Dracula: Prince of Many Faces*, p. 219.

*Chapter Seven*

1. Robert W. Thurston, 'The Spawning of Satan', *BBC History Magazine*, Vol. 3, No. 5, May 2002.

2. Quoted in Stephen Friar, *A New Dictionary of Heraldry*, Alpha Books, 1987, p. 380.

3. Genesis 3:14.
4. *The Anglo Saxon Chronicle.*
5. Peter Dickinson, *The Flight of Dragons*, Pierrot Publishing Ltd, 1979, p. 128.
6. By the sixteenth century, *dragon* was the name given to the ornately carved dragon's head or serpentine that formed the firing mechanism of wheel-lock pistols.
7. Revelations, 12: 1–9.
8. Quoted in Florescu and McNally, *Dracula: Prince of Many Faces*, p. 34.
9. Jason Goodwin, *Lords of the Horizons*, Vintage, 1999, p. 12.
10. The *Holy Qur'an* Surah 2 Al-Baqarah trs. Abdullah Yusuf Ali. Wordsworth Editions, Brighton, 2000.
11. Quoted in McNally, 'Vlad Tepes in Romanian folklore', in Treptow, *Dracula: Essays.*
12. A promise, astonishingly, still being offered to the hijackers of the aircraft that attacked the World Trade Center in New York on 11 September 2001.
13. Similar weaknesses and divisions in England would lead in the next century to the highly destructive Wars of the Roses.
14. Quoted in D'Arcy Boulton, *The Knights of the Crown*, p. 350.
15. Christopher Marlowe, like many educated Elizabethans, was fascinated by the man. His play *Tamburlaine,* the second in history to be written in blank verse, took London's theatrical world by storm in 1585.
16. Quoted in Florescu and McNally, *Dracula: Prince of Many Faces*, p. 38.

*Chapter Eight*

1. Goodwin, *Lords of the Horizon*, p. 8.
2. Halil Inalcik, *The Ottoman Empire*, Phoenix, London, 2000.
3. Anon, *Slavs and Turks: the Borderlands of Islam in Europe*, London, 1880, p. 26.
4. Quoted in Inalcik, *The Ottoman Empire*, p. 8.
5. Adam of Usk, *Chronicon*, quoted in Steven Runciman, *The Fall of Constantinople*, Cambridge University Press, 1965, p. 1.
6. Goodwin, *Lords of the Horizon*, p. 15.
7. From the *Annales* of William of Worcester, quoted in Paul Murray Kendall, *Richard the Third*, George Allen and Unwin 1955, p. 28.
8. Quoted in Burford, *Hiking Guide to Romania*, p. 286.
9. For instance Constantin Rezachevici, who also claims that the boy was legitimate.
10. Even in the West, kings and scions of great houses acknowledged and looked after their bastards. In late seventeenth-century England, Charles II saw all thirteen of his handsomely taken care of.

# NOTES

11. Florescu and McNally, *Dracula: Prince of Many Faces*, p. 46.
12. Quoted in Halil Inalcik, *The Ottoman Empire*, p. 90.
13. Documents 80–99 in *Documenta Romanice Historica*, Vol. 1, quoted in Treptow, *Vlad III: Dracula*, p. 46.
14. The epithet came from the fact that Hunyadi was a Vlach. This, in the welter of languages used in the various courts of Europe, became corrupted to 'blanche', i.e. white.
15. Marsden, *The Journal of a Ghosthunter*, p. 104.
16. Marsden, *The Journal of a Ghosthunter*, p. 105–6.
17. Allen Brown, ed., *Castles: a History and Guide*, Blandford Press, 1985.
18. See Chapter Ten for details of the rigorous training of these boys; see Halil Inalcik, *The Ottoman Empire*, p. 78–88.
19. Unattributed source in Florescu and McNally, *Dracula: Prince of Many Faces*, p. 54.
20. Quoted in Florescu and McNally, *Dracula: Prince of Many Faces*, p. 59.
21. Alexander (356–323 BC) was the king of Macedonia, north of Greece. A pupil of the philosopher Aristotle, he may or may not have been involved in the death of his father, Philip, in order to seize the throne. He defeated the Persian Empire, then marched south through Palestine to take Egypt, founding Alexandria. He crossed into India and had plans to conquer Arabia before he died, possibly of food poisoning after a banquet. His military feats are astonishing and it was no doubt seeing Kastrioti in action in the field that led to Murad's nickname for him.
22. All these details can be found in Halil Inalcik, *The Ottoman Empire*, p. 79–83.
23. See *Malleus Maleficarum*, 1486, for one of the most anti-feminist books ever written.
24. Quoted in Malise Ruthven, *Islam in the World*, Penguin, 1984, p. 169.
25. Quoted in Halil Inalcik, *The Ottoman Empire*, p. 89.
26. Typical of Britain's obsession with the supposedly appalling behaviour of the East is well illustrated in the 1828 novel *The Lustful Turk*. Admittedly, the evil Dey is an Algerian pirate and the sex 'normal' – 'indeed, my cries seemed only to excite him to the finishing of my ruin' – but it is followed up with black eunuchs administering floggings and the reader is left with the idea that such people are capable of anything.
27. Florescu and McNally, *Dracula: Prince of Many Faces*, p. 32.
28. Quoted in Kendall, *Richard III*, p. 56.
29. Quoted in John Carey ed. *The Faber Book of Reportage*, 1987, p. 391.
30. Quoted in Carey, *Reportage*, p. 284.
31. Lit. a ride out, the term was widely used in Europe at the time for a campaign.
32. Quoted in Florescu and McNally, *Dracula: Prince of Many Faces*, p. 62.

# Vlad the Impaler

## Chapter Nine

1. *Expuneia istorice*, Chalkondyles. The Greek confuses, as several contemporaries did, Dracula and his father. At this stage, with Dracula still a boy in Hunyadi's eyes and his fate at Turkish hands possibly unknown to him, he did not have any animosity towards him. 'Dracula' here clearly refers to Vlad Dracul.

2. Translated by Nicholae Iorga, quoted as Appendix A. Treptow, *Dracula: Essays*.

3. In a curious abnegation of power, Murad abdicated in favour of the twelve- year-old Mehmed in 1444, ostensibly to avoid the usual bout of murder on a sultan's accession. The plan backfired, however, and a janissary revolt in May 1446 brought Murad back to the throne.

4. Quoted in Treptow, *Vlad III: Dracula*, p. 58.

5. Quoted in Treptow, *Vlad III: Dracula*, p. 60.

6. Quoted in Florescu and McNally, *Dracula: Prince of Many Faces*, p. 75.

7. Quoted in Florescu and McNally, *Dracula: Prince of Many Faces*, p. 77.

8. Despatch from Niccolò Modrussa to Pope Pius II, *c.* 1466, quoted in Florescu and McNally *Dracula, Prince of Many Faces*, p. 85.

9. If we accept 1431 as the accurate date of Ţepeş' birth, he was forty-five when he died.

10. Gonsalvus's condition is the first recorded example of a hirsute child. In terms of eastern and western philosophies, journalists in America and Europe use hysterical phrases to describe later examples of the condition – 'freak', 'mutant', wolf-boy', 'monkey-boy'. The Chinese just call them *mao hai*, 'hairy children'.

11. All this information is contained in Treptow, *Vlad III: Dracula* and originates from Romanian historian Nicolae Stoicescu, *Sfatul domnesc so marii dregatori din Tara Romanesca şi Moldova, sec XIV–XVII* (The Council and officials of Romania and Moldavia from the fourteenth to the seventeenth centuries) Bucharest, 1968.

12. The twelve- or thirteen-man firing squad was composed largely of Lithuanians or Latvians.

13. These were issued to mark the quincentenary of Dracula's death in 1976.

14. Quoted in Florescu and McNally, *Dracula: Prince of Many Faces*, p. 119.

15. Quoted in Nicolae Stoicescu, 'Relations with Transylvania' *Essays*, ed. Treptow, p. 93.

16. Quoted in Florescu and McNally, *Dracula: Prince of Many Faces*, p. 101.

17. The use of this word is fascinating. It emanates from the Athenian law-giver Draco who in 621 BC revised the city's laws so that death was the penalty for almost any offence. Its similarity to the dragon epithet is merely a coincidence, but an extraordinary one.

# Notes

18. All quotations here are from Treptow, *Vlad III: Dracula*, p. 116–17.
19. Quoted in Florescu and McNally, *Dracula: Prince of Many Faces*, p. 188.
20. Kuritsyn.

*Chapter Ten*

1. Quoted in Goodwin, *Lords of the Horizons*, p. 41.
2. Goodwin, *Lords of the Horizons*, p. 54.
3. Quoted in Florescu and McNally, *Dracula: Prince of Many Faces*, p. 127.
4. Quoted in Florescu and McNally, *Dracula: Prince of Many Faces*, p. 128.
5. Quoted in Florescu and McNally, *Dracula: Prince of Many Faces*, p. 132.
6. Tursun Bey, *Tarih-i Ebu-i Feth-I Sultan Mehmed-an*, *c.* 1497.
7. Konstantin Mihailović, *Memoirs of a Janissary*.
8. Quoted in Florescu and McNally, *Dracula: Prince of Many Faces*, p. 132.
9. Letter from Vlad Ţepeş to Matthias Corvinus, 11 February 1462, quoted in Treptow, *Vlad III Dracula*, p. 183.
10. Quoted in Treptow, *Essays*, p. 316.
11. Quoted in Treptow, *Essays*, p. 184.
12. Quoted in Treptow, *Essays*, p. 316.
13. Quoted in Treptow *Essays*, p. 316.
14. Quoted in Florescu and McNally, *Dracula: Prince of Many Faces*, p. 136.
15. From the account of Laonic Chalkondyles.
16. Tursun Bey, *Tarih-i Ebu-i Feth-I Sultan Mehmed-an*, *c.* 1497.
17. Quoted in Goodwin, *Lords of the Horizons*, p. 66.
18. Compare Richard III's 'fellowship of steel' at Bosworth and the elite gentlemen corps of the Household Cavalry created on Charles II's restoration in 1660.
19. For the Turkish names of all these ranks, see David Nicolle, *The Janissaries*, Osprey Elite Series No. 58, p. 18–19.
20. Nicolle, *The Janissaries*, p. 20.
21. Bertrand de la Brocquière, quoted in David Nicolle, *The Janissaries*, p. 29.
22. Nicolle, *The Janissaries*, p. 32.
23. Quoted in J.M. Brereton, *The Horse in War*, David and Charles, 1976, p. 39.
24. The *Landsknechtes'* distinctive strips of coloured cloth were traditionally first worn in the year of Dracula's death in battle with Charles the Bold of Burgundy. The cloth came from the tents of his ransacked camp.
25. Quoted in Gerry Embleton and John Howe, *The Medieval Soldier*, Windrow and Greene, 1994, p. 24.

26. Quoted in Gerry Embleton and John Howe, *The Medieval Soldier*, p. 24.
27. Quoted in McNally and Florescu, *In Search of Dracula*, p. 198.
28. Quoted in Gerry Embleton and John Howe, *The Medieval Soldier*, p. 75.

*Chapter Eleven*

1. From the account of Laonic Chalkondyles.
2. Quoted in Treptow, *Essays*, p. 129.
3. Quoted in Treptow, *Essays*, p. 130.
4. Quoted in Treptow, *Essays*, p. 130.
5. Quoted in Florescu and McNally, *Dracula: Prince of Many Faces*, p. 144.
6. Tursun Bey, *Tarih-i Ebu-i Feth-i Sultan Mehmed an*.
7. Quoted in Florescu and McNally, *Dracula: Prince of Many Faces*, p. 144.
8. Tursun Bey, *Tarih-i Ebu-i Feth-i Sultan Mehmed an*.
9. From the account of Laonic Chalkondyles.
10. Tursun Bey, *Tarih-i Ebu-i Feth-i Sultan Mehmed an*.
11. Konstantin Mihailović, *Memoirs of a Janissary*.
12. Tursun Bey, *Tarih-i Ebu-i Feth-i Sultan Mehmed an*.
13. From the account of Laonic Chalkondyles.
14. Tursun Bey, *Tarih-i Ebu-i Feth-i Sultan Mehmed an*.
15. Quoted in Treptow, *Dracula: Essays*, p. 253–63.
16. Quoted in Treptow, *Essays*, p. 218.
17. In fact, the *direct* line of Vlad Dracula, via the offspring of his first and second marriages, died out in the early seventeenth century.
18. Quoted in Florescu and McNally, *Dracula: Prince of Many Faces*, p. 168.
19. Quoted in Florescu and McNally, *Dracula: Prince of Many Faces*, p. 169.
20. Quoted in Treptow, *Essays*, p. 319.
21. Quoted in Treptow, *Essays*, p. 320.
22. Quoted in Treptow, *Essays*, p. 320.

*Chapter Twelve*

1. Quoted in an article by Paul Harris, *Daily Mail*, 19 February 2002.
2. Brian Masters, 'The Banality of Evil', *Daily Mail*, 19 February 2002.
3. William Shakespeare, *Henry V* Act IV Sc. VIII.
4. These figures are quoted in William Seymour, *Battles in Britain*, Wordsworth Military Library, 1997, pp. 134 and 149.
5. The Dun Cow was originally a fairy beast that terrorised the

# Notes

Warwickshire countryside. Guy, according to folklore, was a squire to the Earl of Warwick in the tenth century. The Lambton worm was a dragon terrifying the locals near Penshaw in Durham at some vague time in the thirteenth century.

6. In the recent, *The Most Evil Men and Women in History*, Michael O'Mara, 2002.
7. All the translations of the 'Saxon' stories in this chapter are by Peter Panaitescu from *Dracula: Essays*, ed. Kurt Treptow, p. 188–96.
8. From a book written in 1583 by Sir Thomas Smith, quoted in *Rack, Rope and Red-hot Pincers*, Geoffrey Abbott, London, 1993, p. 3.
9. Quoted in Abbott, *Rack, Rope and Red-hot Pincers*, p. 70.
10. So too, in the Far West. There are photographs from the 1870s showing Apache adulterers with nose-tips missing.
11. Quoted in Abbott, *Rack, Rope and Red-hot Pincers*, Bouldhampton Press, p. 75.
12. Quoted in Abbott, *Rack, Rope and Red-hot Pincers*, p. 76.
13. The Dracula Conference was held in May 1995 at a number of venues throughout Romania.
14. All quotations from Worley are from the Dracula conference website http://members.tripod.com/_Baron91/WorleyImpaling.html.
15. Both quotations from Florescu and McNally, *Dracula: Prince of Many Faces*, p. 163.
16. Quoted in Robbins, *The Encyclopedia of Witchcraft and Demonology*.
17. Colin Wilson, *The Mammoth Book of Murder*, Robinson, 1990, p. 59.
18. In his political novel, *The Young Duke*.
19. Quoted in *The Mail on Sunday*, byline Emma Hartley, 18 November 2001.
20. John Symonds, *Renaissance in Italy* quoted in Brian Marriner, *A Century of Sex Killers*, Foreword by Colin Wilson. True Crime Library, 1992.

## Chapter Thirteen

1. Jessica Douglas-Home, *The Spectator*, 12 January 2002.
2. Quoted in *The Spectator*, 12 January 2002.
3. *Documente istorice slavo-române*, quoted in Treptow, *Vlad III: Dracula*, p. 111.
4. Quoted in J.J. Bagley, *Historical Interpretation*, Penguin Books, 1965, p 191.
5. Bagley, *Historical Interpretation*, p. 192.
6. Bagley, *Historical Interpretation*, p. 197.
7. Quoted in Bagley, *Historical Interpretation*, p. 199.
8. Jean Benedetti, *The Real Bluebeard*, Dorset Press 1971, p. 12.
9. Benedetti, *The Real Bluebeard*, p. 15.
10. Quoted in Benedetti, *The Real Bluebeard*, p. 17.

11. In Treptow, *Essays*, p. 163.
12. Treptow, *Essays*, p. 24.
13. Treptow, *Essays*, p. 167.
14. Quoted in Miranda Twiss, *The Most Evil Men and Women in History*, Michael O'Mara, 2002, p. 106.
15. Quoted in Thorne, *Children of the Night*, p. 186.
16. Edward Young, *The Complaint: Night Thoughts*, 1742–5.
17. Leviticus 17: 10–14.

# BIBLIOGRAPHY

Abbott, Geoffrey, *Rack, Rope and Red-hot Pincers*, London, 1933
Abraham, Gerald, *The Concise Oxford History of Music*, Oxford, OUP, 1979
Ahmed, Rollo, *The Black Art*, London, Arrow Books, 1996
Alder, L. and Dalby, R., *The Dervish of Windsor Castle*, London, Bachman & Turner, 1979
Ali, Abdullah Yusuf, (tr.), *Holy Qur'an*, Birmingham, Wordsworth, 2000
Anon, *The Real Prince Dracula*, www.geocites.com/athens/agean/7545/dracula.html
Aston, Margaret, *Panorama of the Renaissance*, London, Thames & Hudson, 2000
Bagley, J.J., Historical Interpretation
Barclay, Glen St John, *Anatomy of Horror*, London, Weidenfeld and Nicolson, 1978
Barraclough, Geoffrey, *The Times Atlas of World History*, London, HarperCollins, 1992
Behr, Edward, *Kiss the Hand You Cannot Bite*, London, Hamish Hamilton, 1991
Benedetti, Jean, *The Real Bluebeard*, New York, Dorset Press, 1971
Bennet, Matthew (ed.), *Hutchinson Dictionary of Ancient and Medieval Warfare*, London, Helicon, 1998
Blackmore, Howard L., *Arms and Armour*, London, Studio Vista, 1965
Blunden, Nigel, *Encyclopedia of Serial Killers*, PRC, London, 1996
Bois, Guy, *The Crisis of Feudalism*, Cambridge, 1984
Bord, Janet and Colin, *Alien Animals*, London, BCA, 1981
Boulton, D'A.J.D., *The Knights of the Crown*, Woodbridge, Suffolk, Boydell Press, 2000
Brady, Thomas et al. (eds), *Handbook of European History 1400–1600*, 2 vols, Michigan, William B. Eerdmans, 1996
Brereton, J.M., *The Horse in War*, Newton Abbott, David and Charles, 1976
Briggs, Asa, *Everyday Life Through the Ages*, London, Reader's Digest, 1992
Briggs, Katherine, *A Dictionary of Fairies*, London, Penguin, 1977
Brown, R. Allen, *Castles: a History and Guide*, Poole, Blandford Press, 1985
Burford, Tim, *A Hiking Guide to Romania*, Chalfont St Peter, Bradt Publications, 1993

Carey, John, *The Faber Book of Reportage*, London, Faber, 1989

Carter, Francis (ed.), *An Historical Geography of the Balkans*, London, Academic Press, 1977

Clark, Victoria, *Why Angels Fall*, London, Picador, 2001

Cohn, Norman, *Europe's Inner Demons*, London, Granada, 1976

Copper, Basil, *The Vampire in Legend, Fact and Art*, London, Corgi, 1973

Corfis, Ivy and Wolfe, Michael (eds), *The Medieval City Under Siege*, Woodbridge, Suffolk, Boydell Press, 1999

Dickinson, Peter, *The Flight & Dragons*, Pierrot Publishing, 1979

Dowley, Tim (ed.), *The History of Christianity*, Tring, Lion Publishing, 1977

Drury, Ian (ed.), *The Times History of War*, London, HarperCollins, 2000

Edge, David and Paddock, John, *Arms and Armour of the Medieval Knight*, London, Guild Publishing, 1988

Embleton, Gerry and Howe, John, *The Medieval Soldier*, London, Windrow and Greene, 1994

Ertug, Ahmet and Koluk, Ibrahim, *Topkapi: The Palace of Felicity*

Farrington, Karen, *Punishment and Torture*, London, Hamlyn, 1996

Farson, Daniel, *Vampires, Zombies and Monster Men*, London, Aldus/Jupiter, 1975

Fields, Bertram, *Royal Blood*, Stroud, Sutton, 1998

Fine, John, *The Late Medieval Balkans*, Michigan, UMP, 1994

Florescu, Radu and McNally, Raymond T., *Dracula: Prince of Many Faces*, Boston, Little Brown, 1989

Florescu, Radu, *In Search of Frankenstein*, London, Robson Books, 1999

Frayling, Christopher, *Nightmare: The Birth of Horror*, London, BBC Books, 1996

Friar, Stephen, *A New Dictionary of Heraldry*, London, A&C Black, 1987

Godley, A.D. (tr.), *Zalmoxis the God of the Gatae*, www.alexm.here.ru/mirrors

Goodwin, Jason, *Lords of the Horizons*, London, Random House, 1999

Hay, Denys, *Europe in the 14th and 15th Centuries*, London, Longman, 1966

Herbert, Rosemary, *The Oxford Companion to Crime and Mystery Writing*, OUP

Hindley, Geoffrey (ed.), *The Larousse Encyclopaedia of Music*, London, Hamlyn, 1993

Hinnells, John H., *A Handbook of Living Religions*, London, Penguin, 1991

Hinnells, John R., (ed.), *The Who's Who of Religions*, London, Penguin, 1991

Inalcik, Halil, *The Ottoman Empire*, London, Phoenix, 1994

Jackson, Nigel, *The Compleat Vampyre*, Chievley, Capall Ban, 1995

Jacob, E.F., *The Fifteenth Century*, Oxford, OUP, 1961

Kaplan, Robert D., *Balkan Ghosts*, New York, Vintage, 1993

Hilton, Rodney, *Class Conflict and the Crisis of Feudalism*, London 1985

Kightly, Charles, *The Perpetual Almanack of Folklore*, London, Thames & Hudson, 1987

# BIBLIOGRAPHY

Kramer, H. and Sprenger, J., *Malleus Maleficarum*, tr. Summers, M., London, Arrow Books, 1971

Laffont, Robert (ed.), *A History of Rome and the Romans*, London, Macdonald, 1960

Leatherdale, Clive, *Dracula: The Novel and the Legend*, Brighton, Desert Island Books, 1993

Macchiavelli, Niccolò, *The Prince*, London, Penguin, 1961

Maclagan, Michael, *Lines of Succession*, London, Little Brown, 1999

Marriner, Brian, *A Century of Sex Killers*, London, True Crime Library, 1992

Marsden, Simon, *Journal of a Ghosthunter*, London, Little Brown & Co, 1994

Marshall, Robert, *Storm from the East*, London, BCA, 1993

McNally, Raymond T. and Florescu, Radu, *In Search of Dracula*, London, Robson Books, 1994

Mellersh, H.E.L., *Hutchinson Chronology of World History*, Oxford, Helicon, 1999

Miller, Elizabeth, *Dracula the History of Myth and the Myth of History*, www.ucs.mun.ca/emiller/vladjotd.htm

Monaco, Richard and Burt, William, *The Dracula Syndrome*, London, Headline, 1993

Morley, John, *Death, Heaven and the Victorians*, London, Studio Vista, 1971

Murray Kendall, Paul, *Richard the Third* George Allen and Unwin, 1955

Newark, Tim, *Warlords*, London, Brockhampton Press, 1998

Nicolle, David, *The Janissaries*, London, Osprey, 1995

Otetea, Andre, *The History of the Romanian People*, Bucharest, Scientific Publishing House, 1970

Parker, Geoffrey (ed.), *The Age of Calamity*, Amsterdam, Time-Life, 1989

Parker-Pearson, Michael, *The Archaeology of Death and Burial*, Stroud, Sutton, 1999

Peterson, Harold L., *The Book of the Gun*, London, Hamlyn, 1962

Picknett, Lynn, *Encyclopaedia of the Paranormal*, London, Guild Publishing, 1990

Pirie, David, *The Vampire Cinema*, London, Galley Press, 1977

Porter, Ray, *The Historical Dracula: Vlad III Ţepeş*, www.nat.vu.nl/radu/Vlad.html

Ramsland, Katherine, *The Vampire Companion*, London, Little Brown, 1993

Raphael, Frederic, *Byron*, London, Thames & Hudson, 1982

Robbins, Rossell, *The Encyclopaedia of Witchcraft and Demonology*, London, Peter Nevill, 1959

Robinson, F.K., *Glossary of Words Used in the Neighbourhood of Whitby*

Ronay, Gabriel, *The Shadow of the Vampire*, www.hungary.com/hungq/no151/117.html

Runciman, Steven, *The Fall of Constantinople*, Cambridge, CUP, 1965

Ruthven, Malise, *Islam in the World*, London, Penguin, 1984

Rymer, *Varney the Vampire*

Schechter, Harold and Everitt, David, *The A to Z Encyclopaedia of Serial Killers*, New York, Pocket Books, 1996

Seymour, William, *Battles in Britain*, Ware, Wordsworth Military Library, 1997

Stoker, Bram, *Dracula*, Ware, Wordsworth, 2000

Sugar, Peter, *A History of East–Central Europe*, Washington, UWP, 1977

Summers, Montague, *The History of Witchcraft and Demonology*, US, Castle Books, 1992

——, *The Vampire*, New York, Dorset Press, 1991

Thorne, Tony, *Children of the Night: Of Vampires and Vamirism*, London, Indigo, 2000

Thurston, Robert, 'The Spawning of Satan', *BBC History Magazine*, May 2002

Tondriau, J. and Villeneuve, R., *A Dictionary of Devils and Demons*, London, Tom Stacey Ltd, 1972

Treptow, Kurt W. (ed.), *Dracula: Essays on the Life and Times of Vlad Ţepeş*, East European Monographs, New York, Columbia University Press, 1991

——, *Vlad III: Dracula*, Iaxi, Centre for Romanian Studies, 2000

Twiss, Miranda, *The Most Evil Men and Women in History*, London, Michael O'Mara Books, 2002

Twitchell, James, *The Living Dead – a Study of the Vampire in Romantic Literarure*, Duke University Press, 1981

Vuksic, V., *Cavalry*, London, Cassell, 1993

Weir, Alison, *The Princes in the Tower*, Pimlico 1992

Wilcox, Peter, *Rome's Enemies: Gallic and British Celts*, London, Osprey, 1985

Wilson, Colin, *The Mammoth Book of Murder*, London, Robinson, 2000

Woodward, Ian, *The Werewolf Delusion*, London, Paddington Press, 1979

Worley, Lloyd, *The Prenatal and Natal Foundations of the Vampire Myth*, www.members.tripod.com/Baron91/worleyPrenatal.html

Wyse, Elizabeth, et al. (eds), *Past Worlds: The Times Atlas of Archaeology*, London, HarperCollins, 1992

Young, Lailan, *Secrets of the Face*, London, Hodder & Stoughton, 1983

# INDEX

# Index

# Index

# INDEX

Wlislocki, Heinrich von 58
Württemberg 94
Wycliffe, John 127

Yorga, Nicholae 9

Zalmoxis 70, 73, 114
Žižka, Jan 127–8, 210
Zopfius, Johann 48
Zoroaster 53